AFRICA

Up Close and Personal

SHARON "SHAZ" SMITH

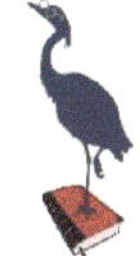

Blue Heron Book Works, LLC
Allentown, Pennsylvania

ISBN:979-8-9913625-6-6
Cover image by Sharon "Shaz" Smith as well as images on page 112

www.blueheronbookworks.com

I hope you enjoy the photos!

Over the past three decades I have been to the northern and southern countries of Africa numerous times to enjoy watching and photographing animals, birds, and scenery. It is my favorite place to be and feels like home when I am there. There is nothing like sitting in a game vehicle surrounded by a herd of curious elephants or watching lions, leopards or cheetahs stalk prey. Every sighting is observing nature in action as they watch you, as you watch them.

I urge everyone to travel to these parks to experience the excitement and joy of seeing nature at its best. You never know what is round the curve of the windy dirt roads, up in a Kigelia or Baobab tree, or just outside your tent. The sights, sounds, and smells are all part of the experience.

Those parks need your support. The list of endangered animals is increasing. Elephants, the Black Rino, African Wild Dog, Cheetahs, Gorillas, African Penguin, and the Ground Penguin are just a few.

This is where the photos were taken:
South Africa-Kruger National Park
Botswana-Chobe National Park, Okavango Delta Region
Zimbabwe-Hwange National Park, Victoria Falls National Park
Zambia-Kafue National Park
Rwanda-Akagera National Park
Tanzania-Tarangire National Park, Serengeti National Park, Ngorongoro Crater
Zanzibar-Jozani Chwaka Bay National Park
Kenya-Masai Mara National Reserve

A special thanks to a family in Victoria Falls, Zimbabwe. They have become more than friends but my African family. Naume and Phanuel Pangidzwa and children, Panashe, Anashe, and Kanashe.

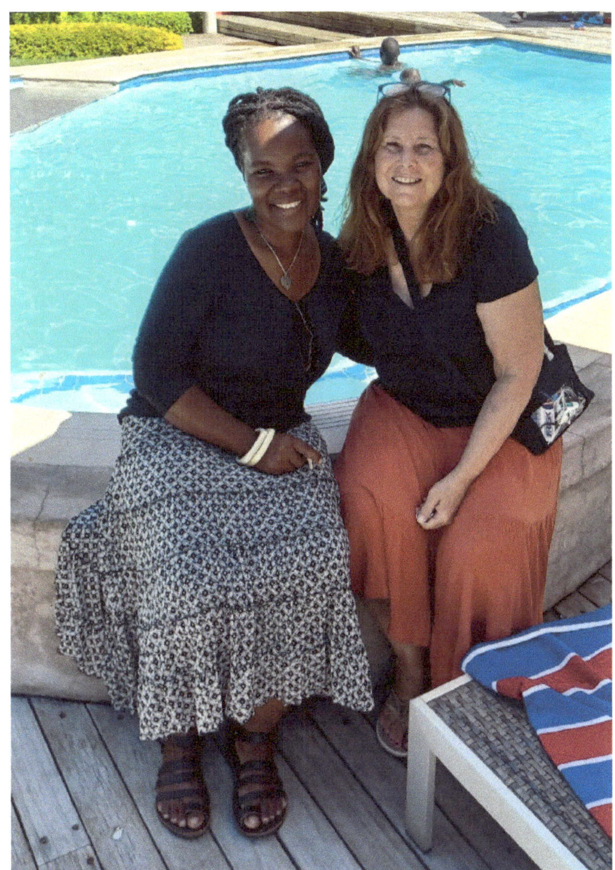

Naume and me at Shearwater Explorers Village in Victoria Fall, Zimbabwe

I like animals. Nothing they do is half-hearted. Everything they do is for the first time: they hunt, they eat, they mate...

Isak Dinesen, OUT OF AFRICA

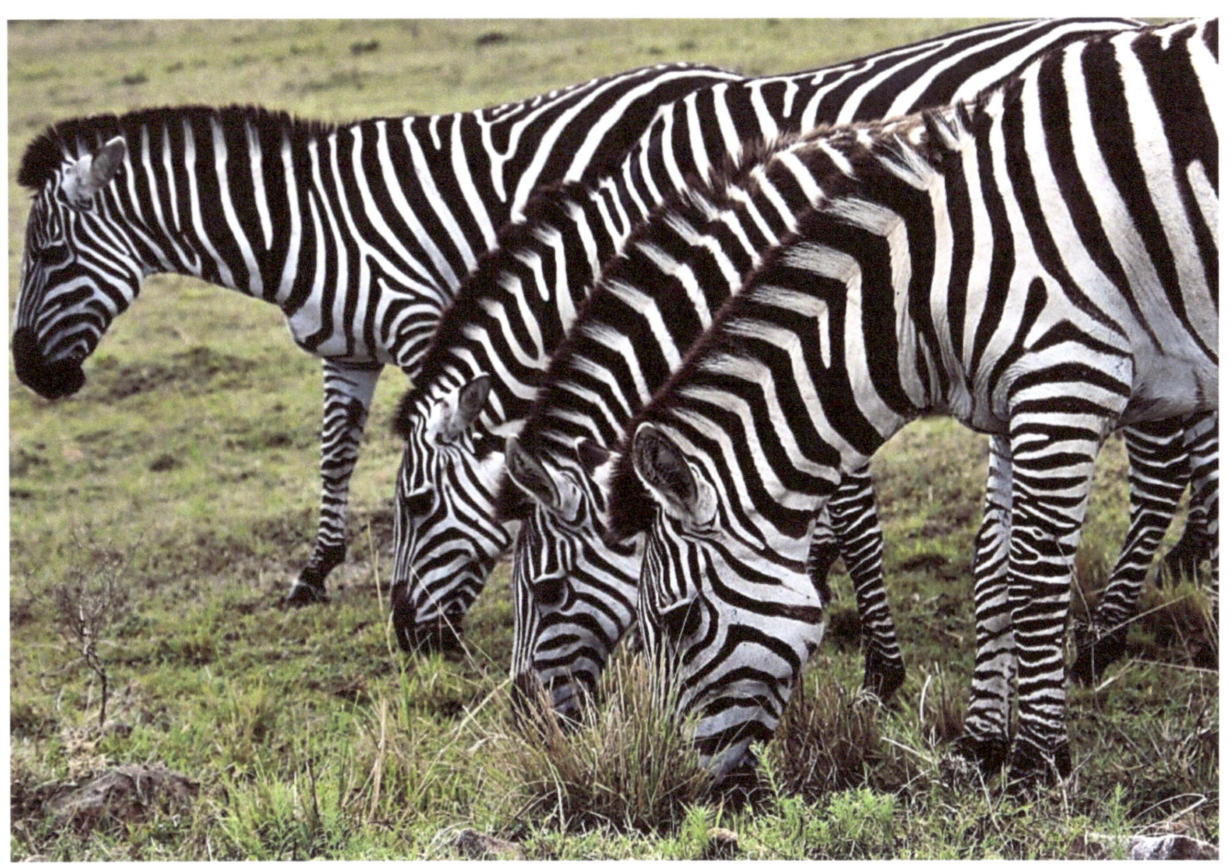

A dazzle of zebras

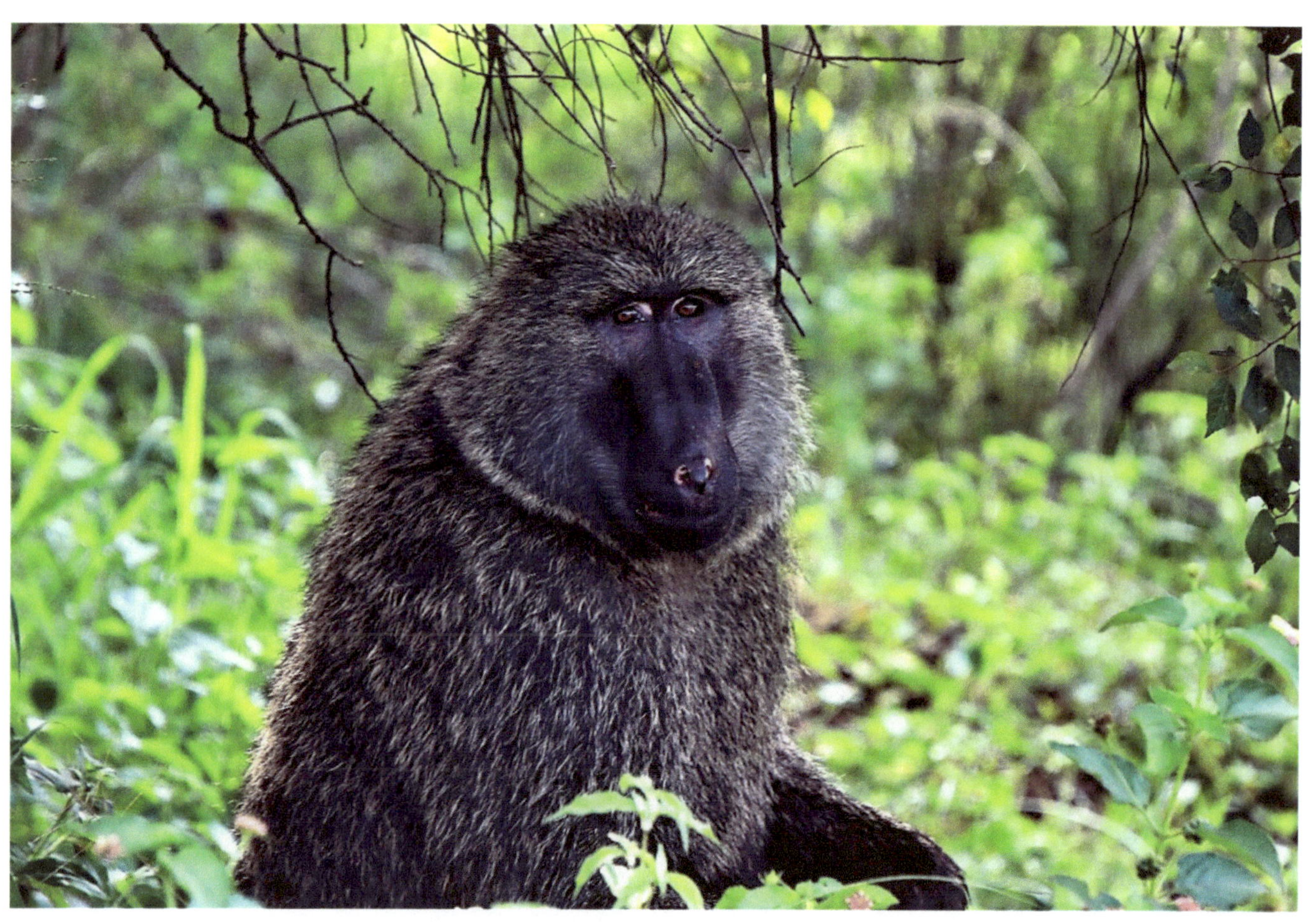

One of the most handsome baboons I have ever seen

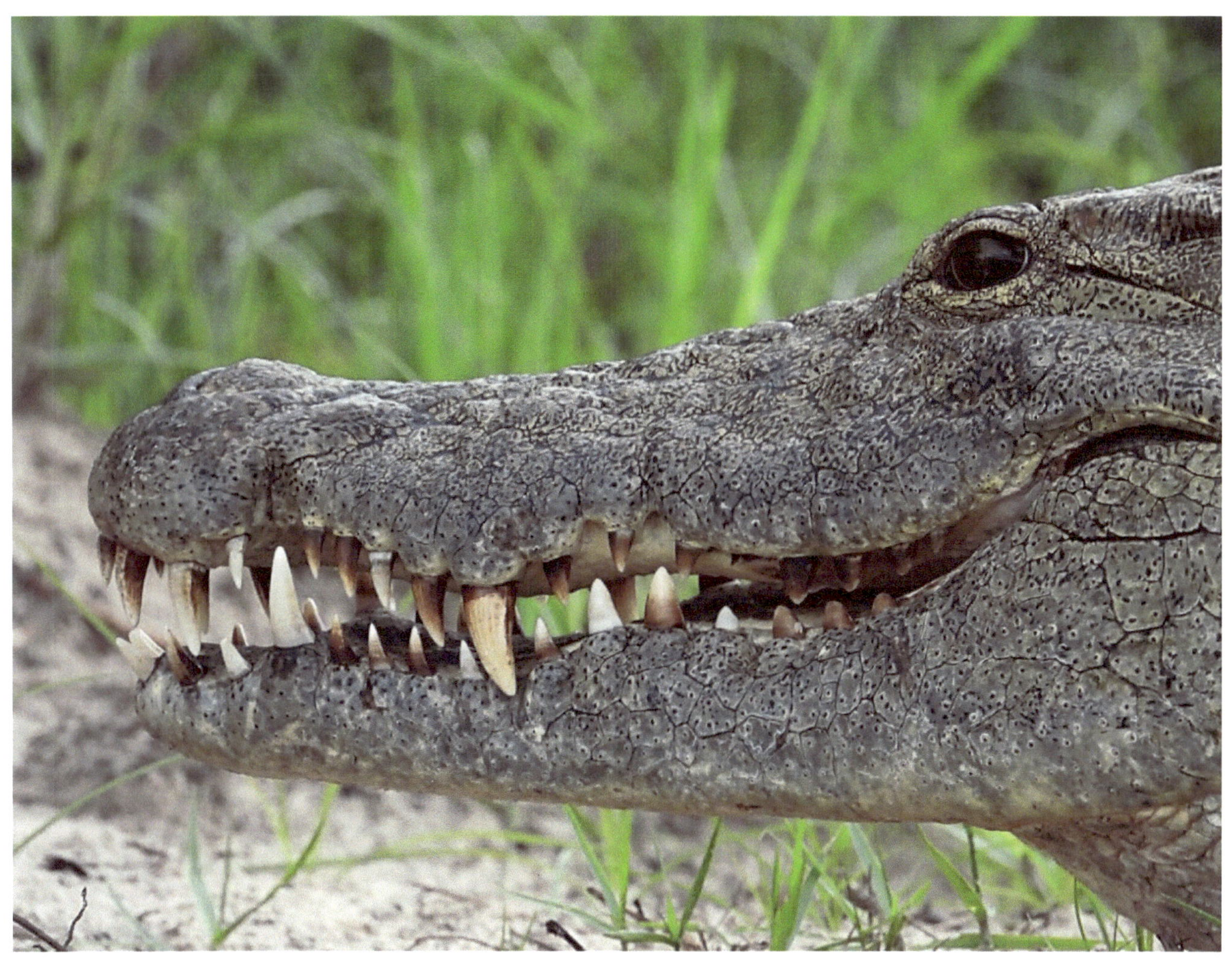

Best "toothy" grin in Zimbabwe

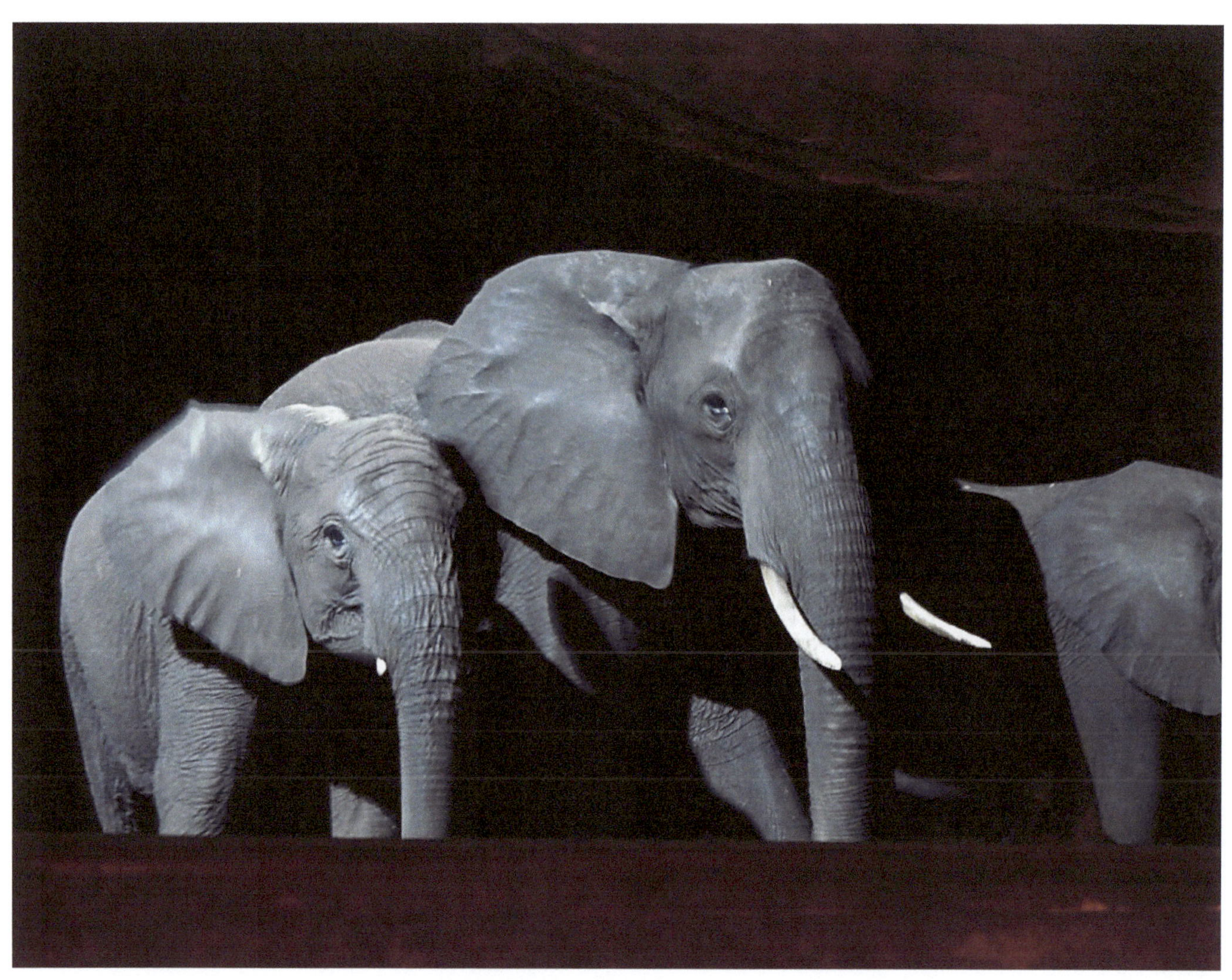

My love of elephants grows every time I spend time with them

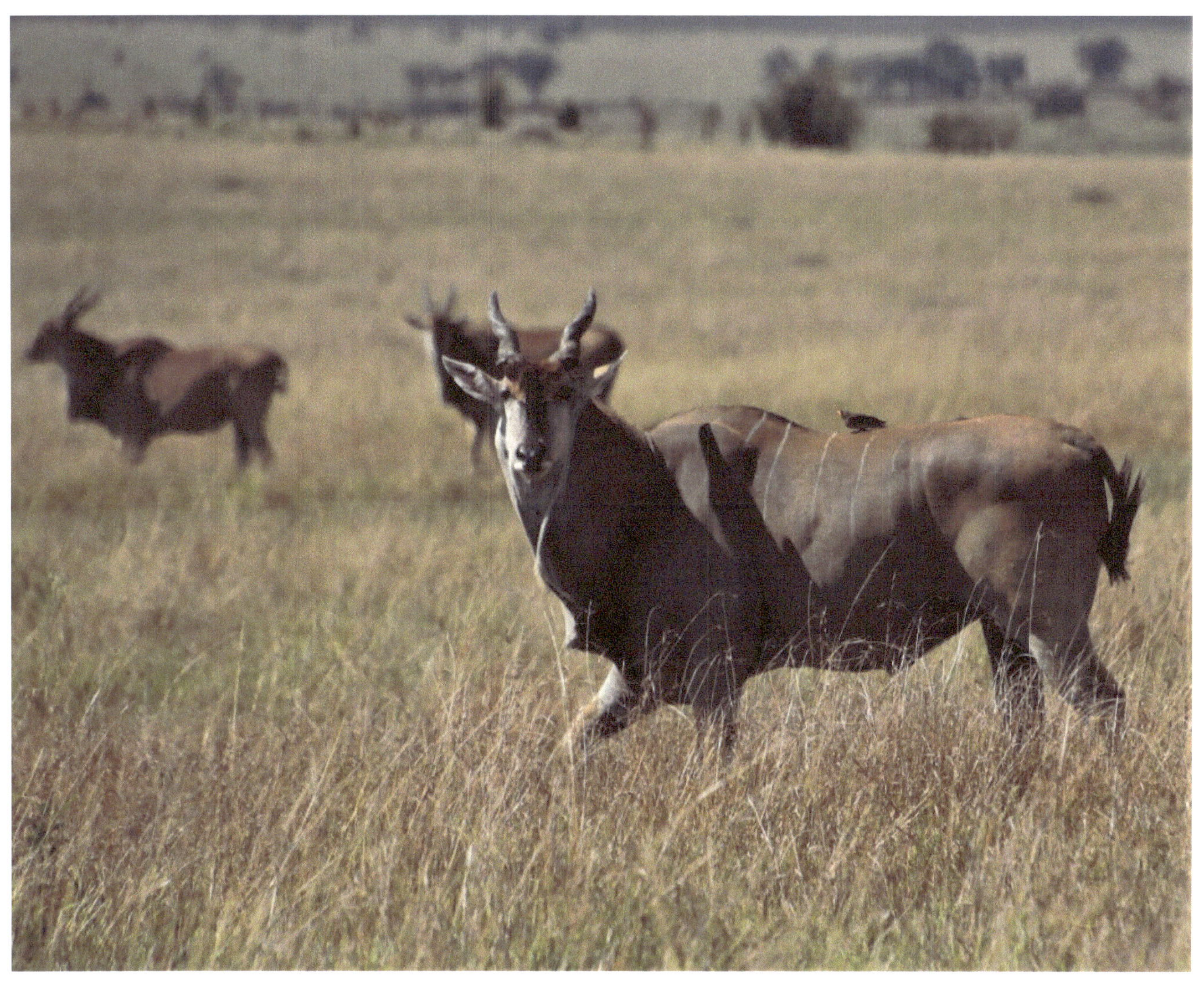

Beautiful eland, the largest of the antelope family, looking back at me

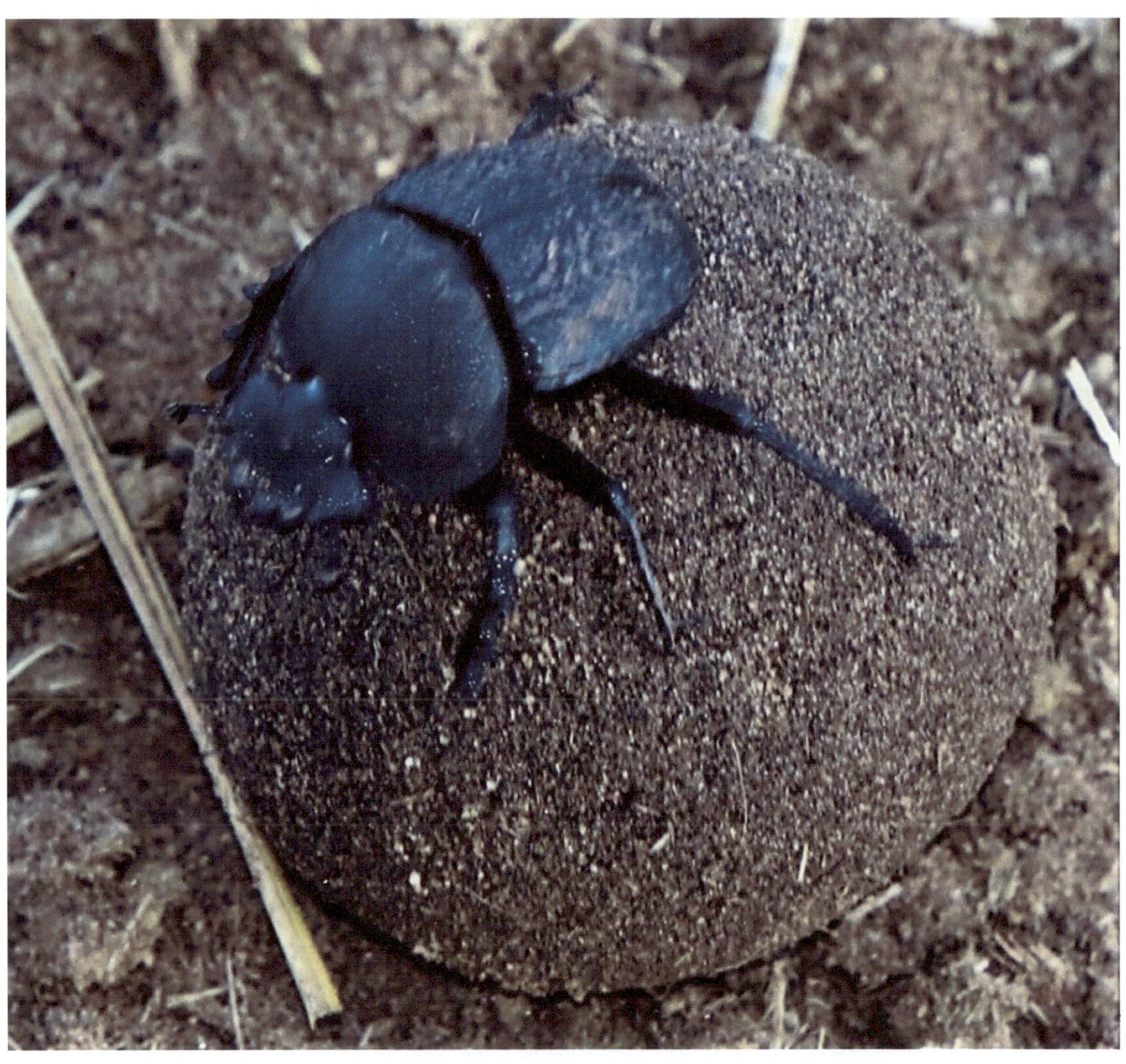

It's challenging work to make a perfect ball out of elephant dung just to attract a female dung beetle.

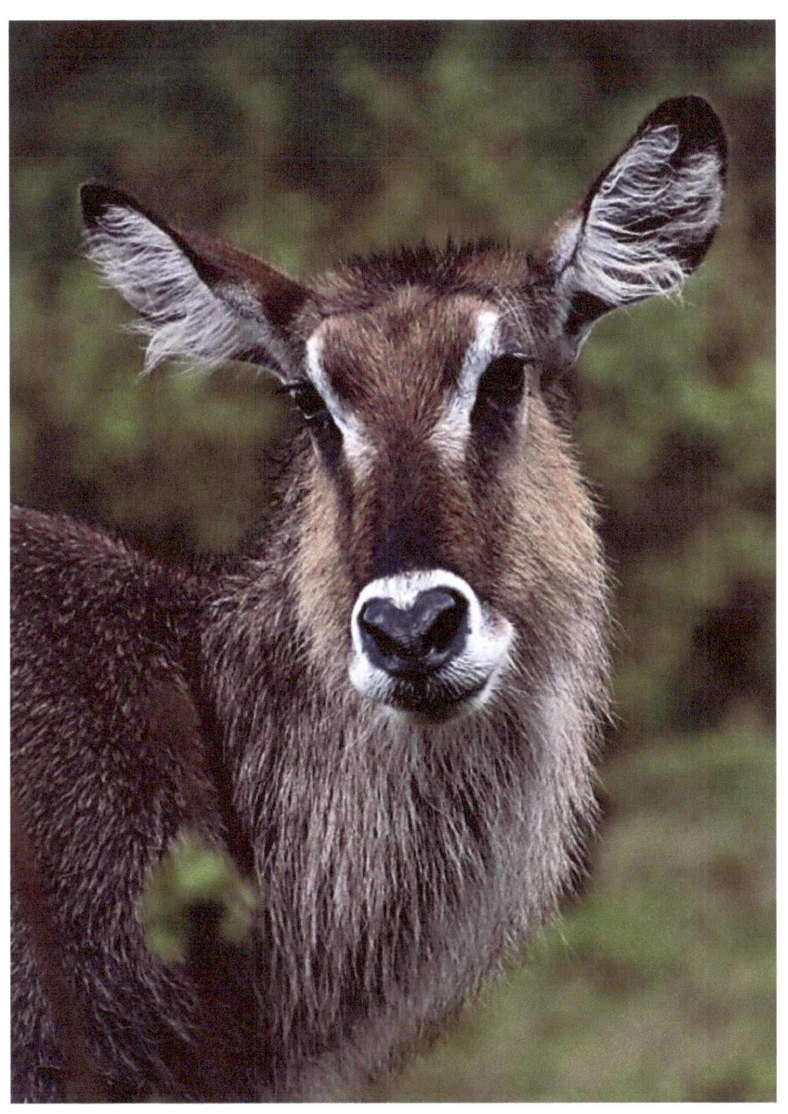

The fluffy face of a water buck, also known as the toilet seat. They have a white circle on their butt.

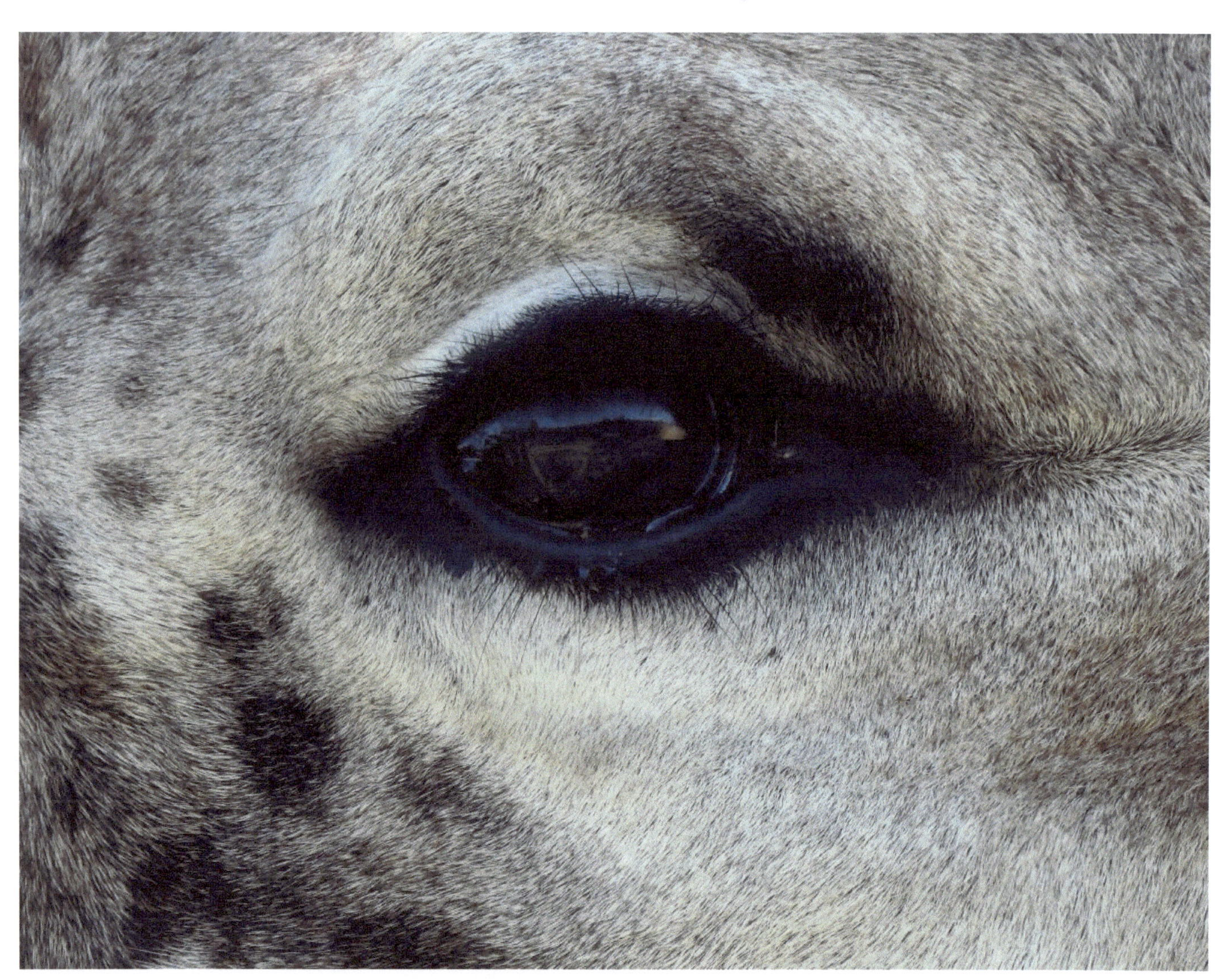

The tallest land animal, they can see movement up to a mile away

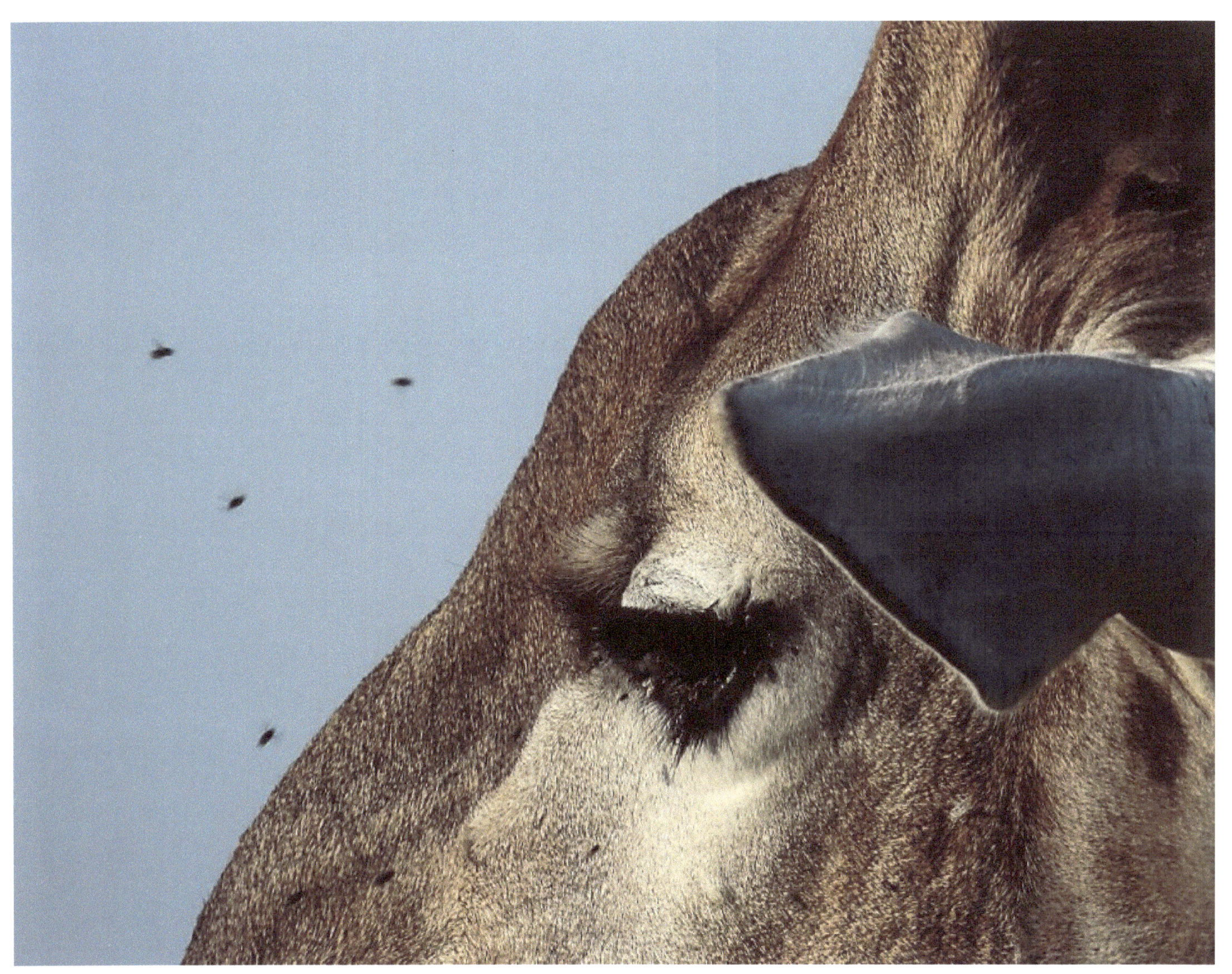

Giraffes have excellent hearing and make grunting, moos, and other sounds to communicate with other giraffes.

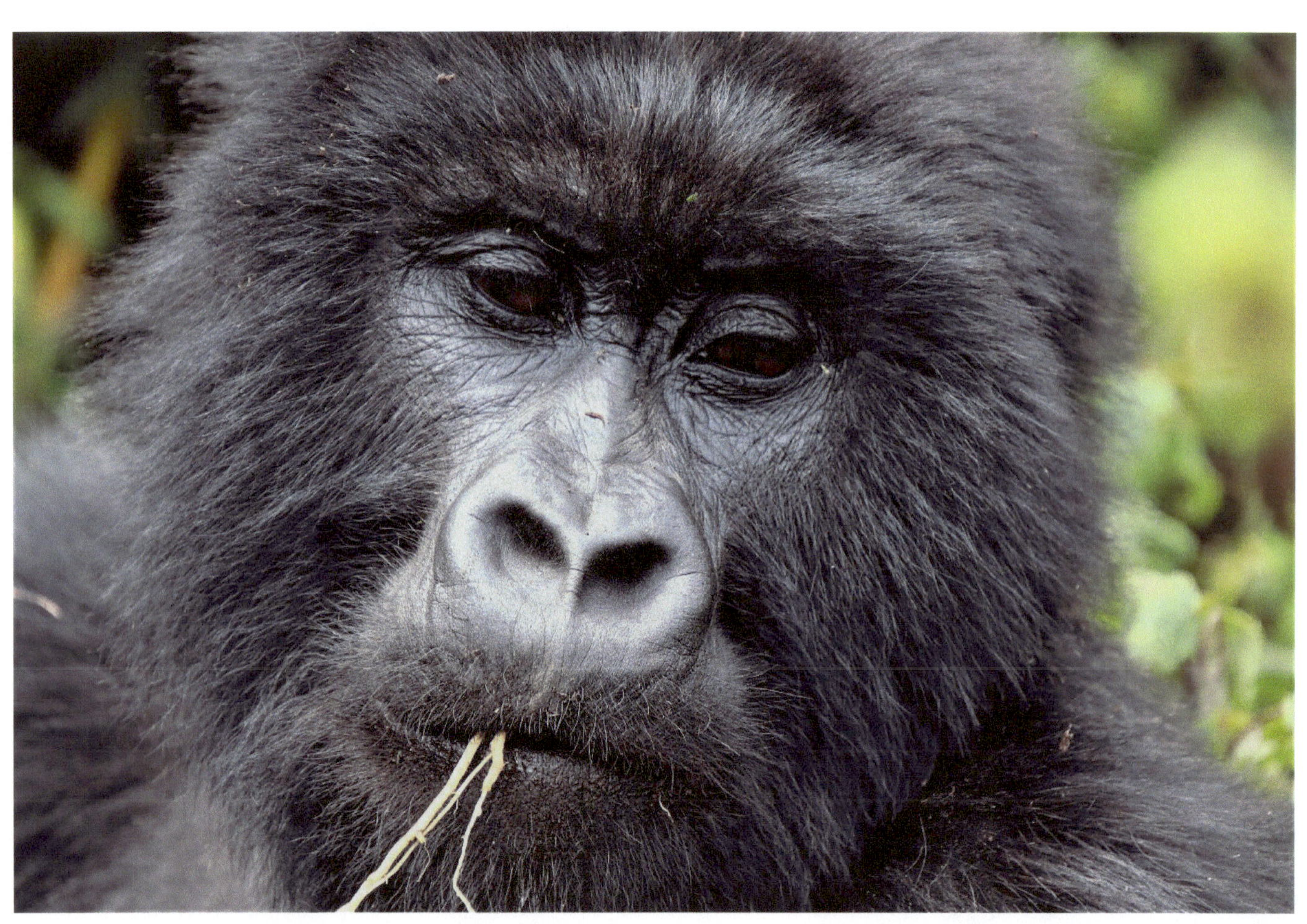

Hiking up to 9,000 ft was no small task with slippery mud and brush but was well worth the effort to sit with the mountain gorillas in Rwanda.

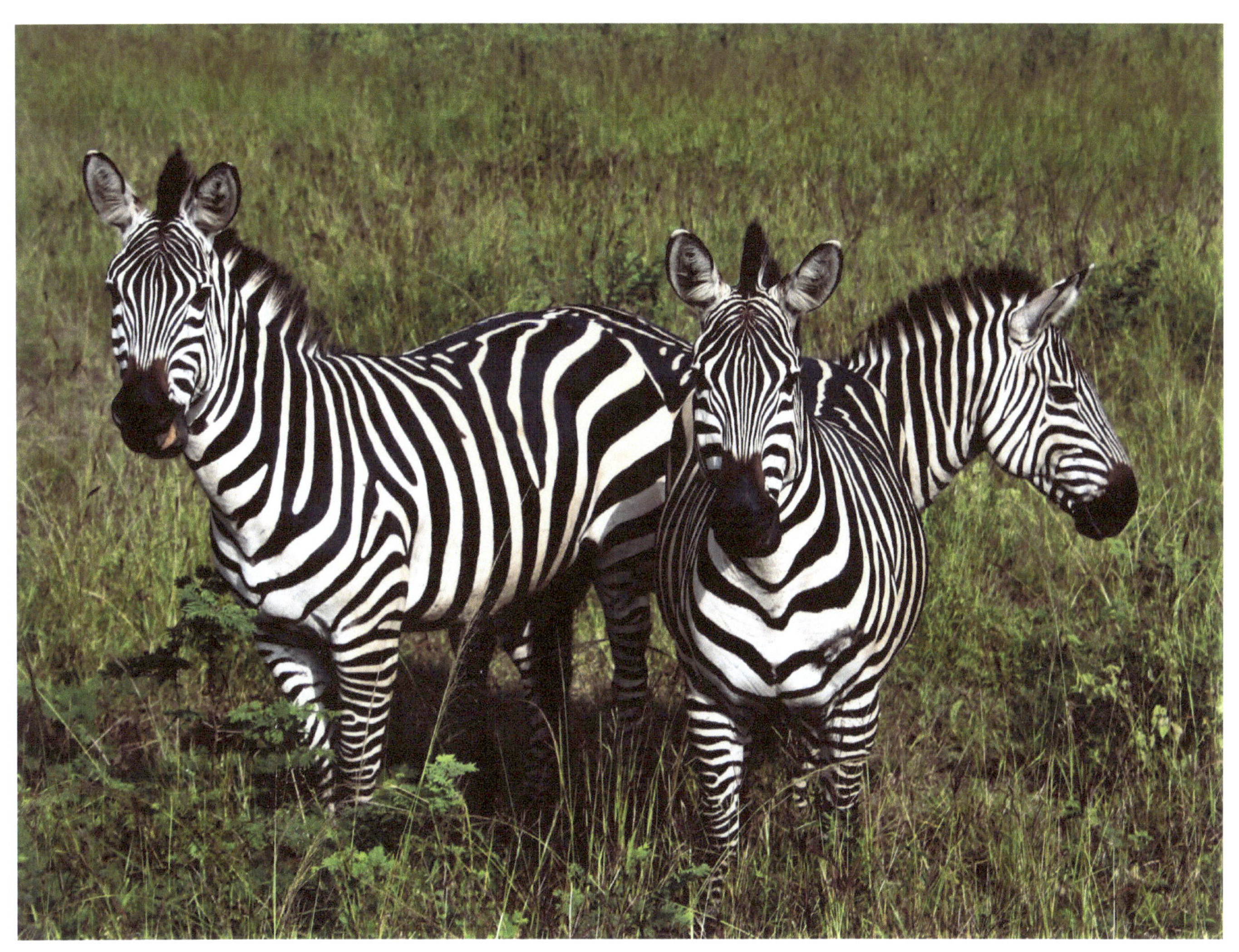

Zebra stripes are like fingerprints, no two are alike.

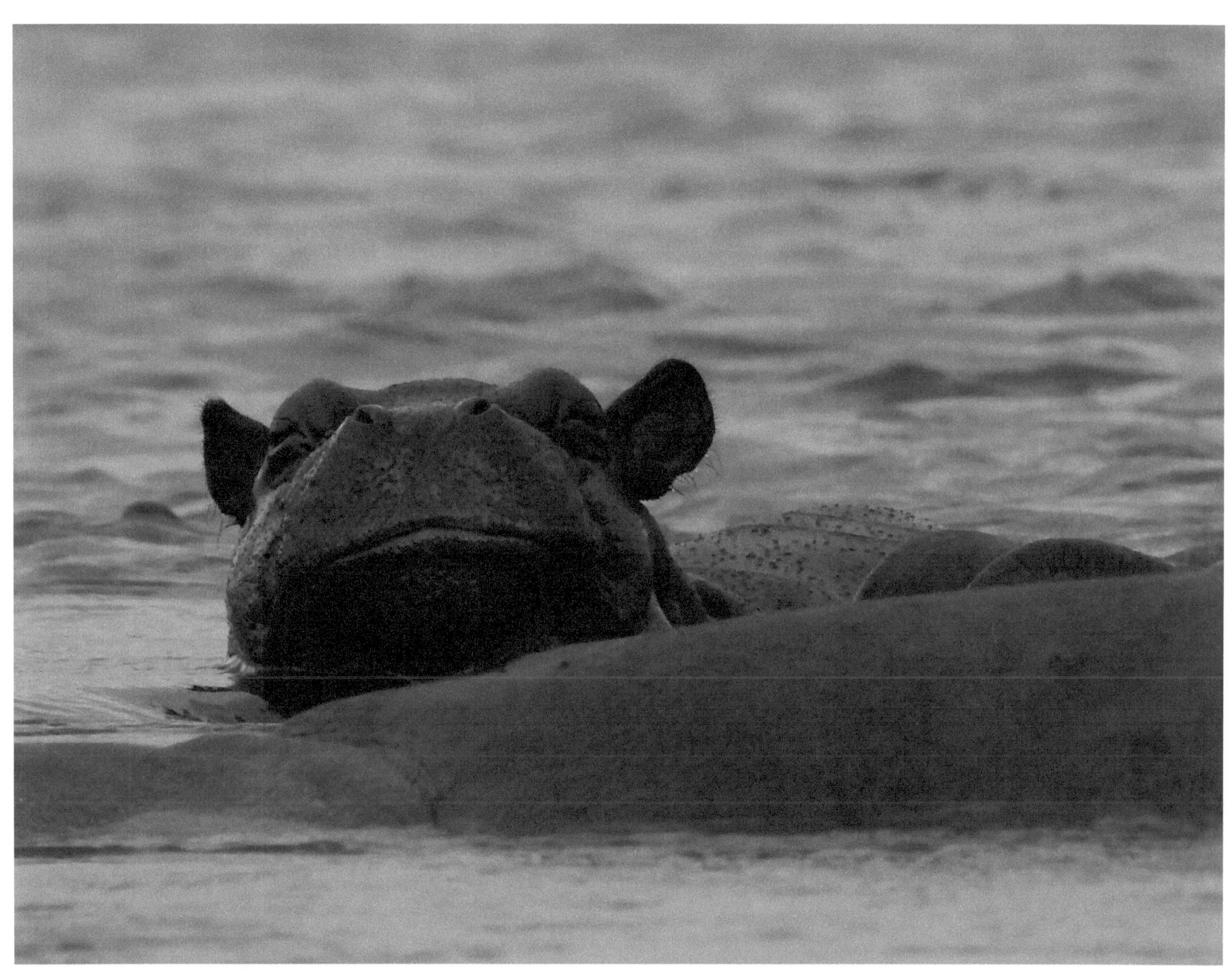

Hippos spend most of the day in the water keeping cool and return to land to graze at night.

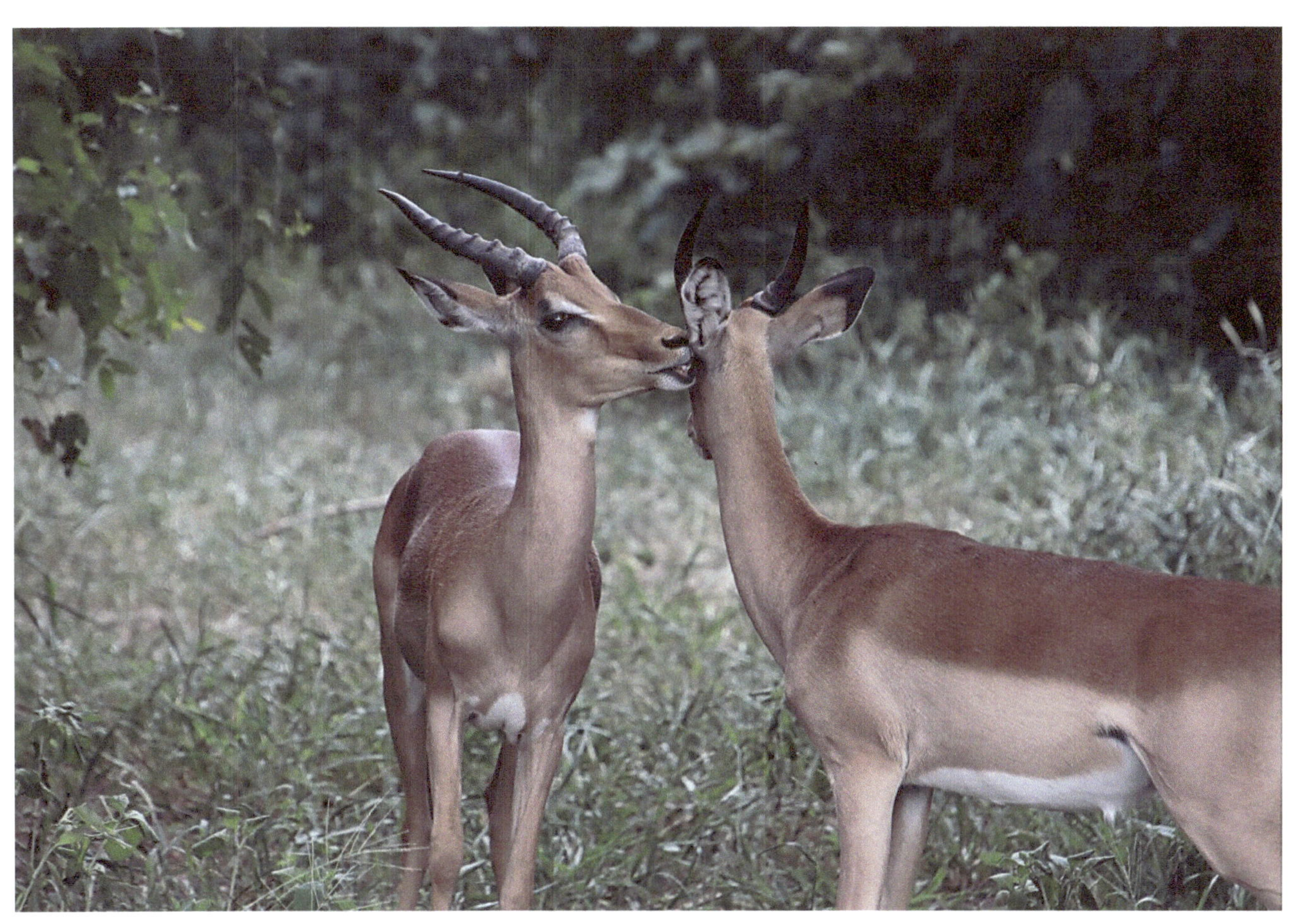

Caught this young male impala telling secrets to his friend

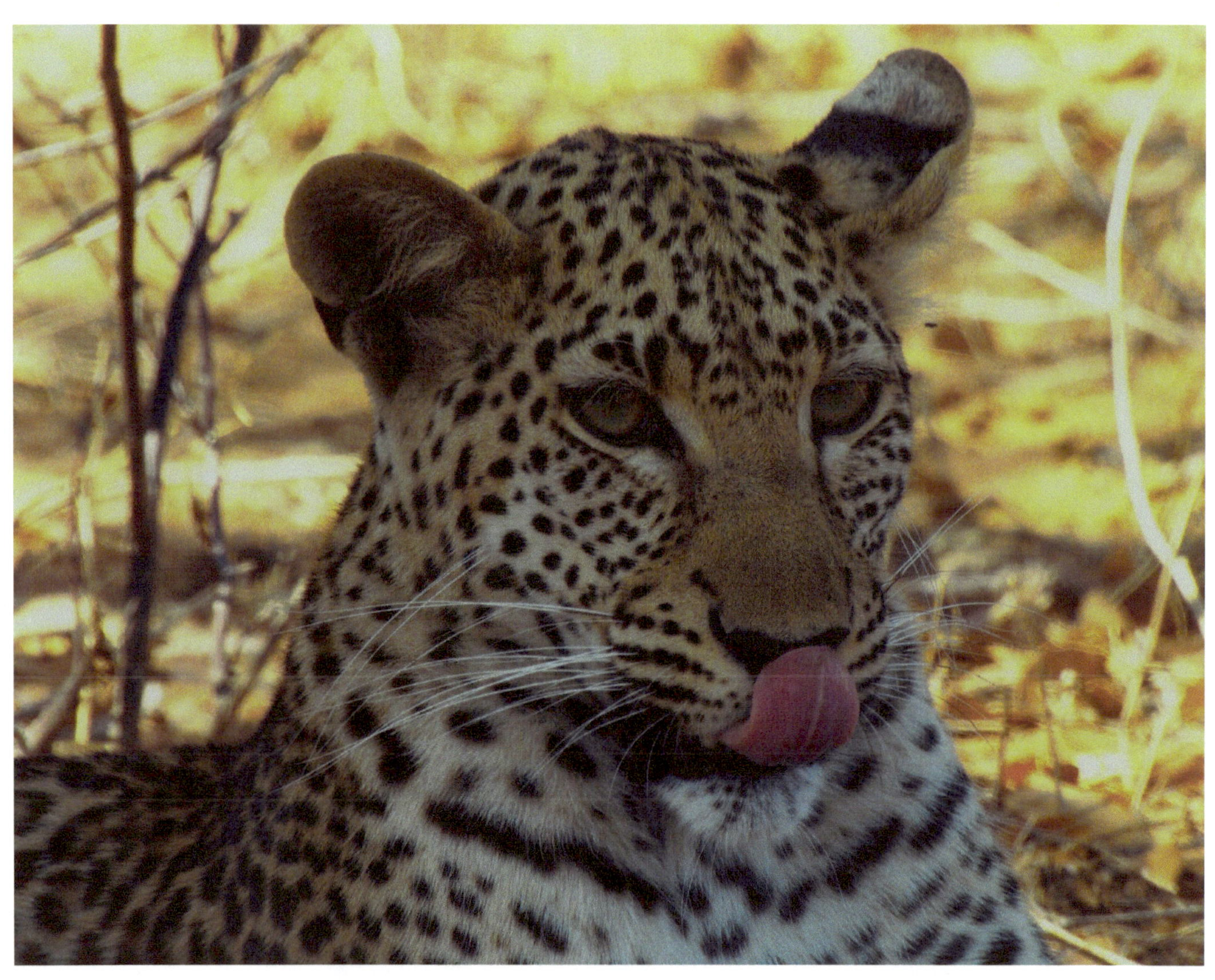

Leopards are carnivores and prey on antelopes, birds, warthogs, and even insects.

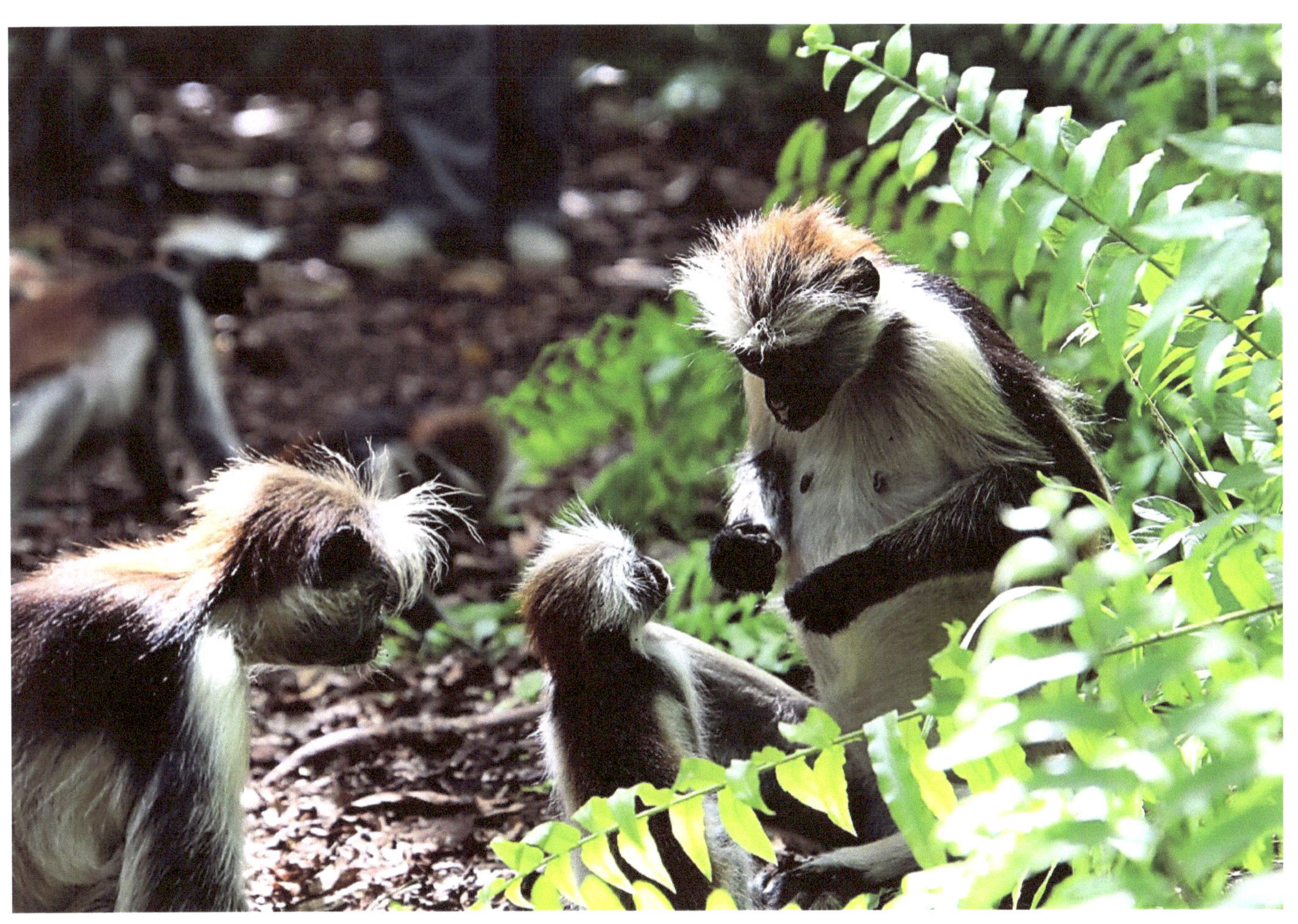

This is a red colobus monkey from Zanzibar. It looks like it's scolding its young.

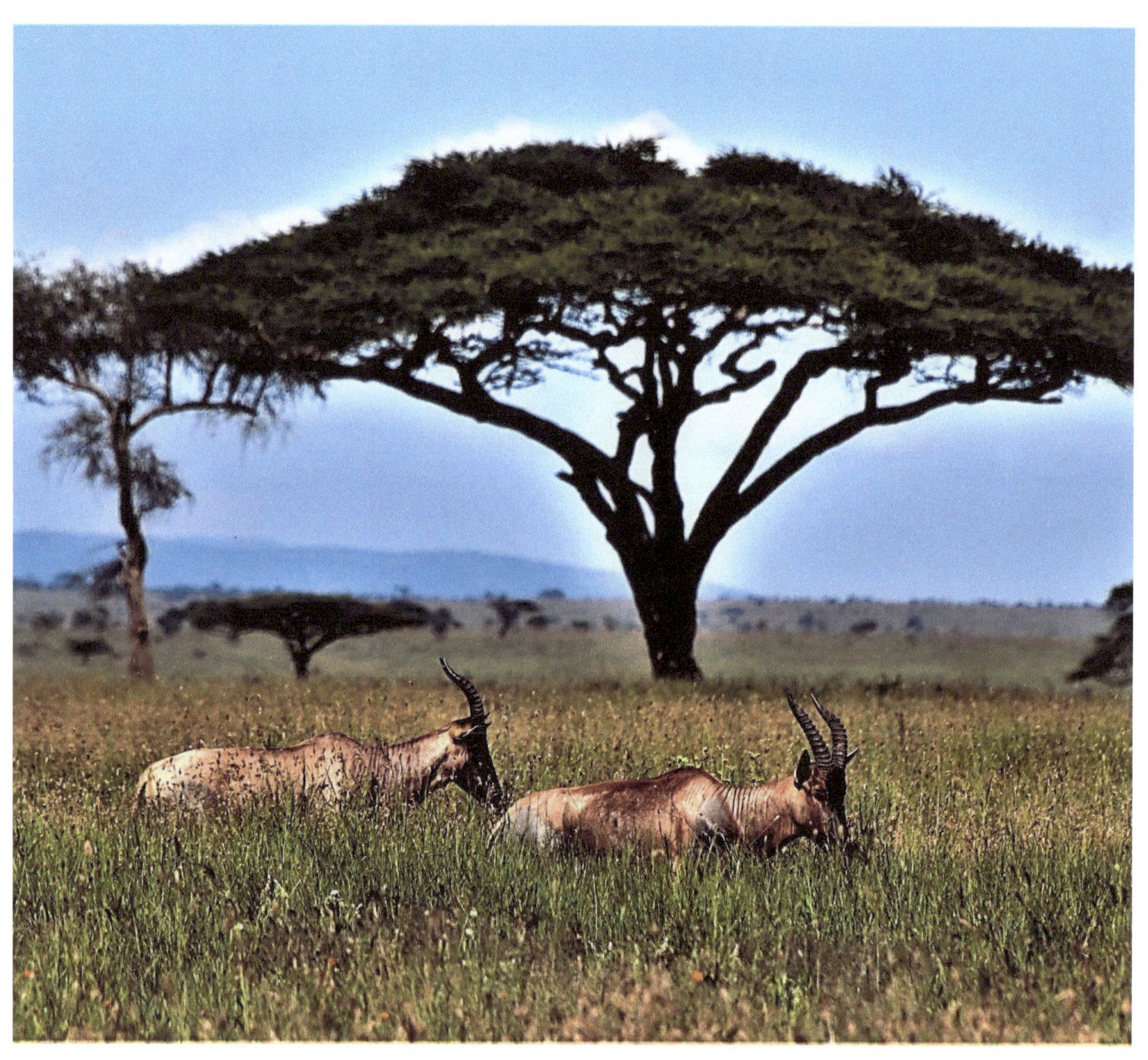

Two young common elands, the largest of the antelope family, found in southern Africa.

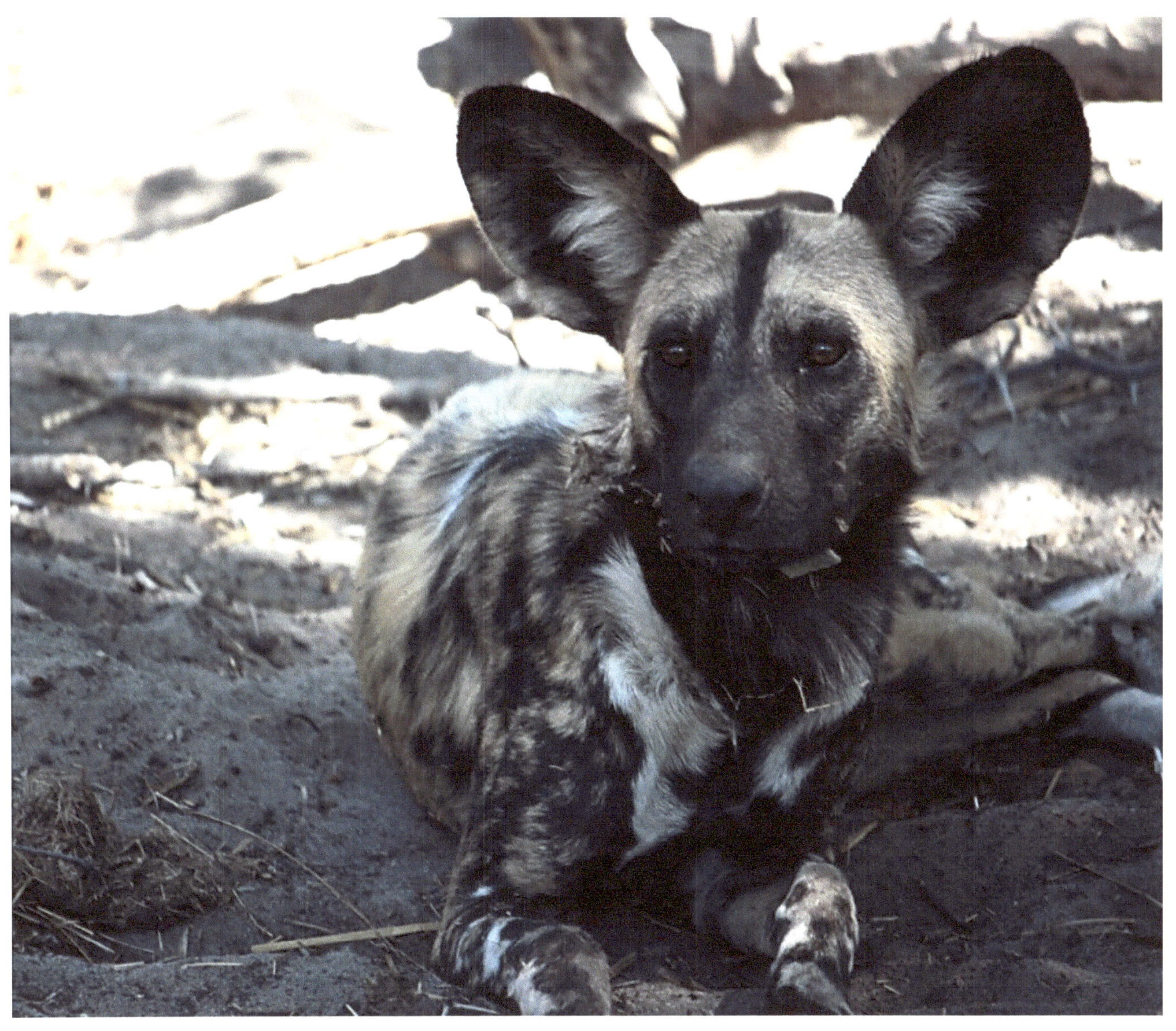

The African wild dog, also known as the painted dog. Fewer than 7,000 remain.

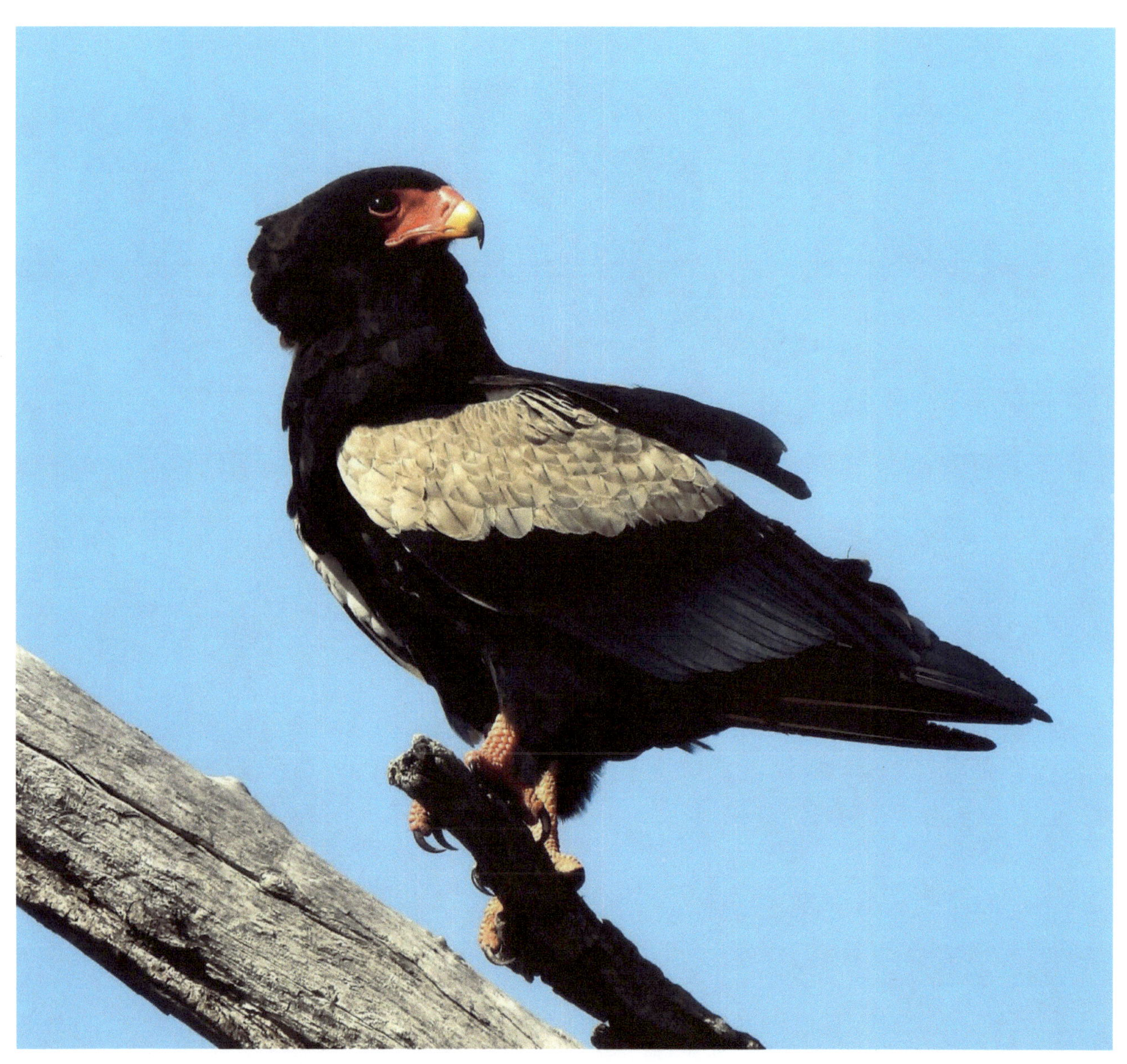

The bateleur eagle is an iconic sight with its orange beak and colorful feathers. My guide was lucky to spot him high in a tree.

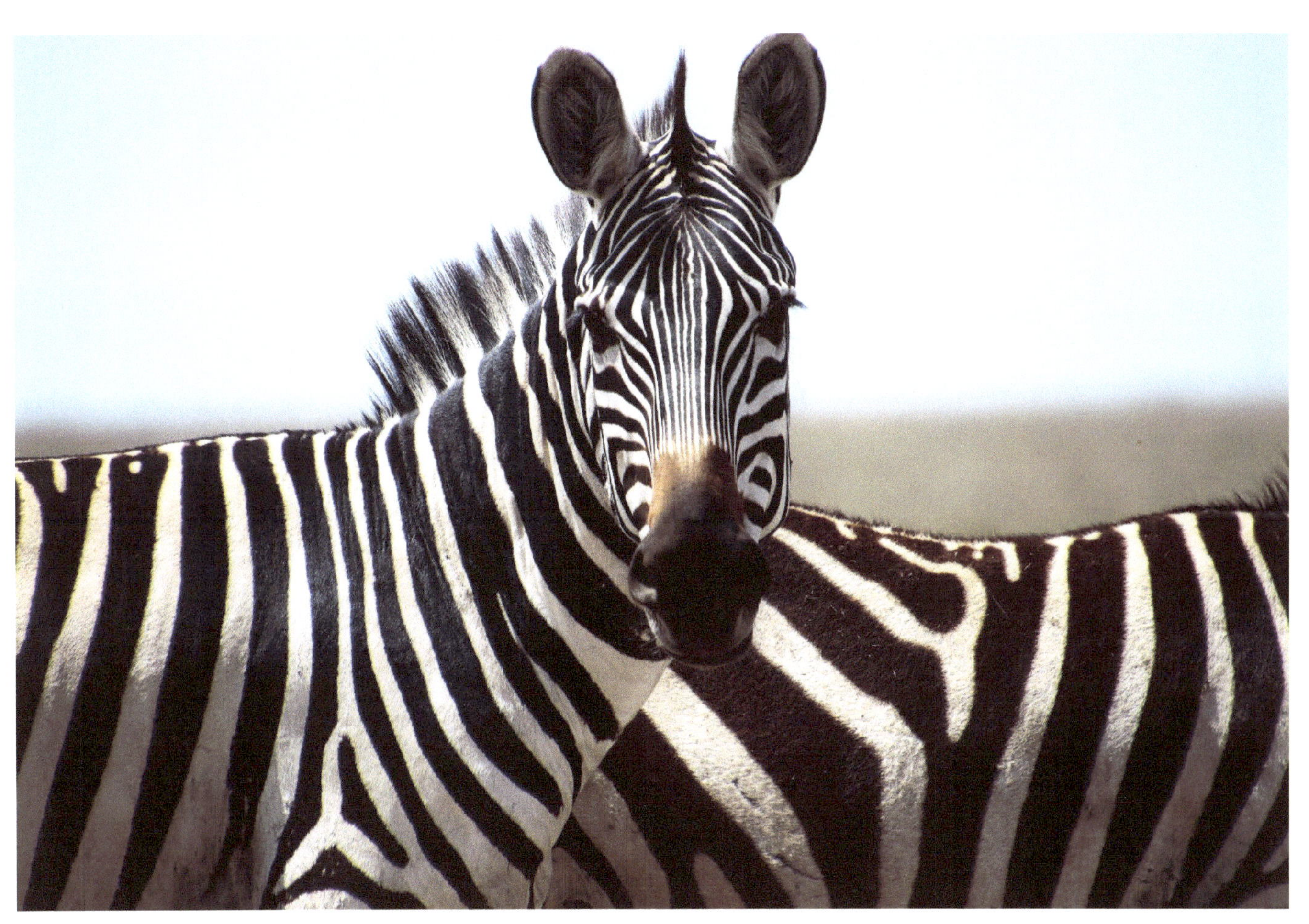

Zebras can live up to 25 years.

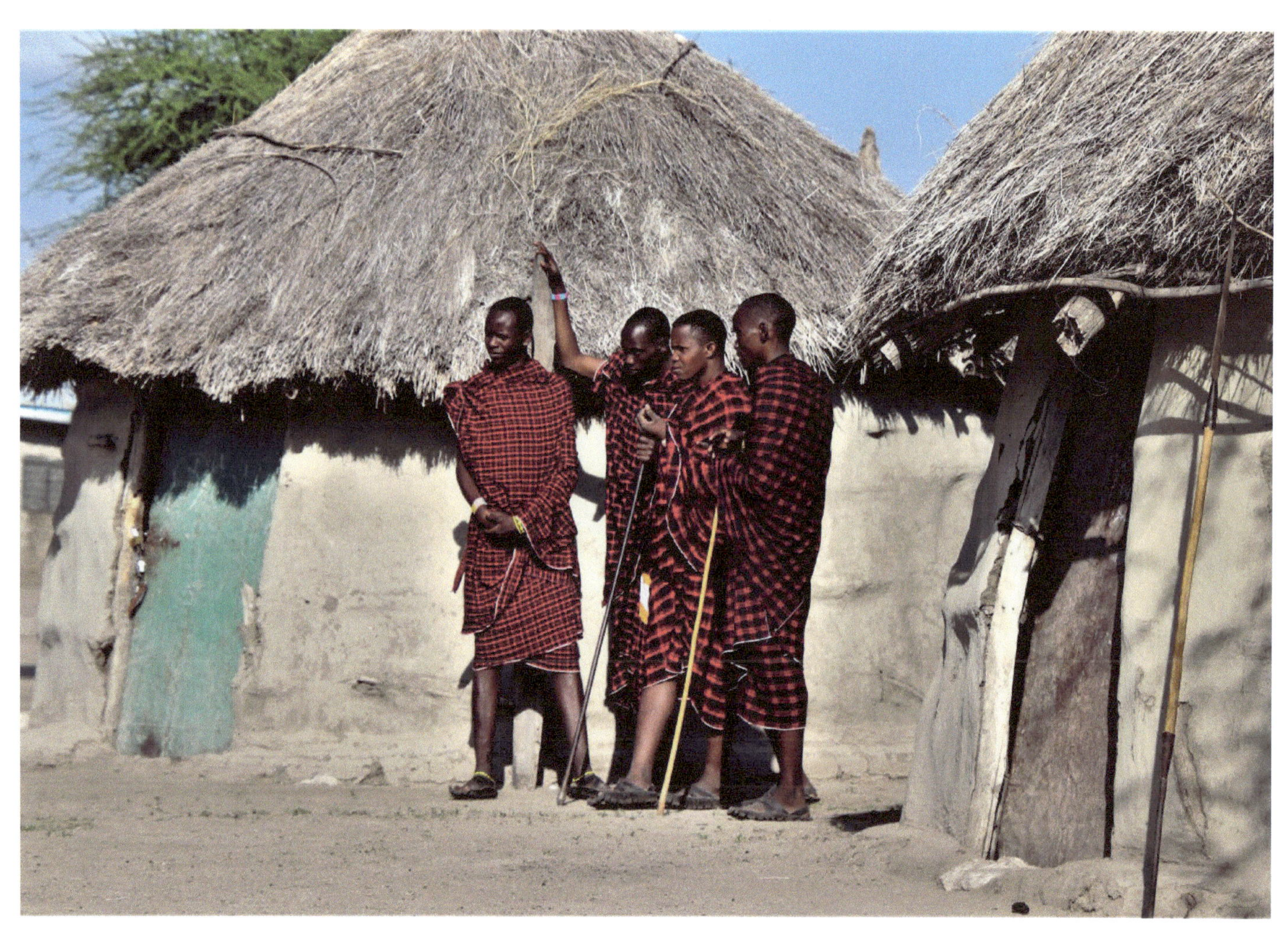

In a local Maasai village, the men gather to discuss the day.

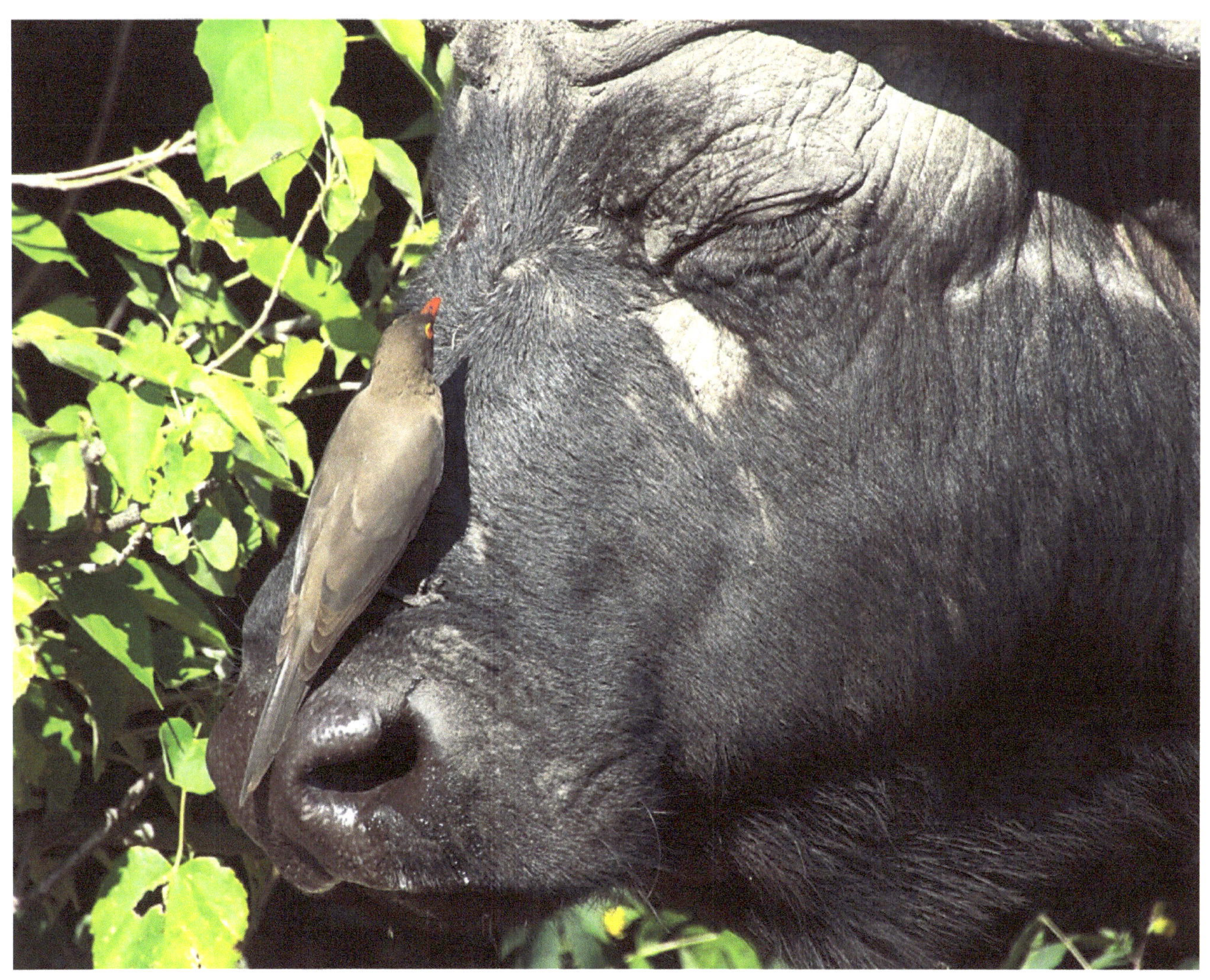

Oxpecker birds eat several varieties of insects on numerous animals as a free cleaning service.

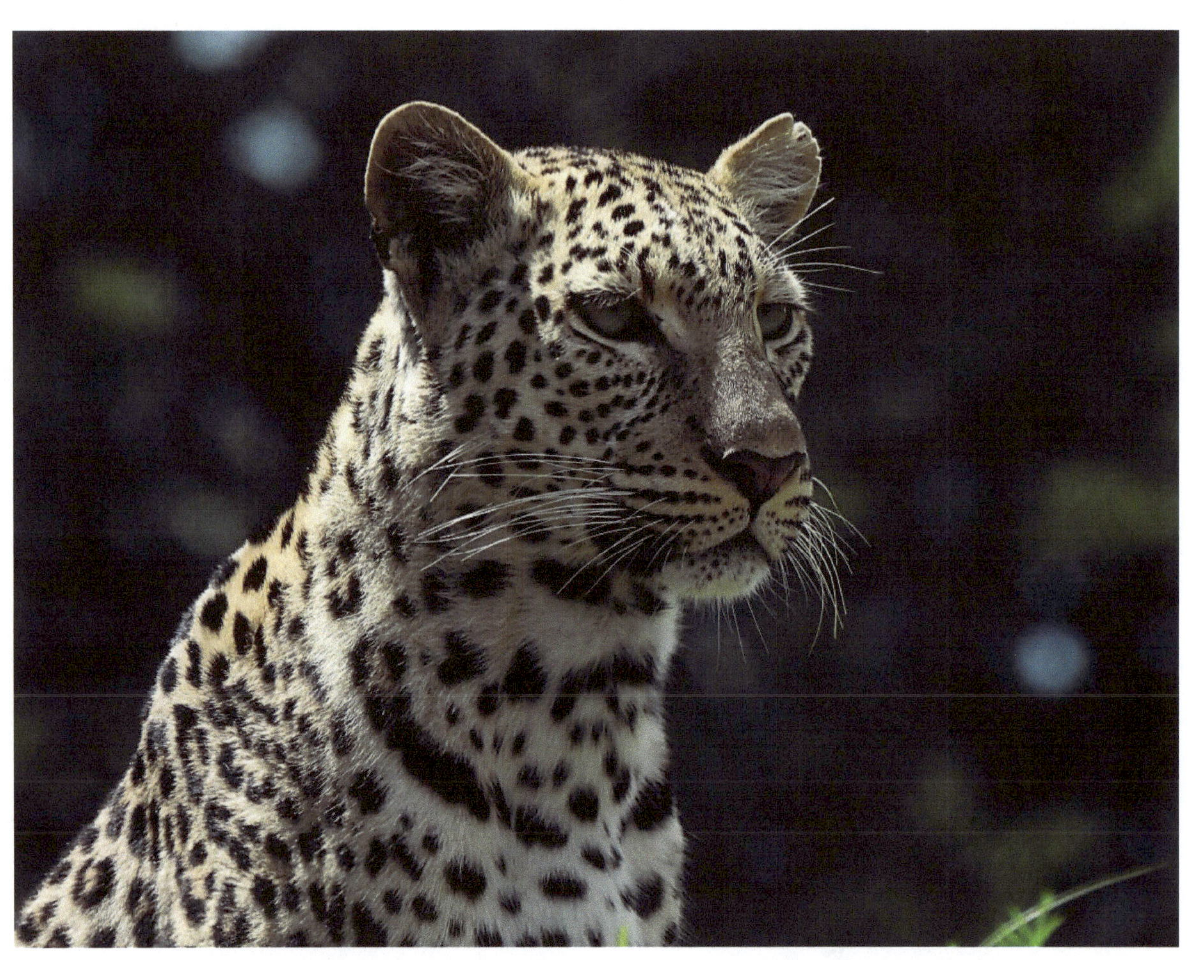

Leopards are solitary cats with excellent hunting and climbing skills.

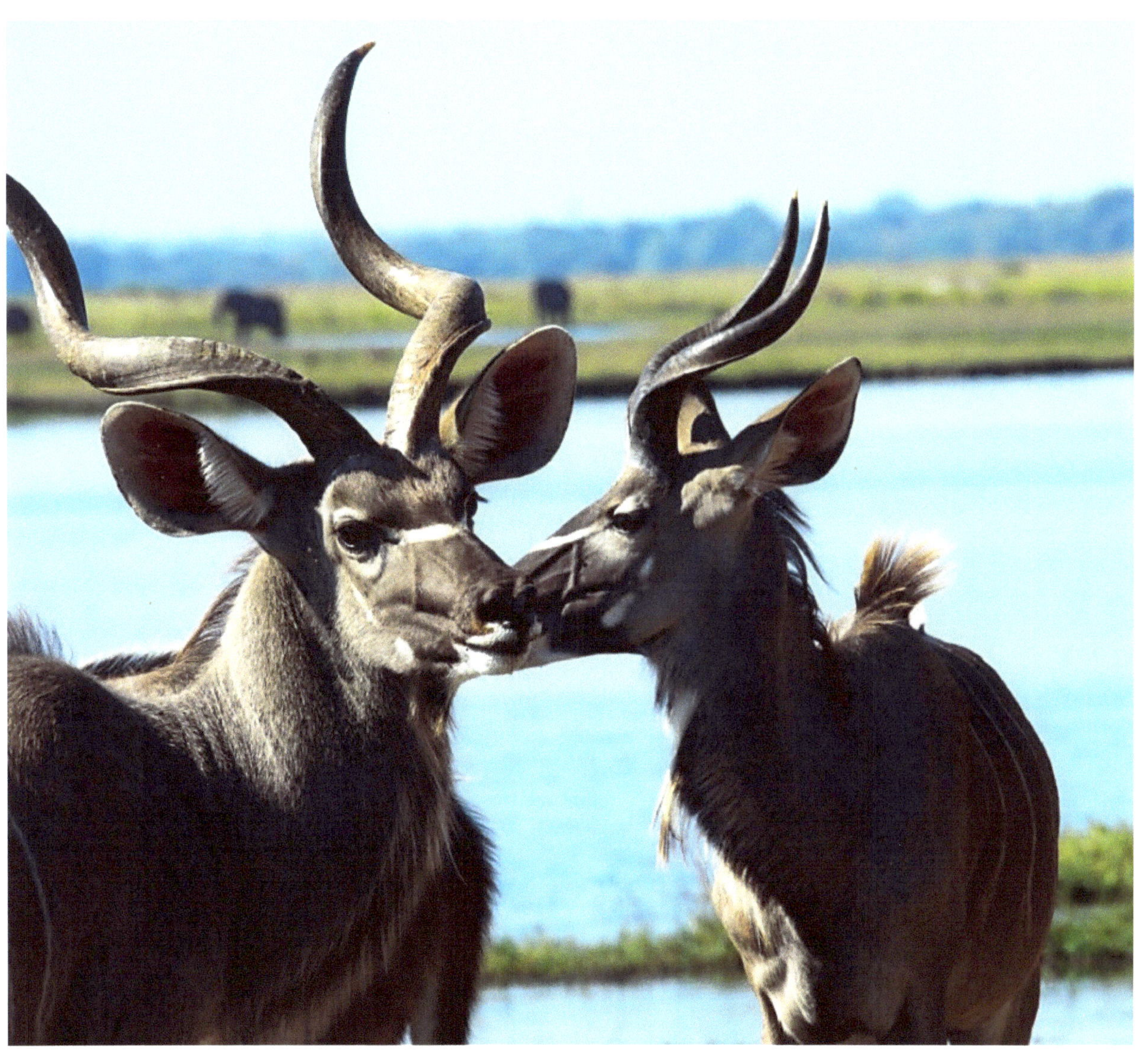

The greater kudu. These antelope can weigh from 400 to more than 600 pounds.

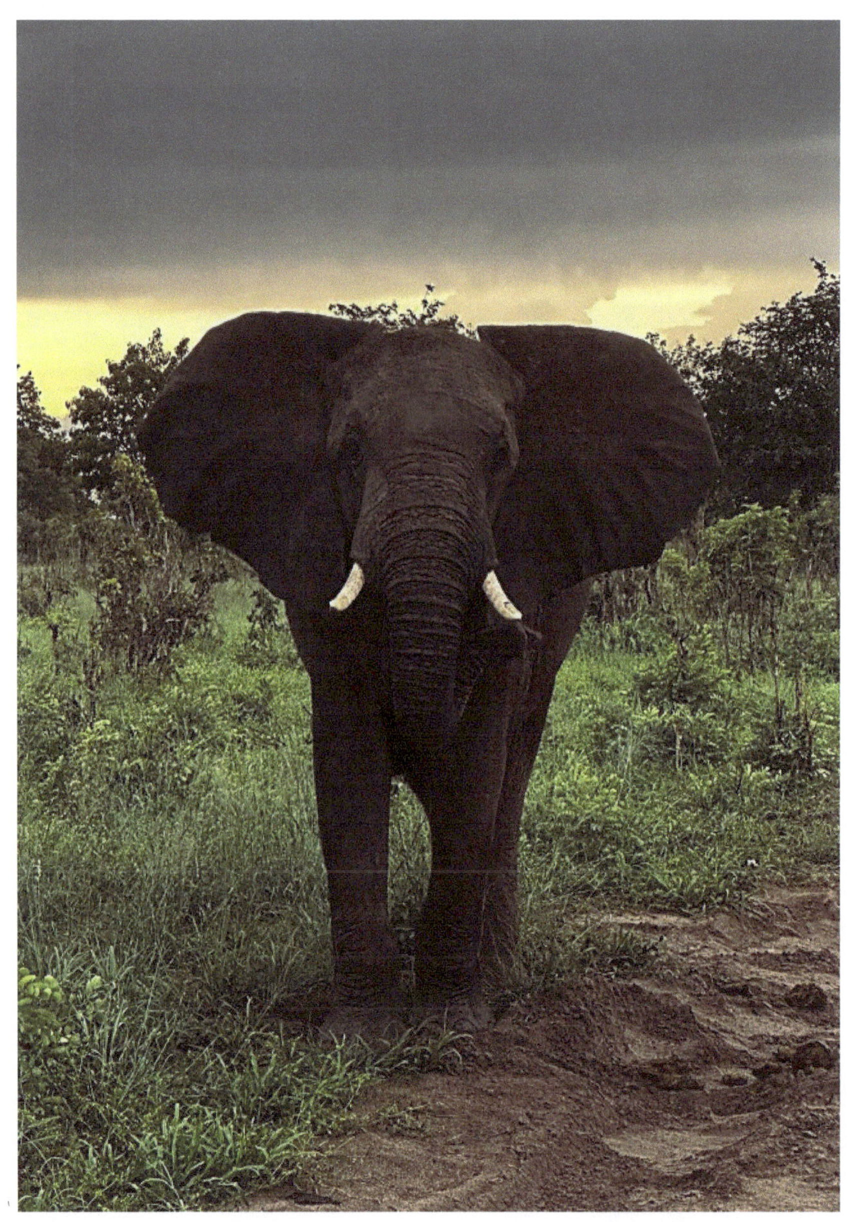

The African elephant. The largest land animal can weigh up to 14,000 pounds and live up to 70 years.

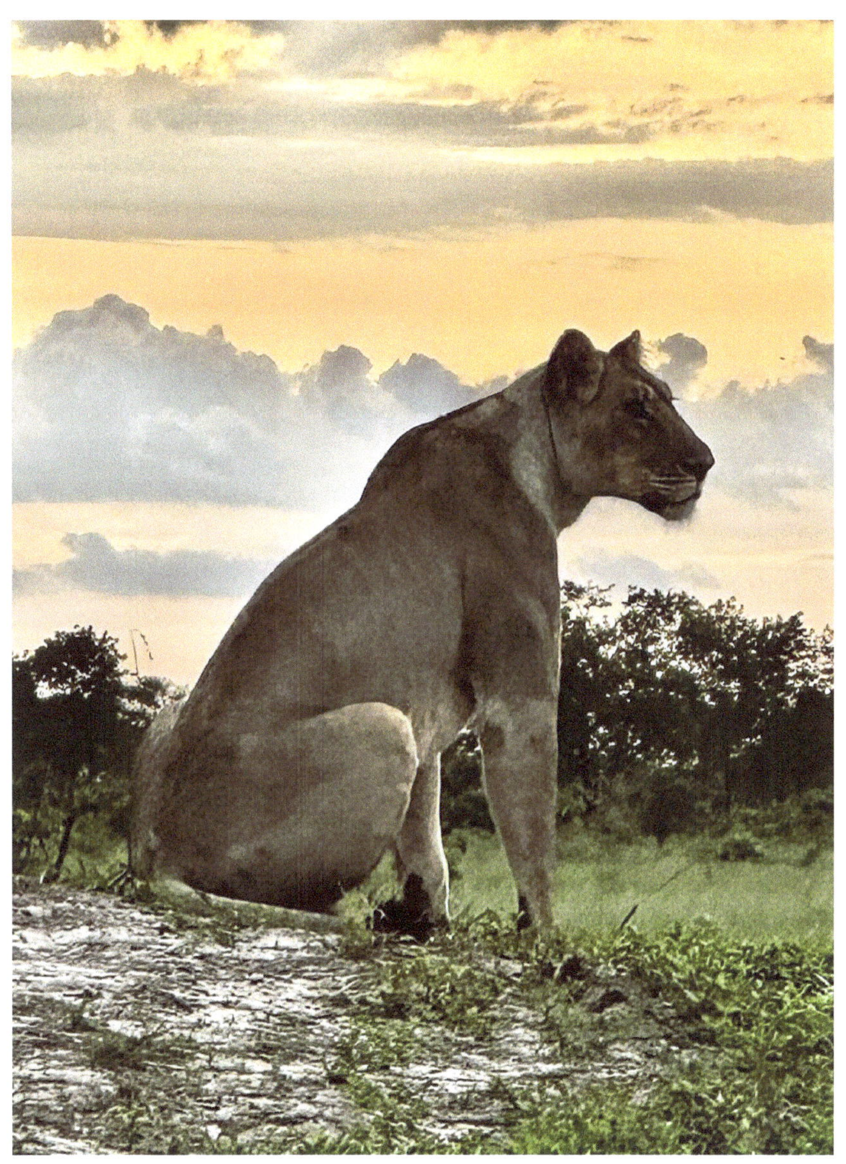

This female lion sat on a mound calling for the four cubs that wandered into the bush.

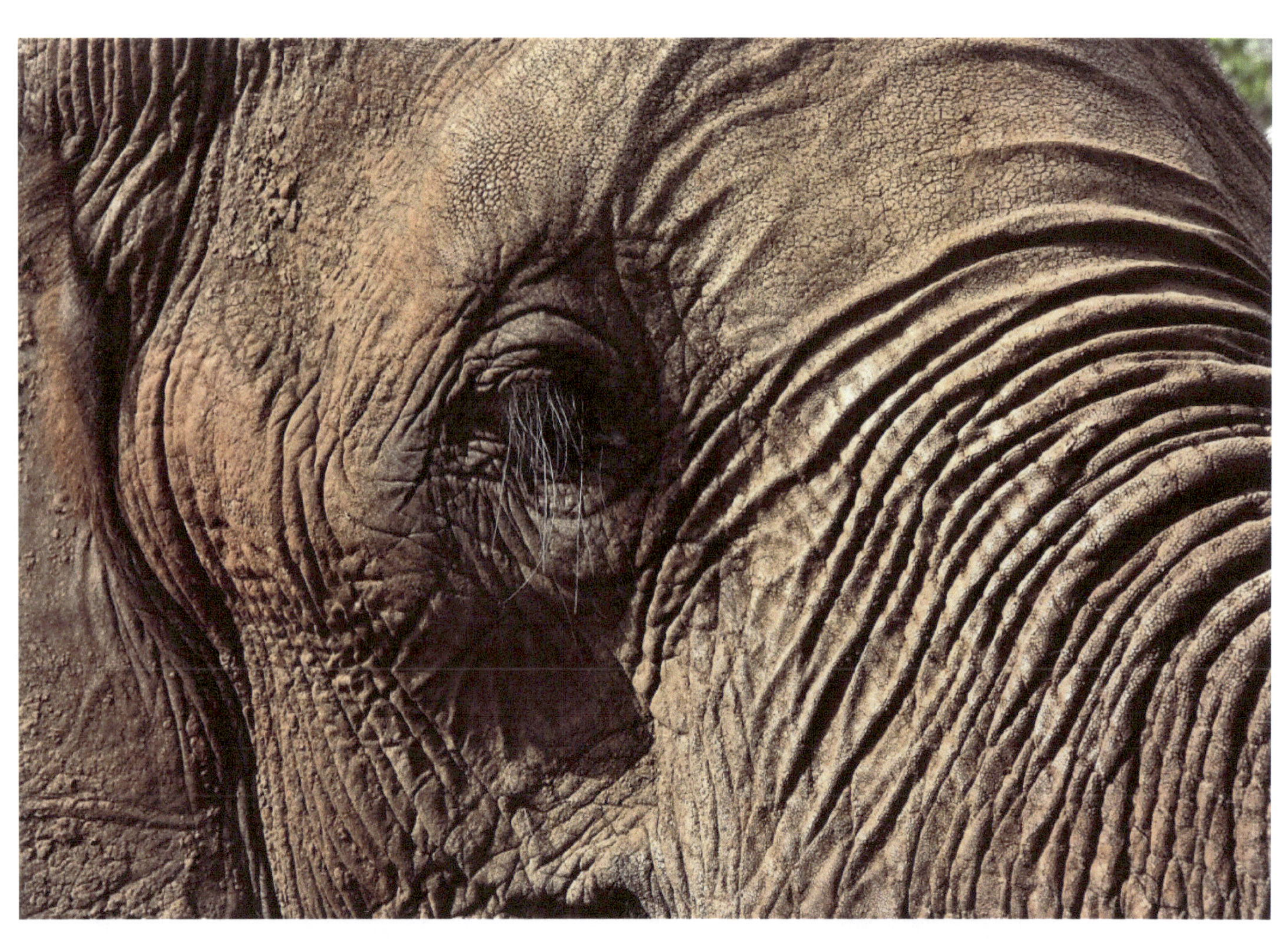

Note the long protective eyelashes on the elephant. This provides protection from dust and debris.

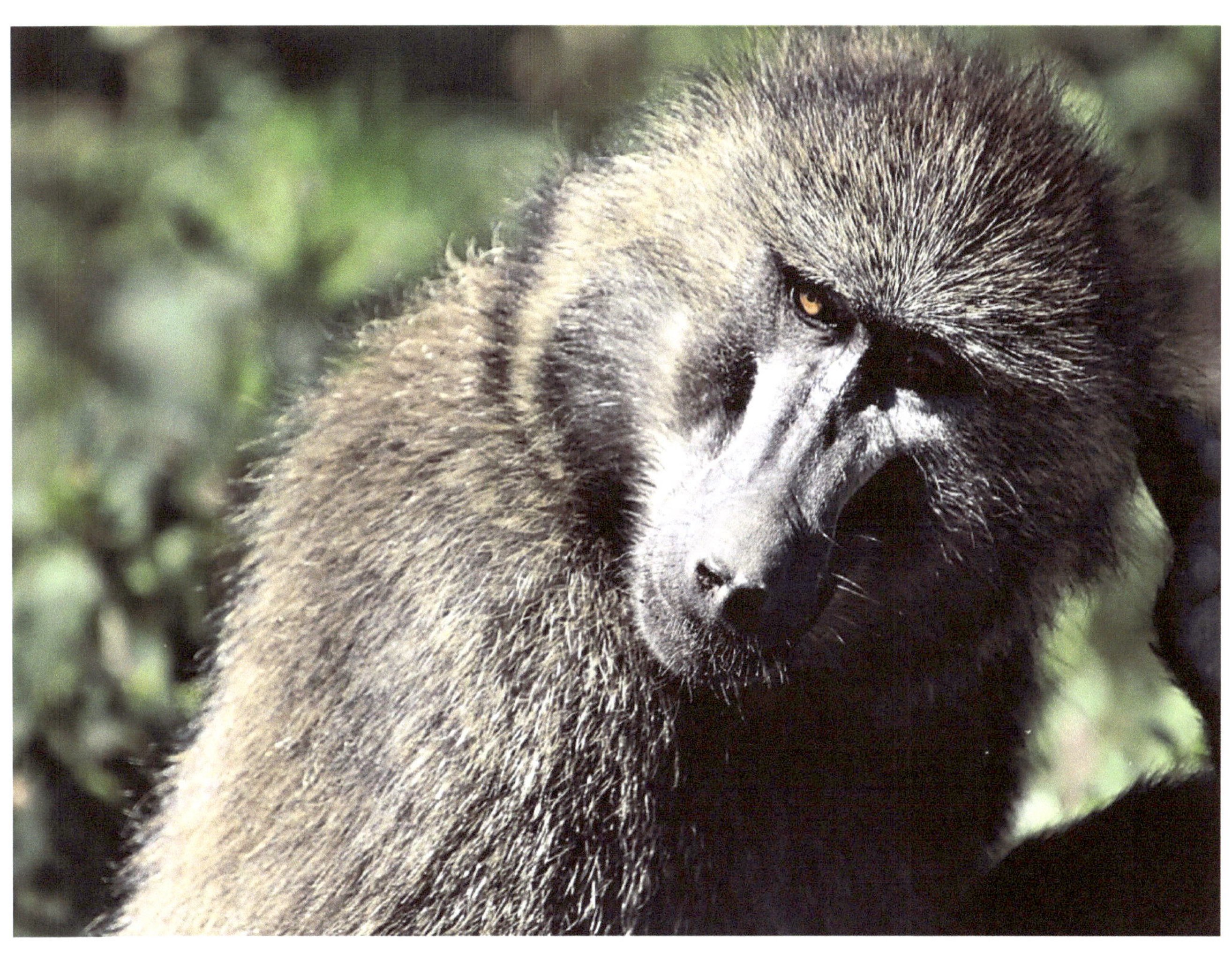

I call this baboon, the "Thinker."

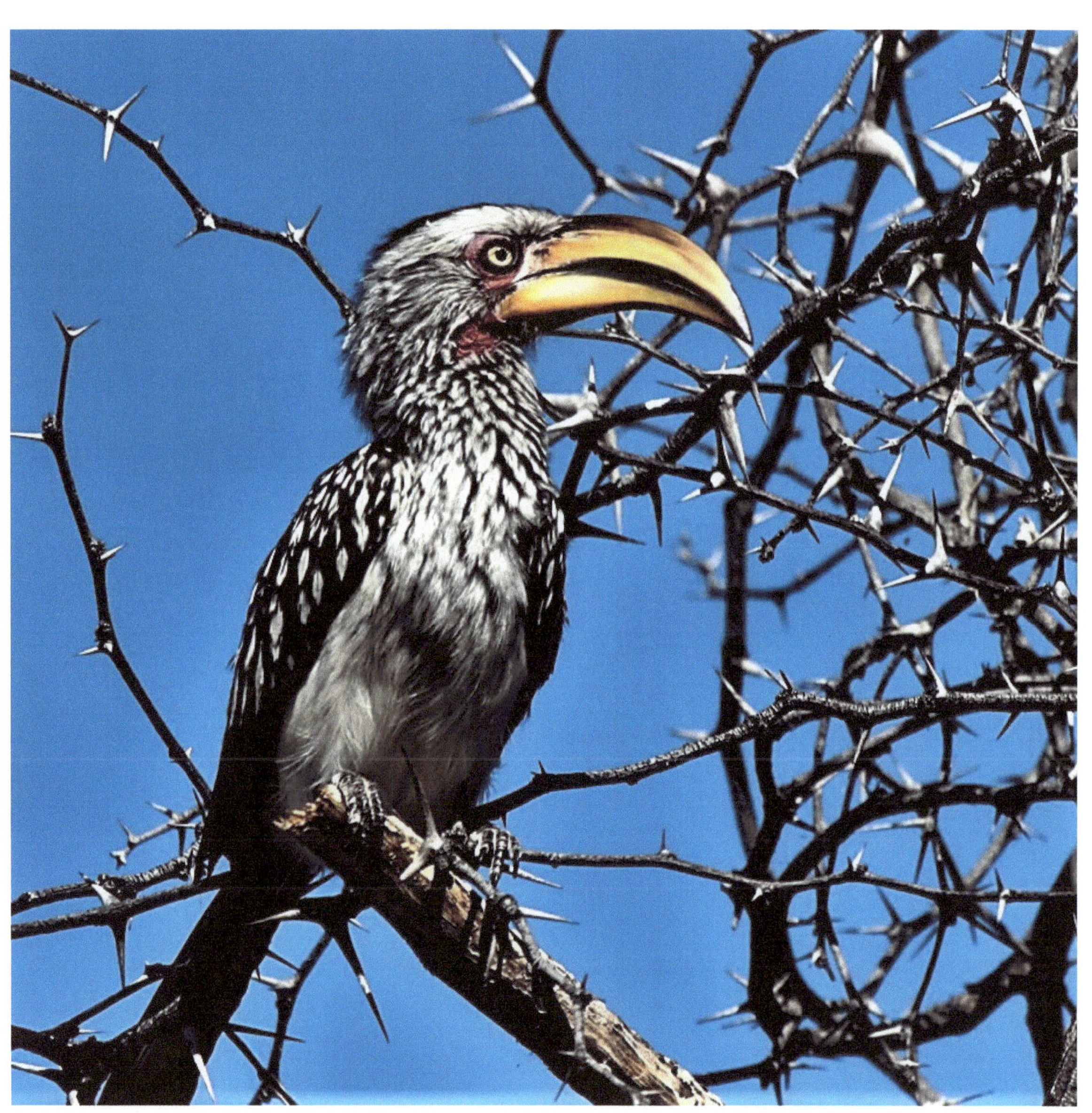

Southern, yellow-billed hornbill is also known as the banana bird.

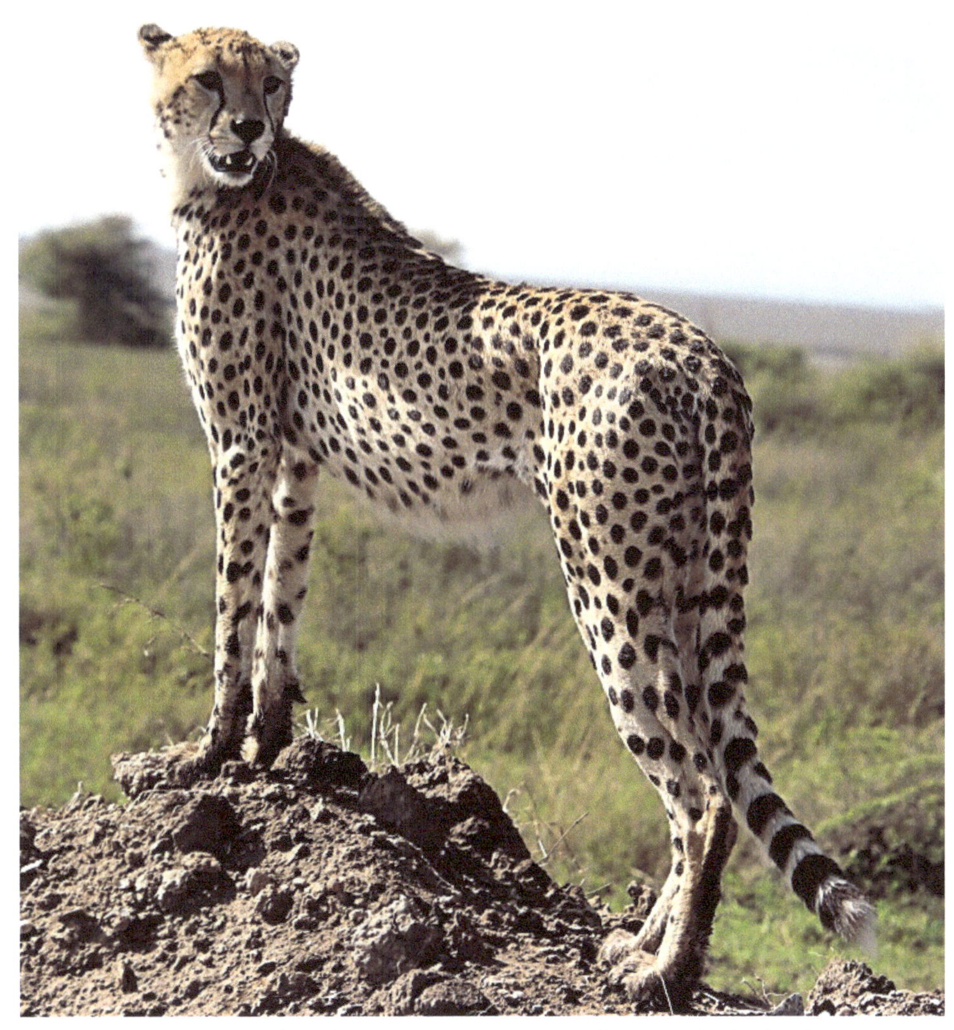

Cheetah posing on a termite mound getting a higher-level view

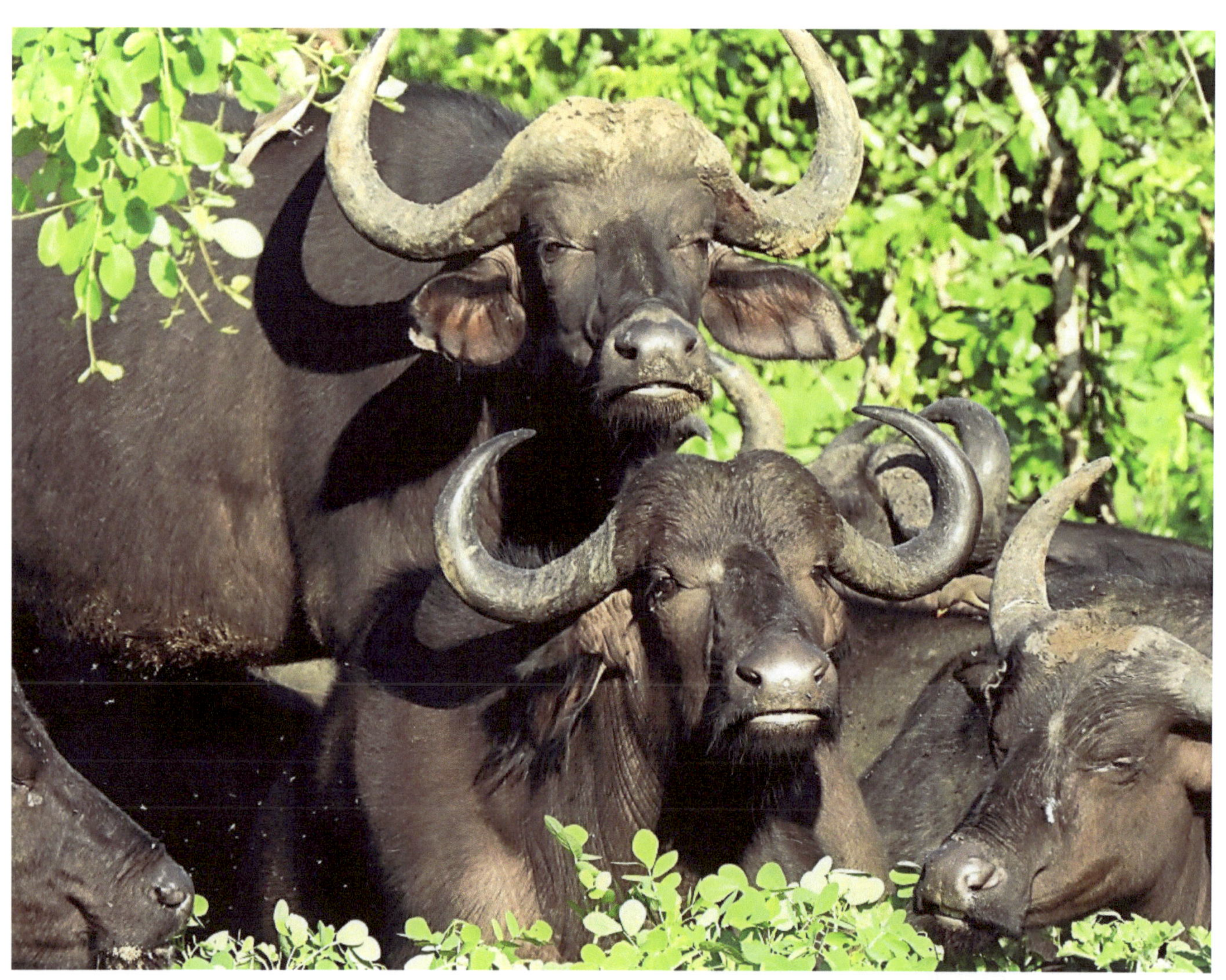

African Cape buffalo are massive with large, curved horns. They travel in herds and are both intelligent and dangerous.

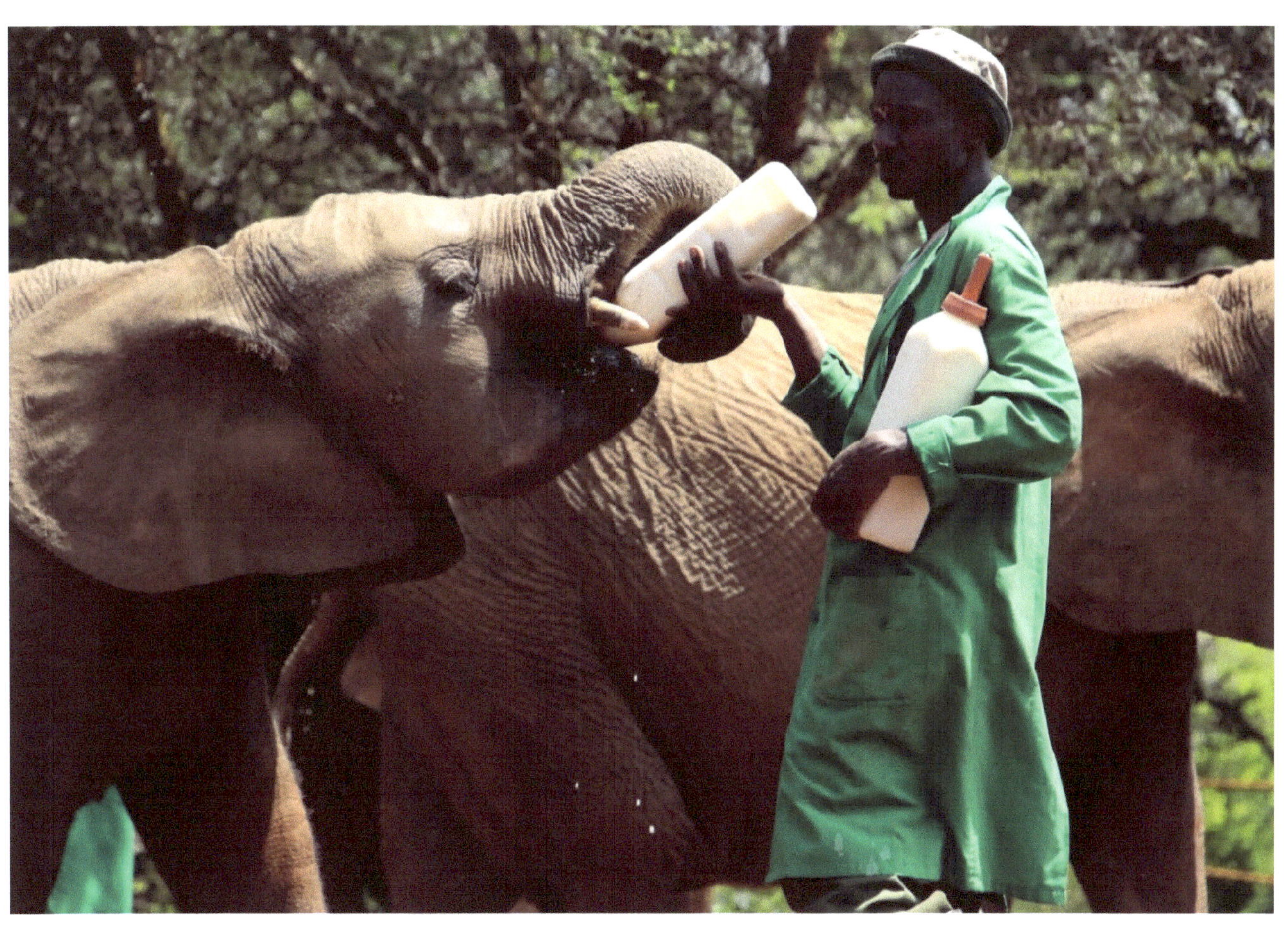

One of my favorite places, feeding time at Sheldrick Wildlife Trust in Nairobi, Kenya

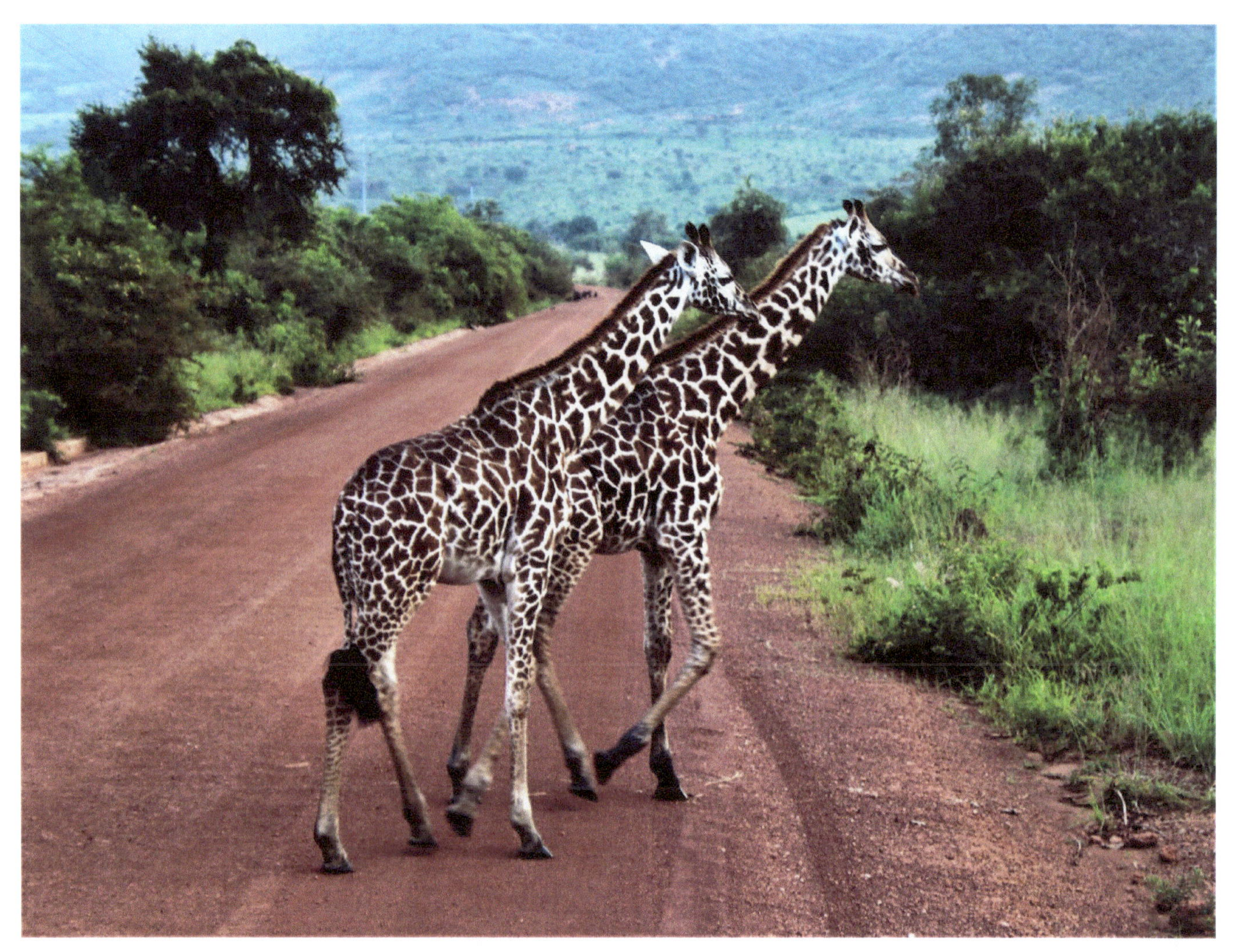

Two giraffes cross the road in Rwanda

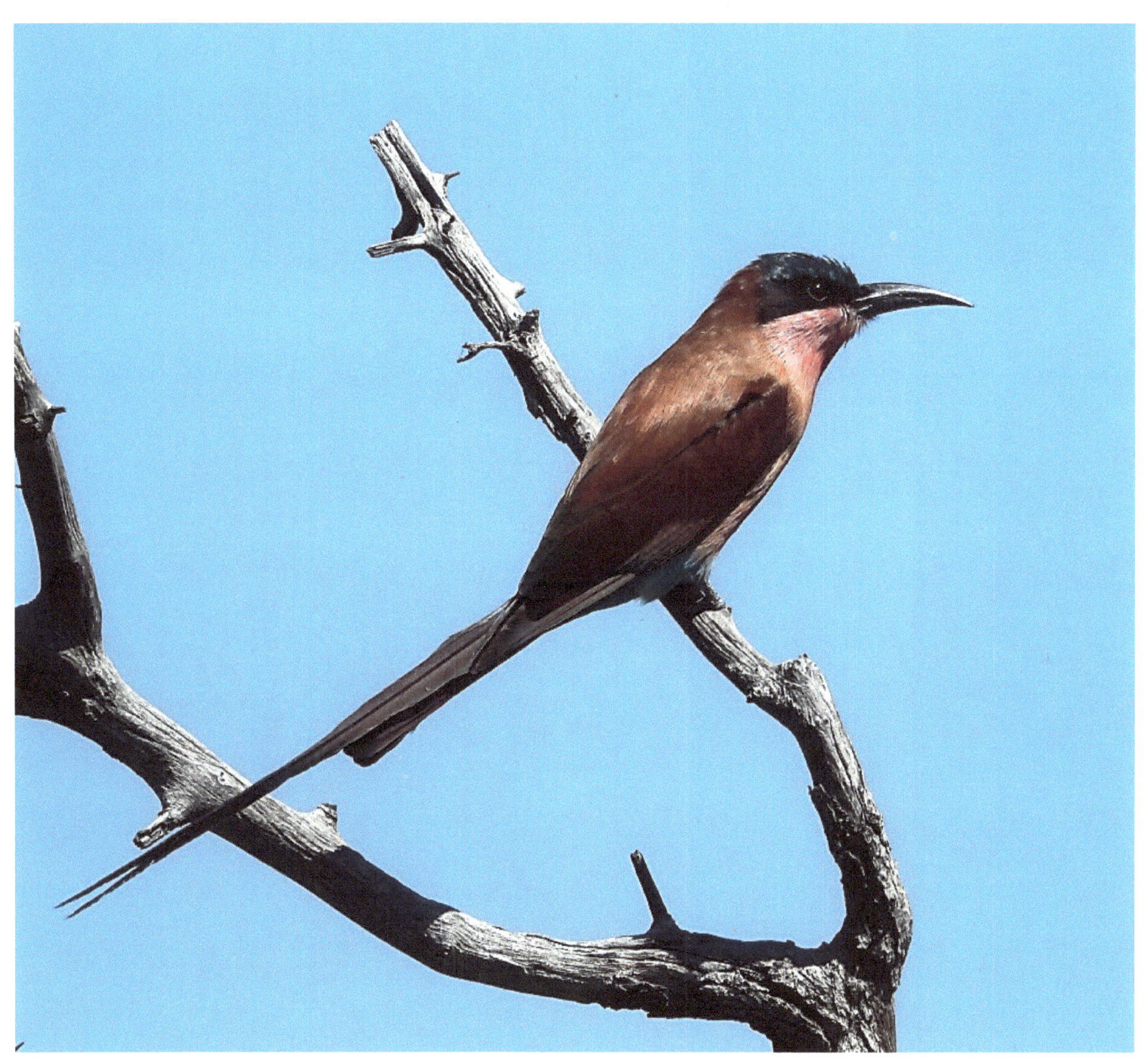

Southern carmine bee-eater. Their excellent acrobatic flying skills enable them to snatch insects.

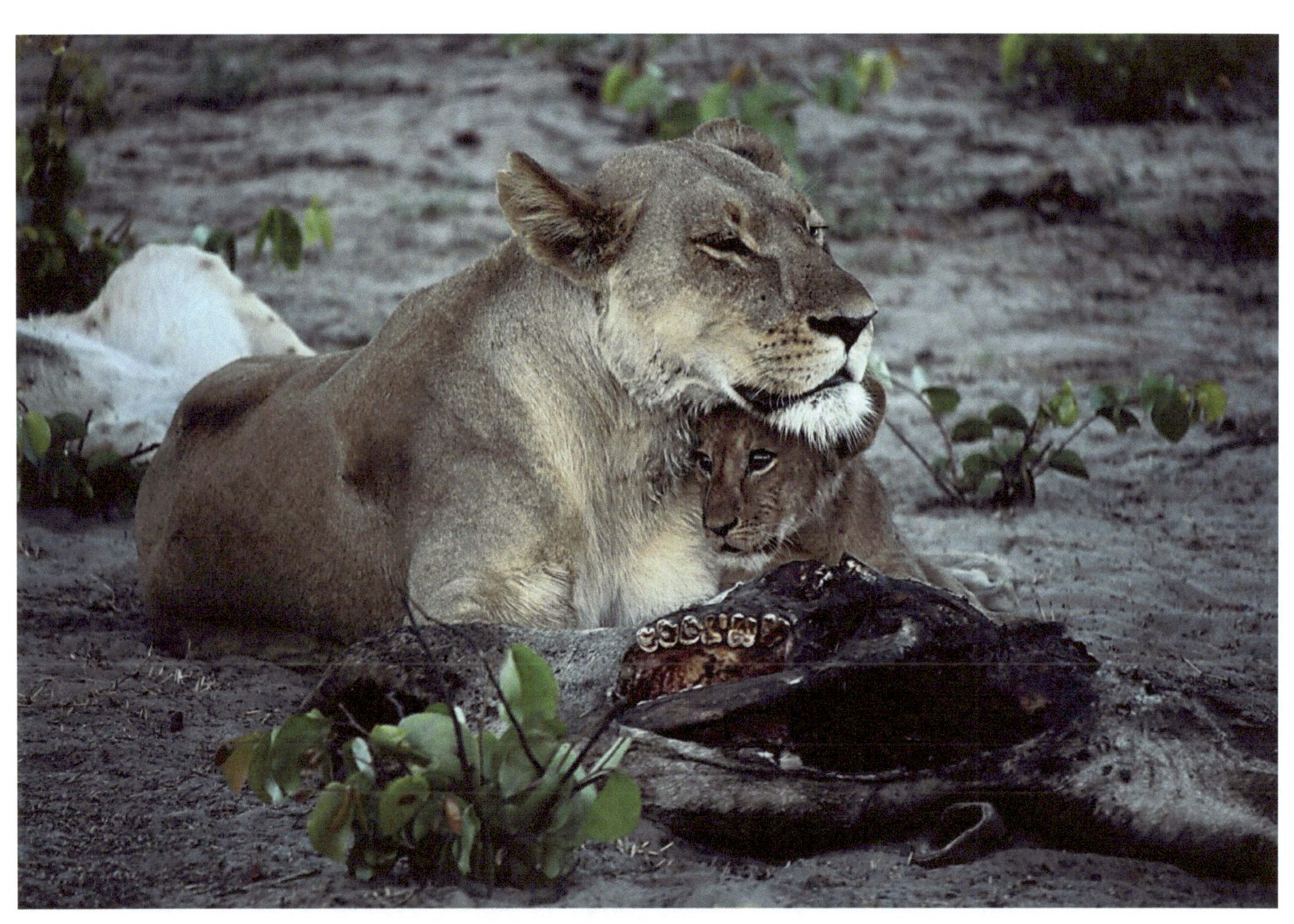

Mother lion and cub after filling their bellies with a giraffe the pride killed

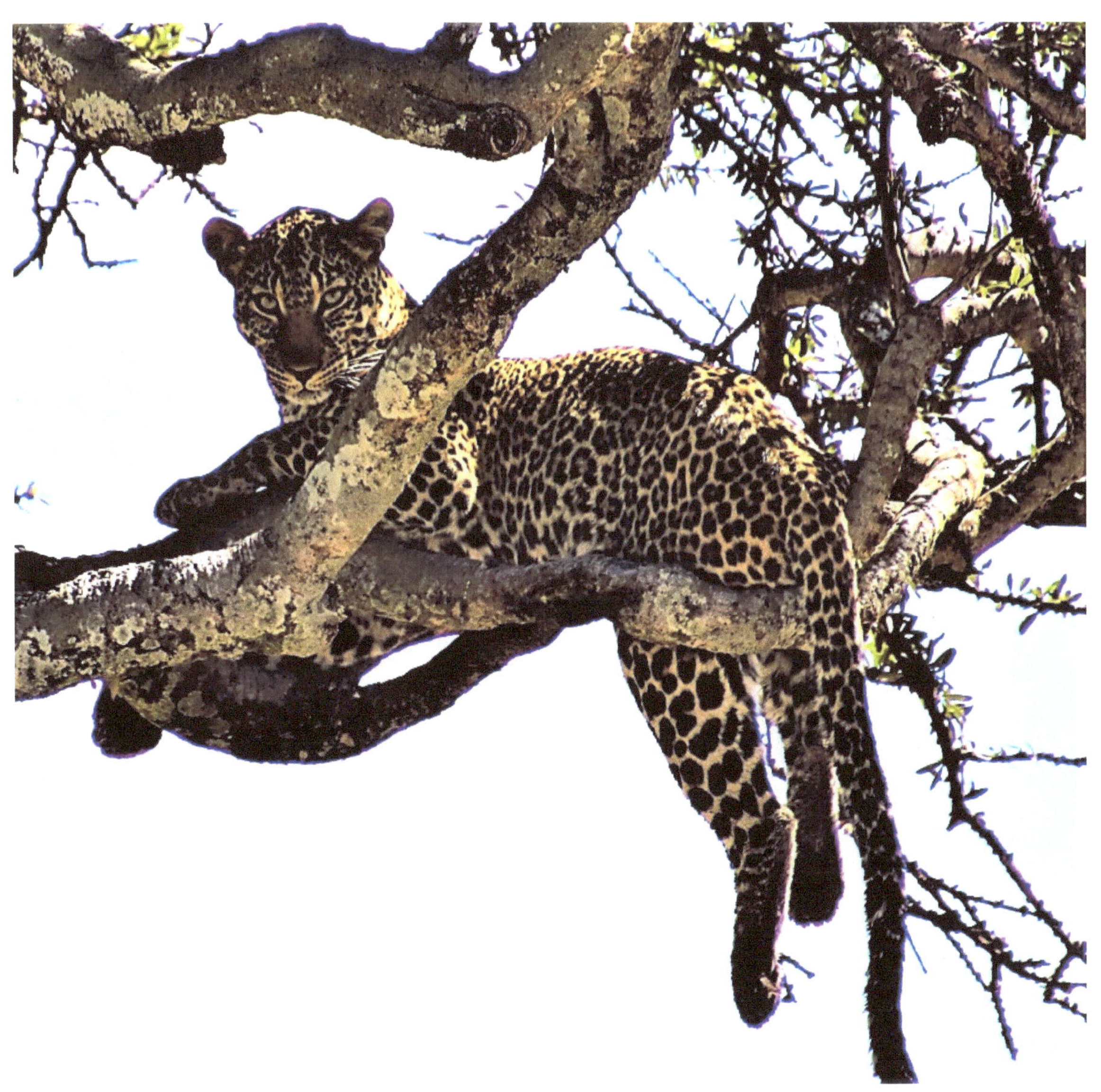

Leopard relaxing high up in a tree wondering why we are taking his photo

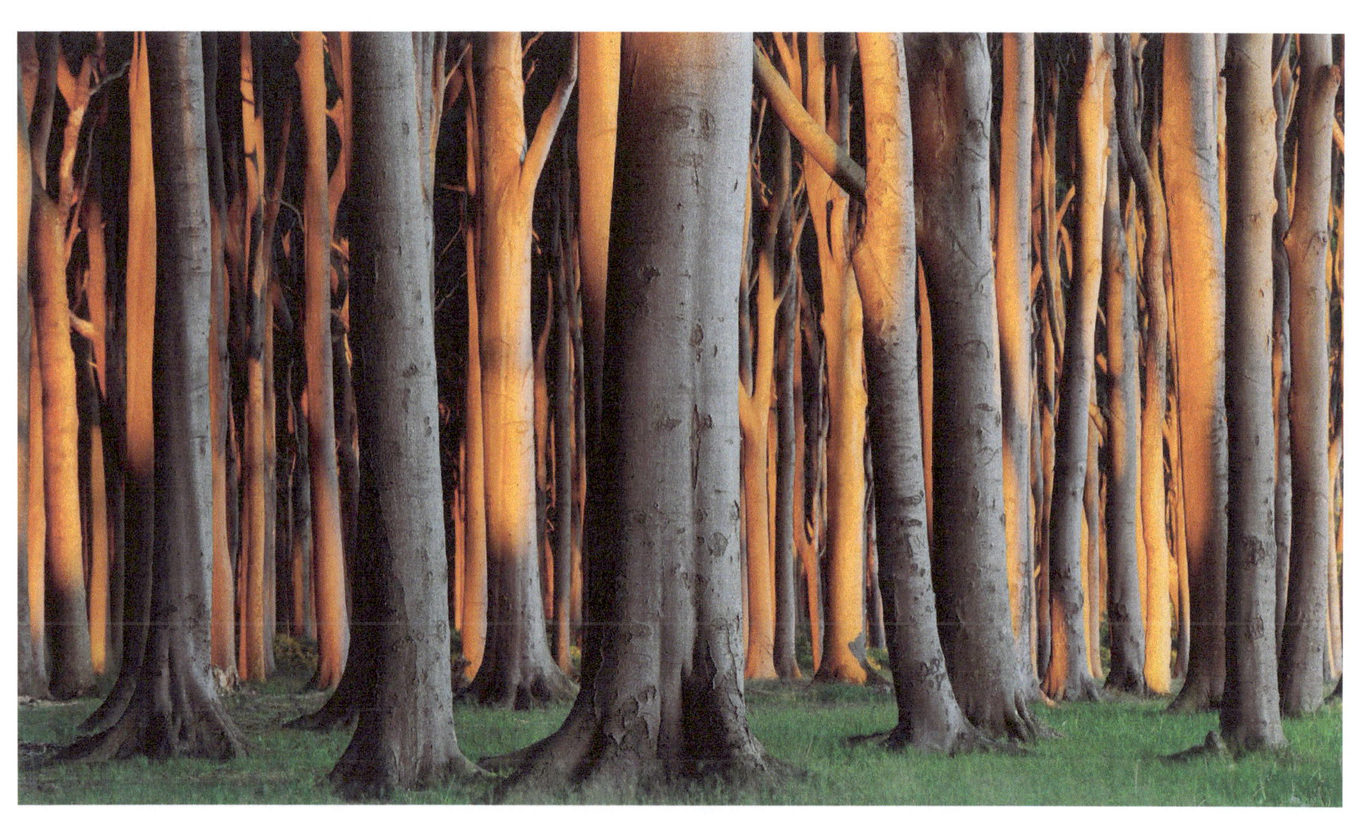

The sun lighting up the forest with vibrant yellow and orange colors

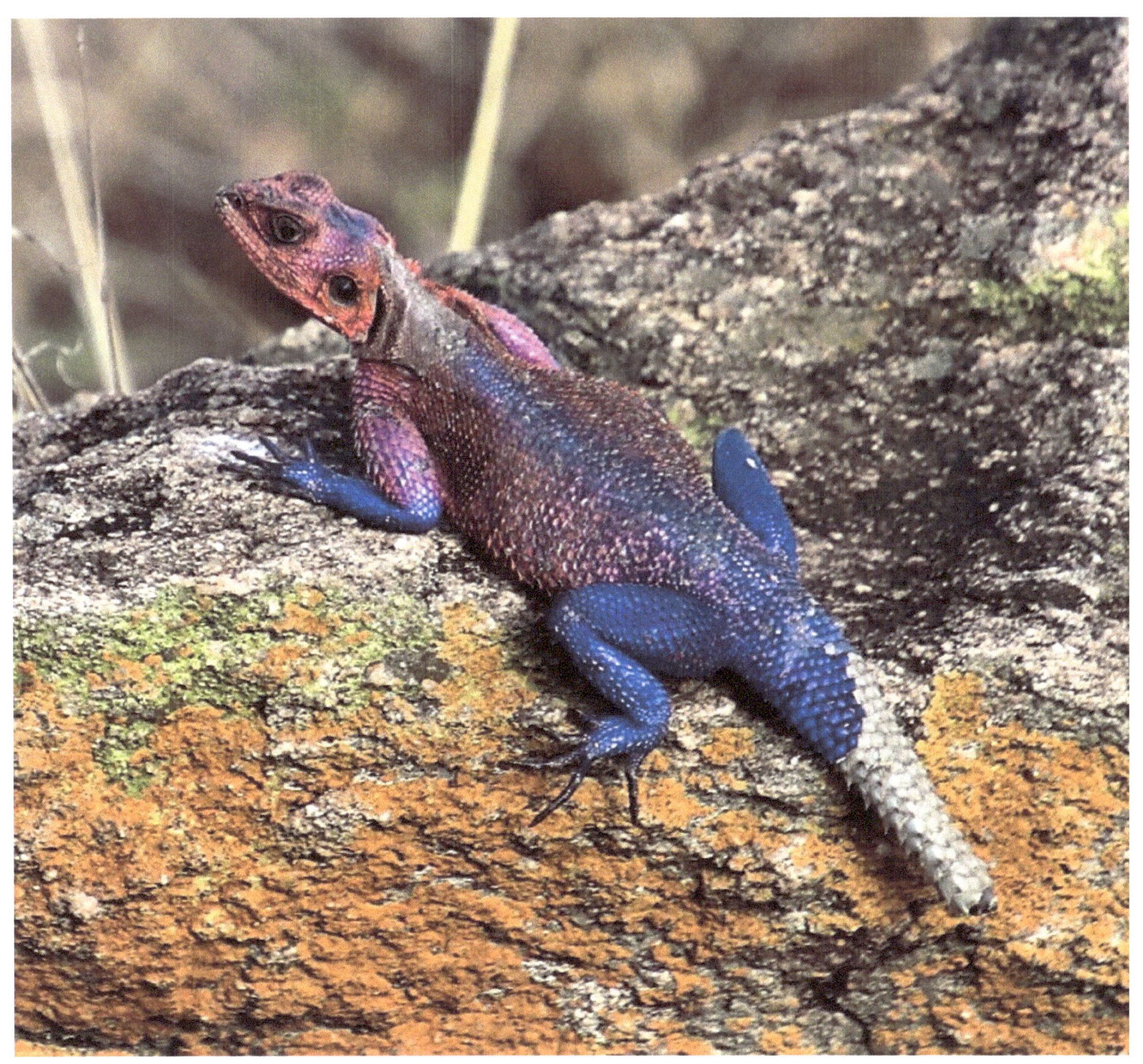

This poor agamas lizard lost part of its tail.

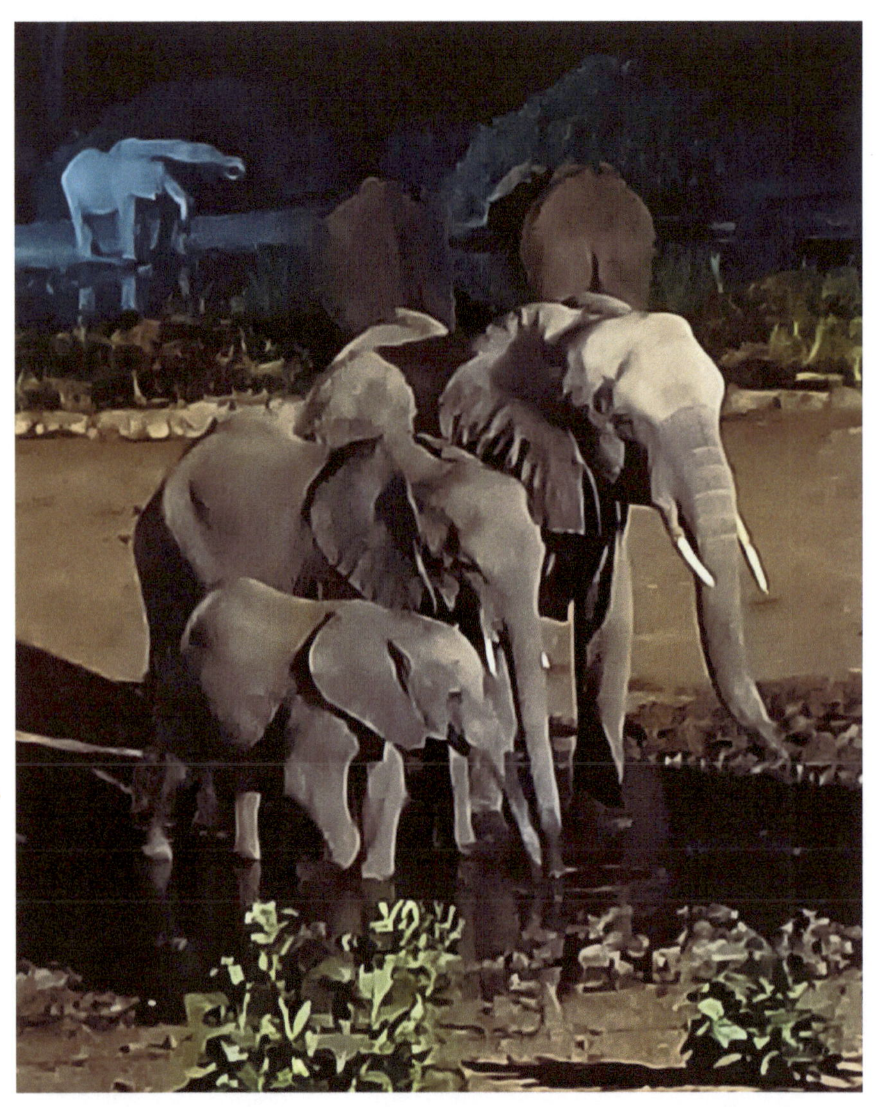

Elephants gather for a nourishing drink at the Elephant Valley Lodge water hole.

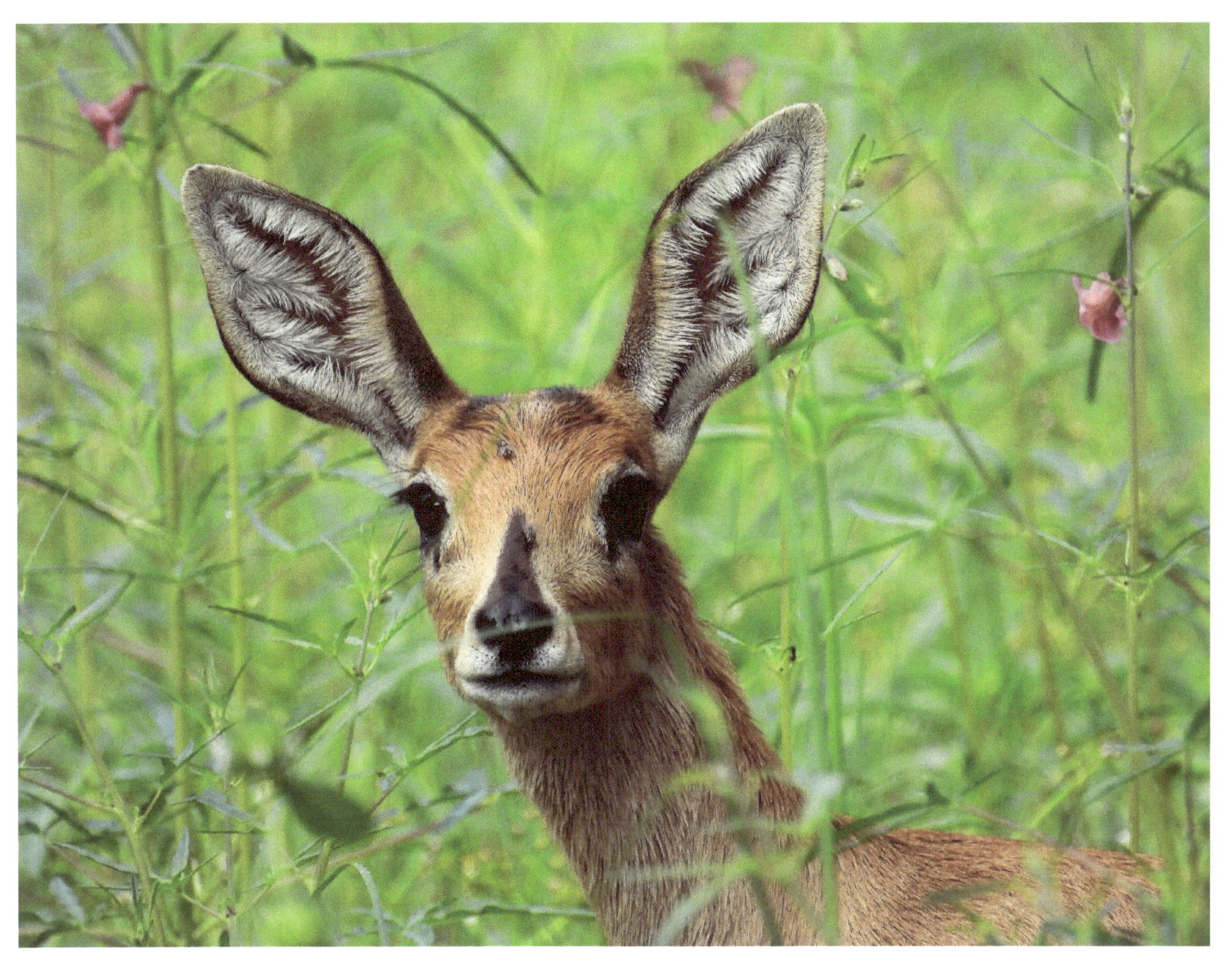

Young female oribi antelope posing for my Nikon

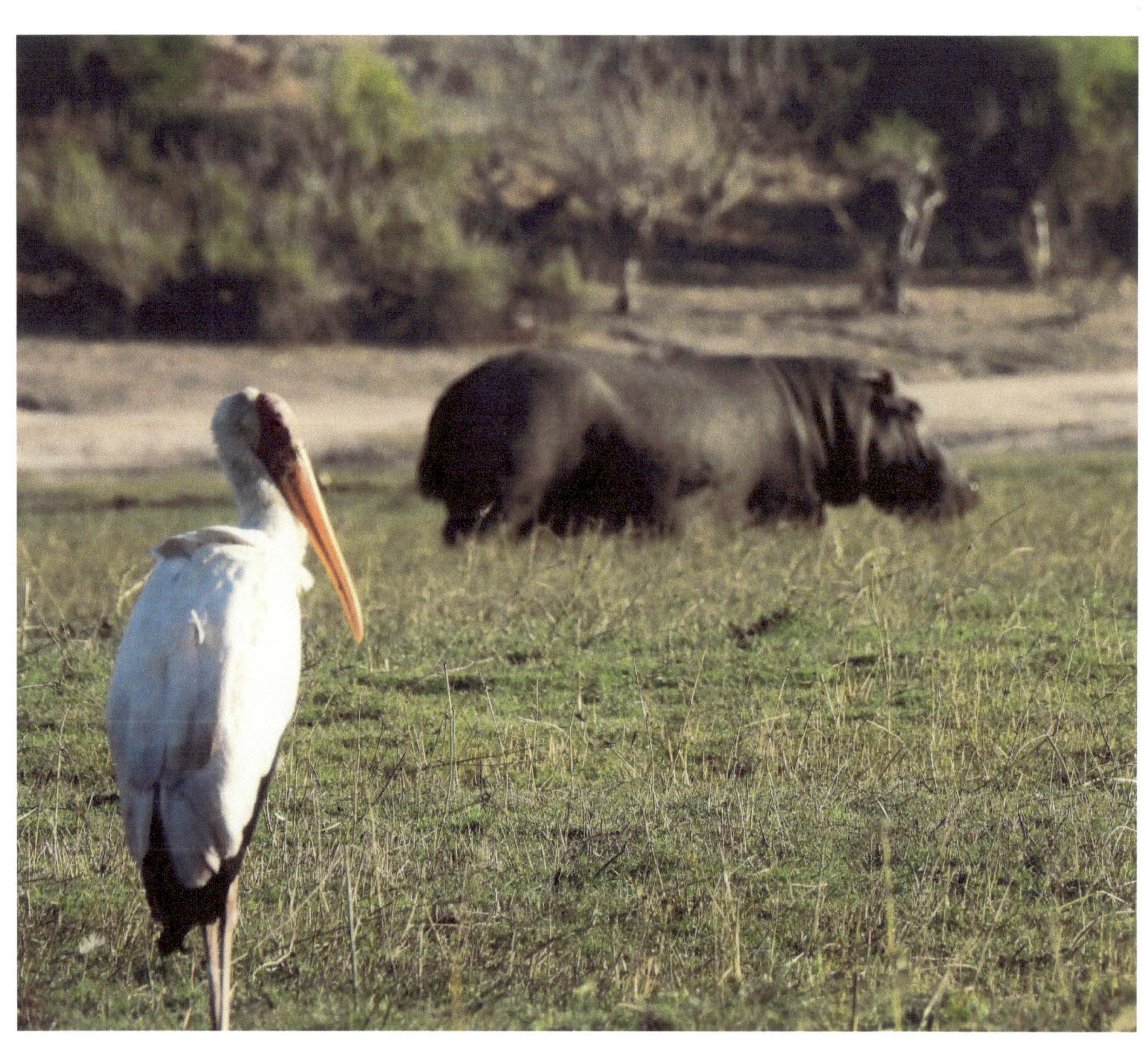

Yellow billed stork and a hippo on the move

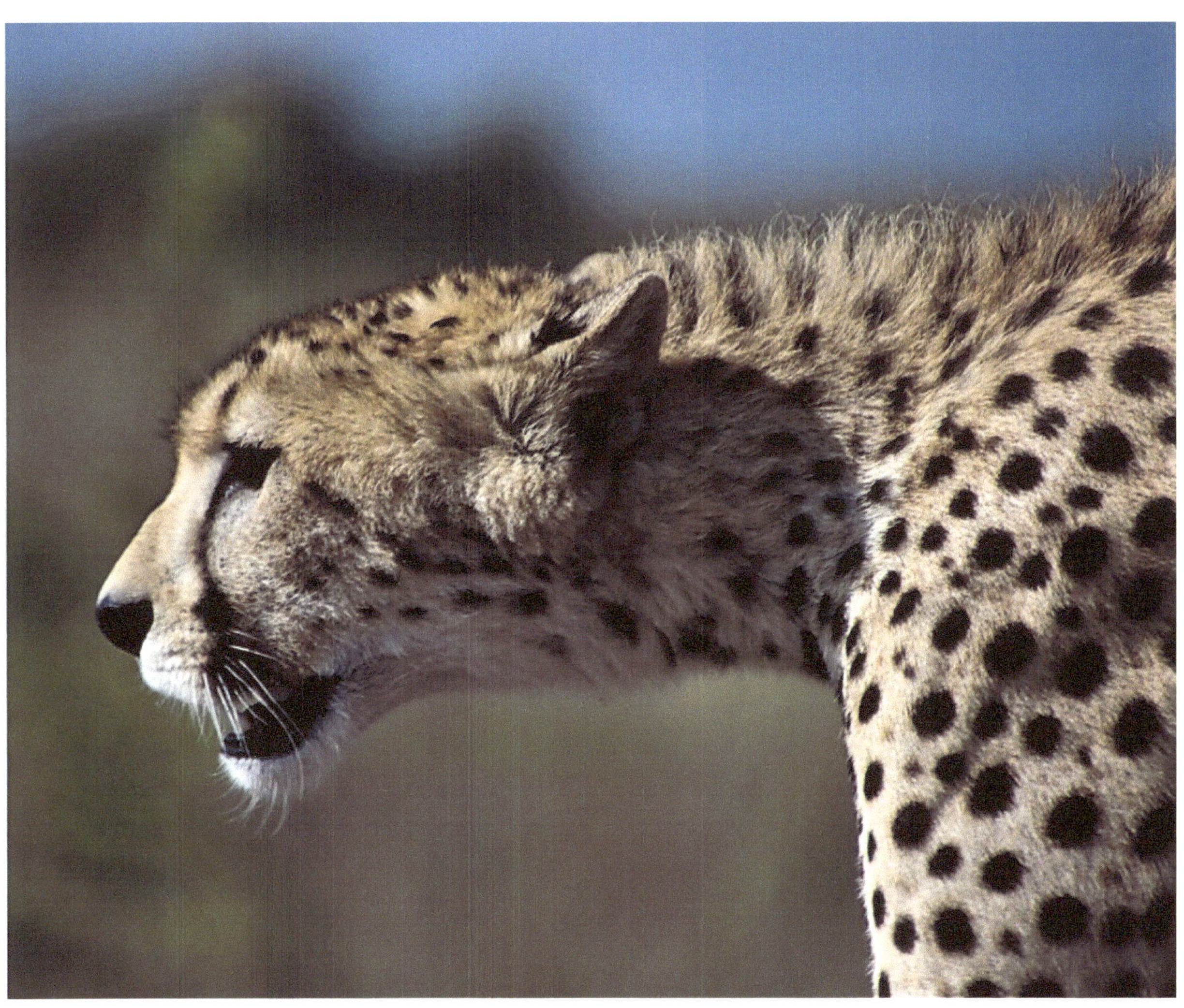

A hungry cheetah stalking prey

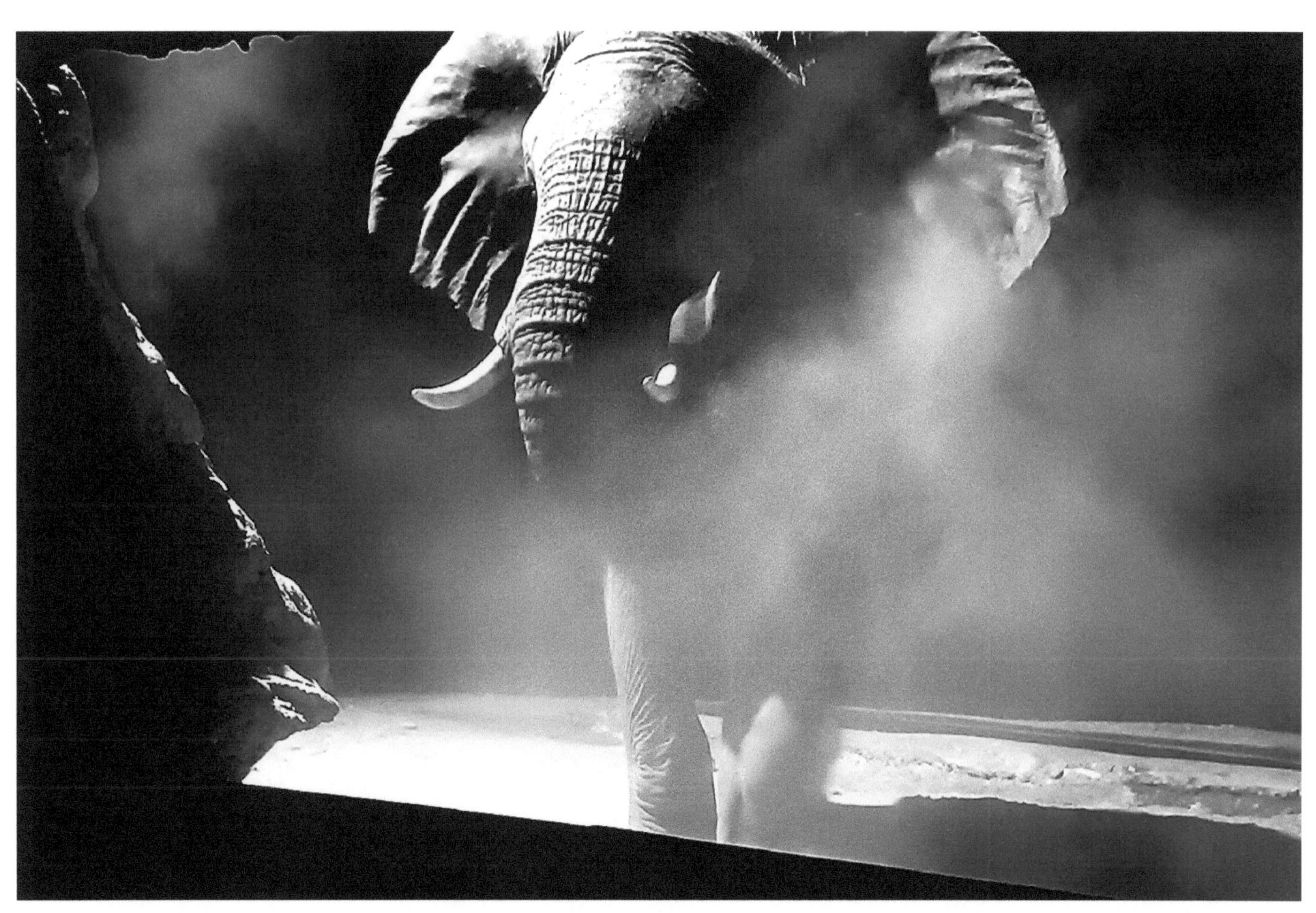

Nighttime at the water hole, one big bull creates a dust storm.

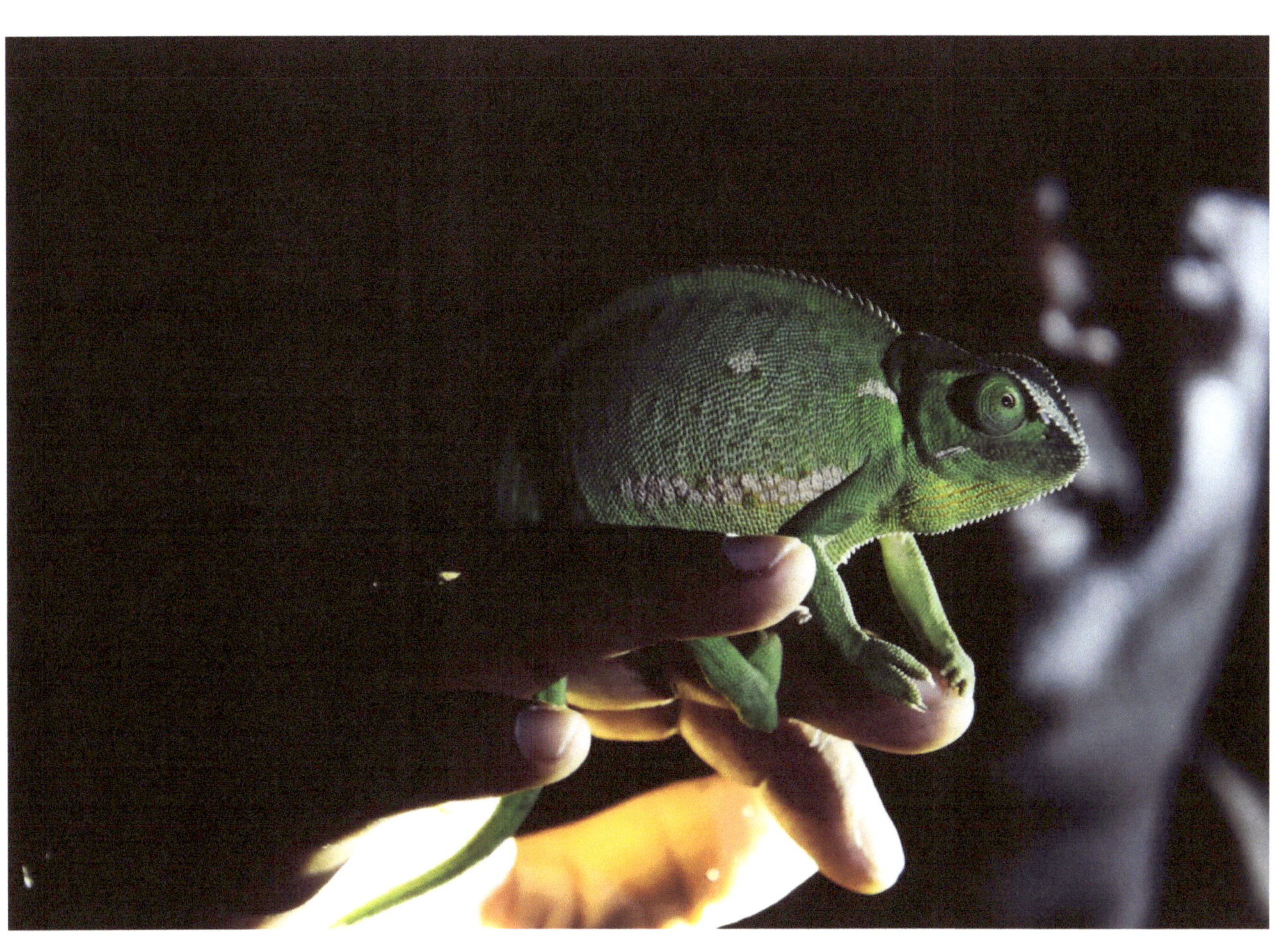

Our guide spotted this flap-necked chameleon on the road. Glad we didn't run over him.

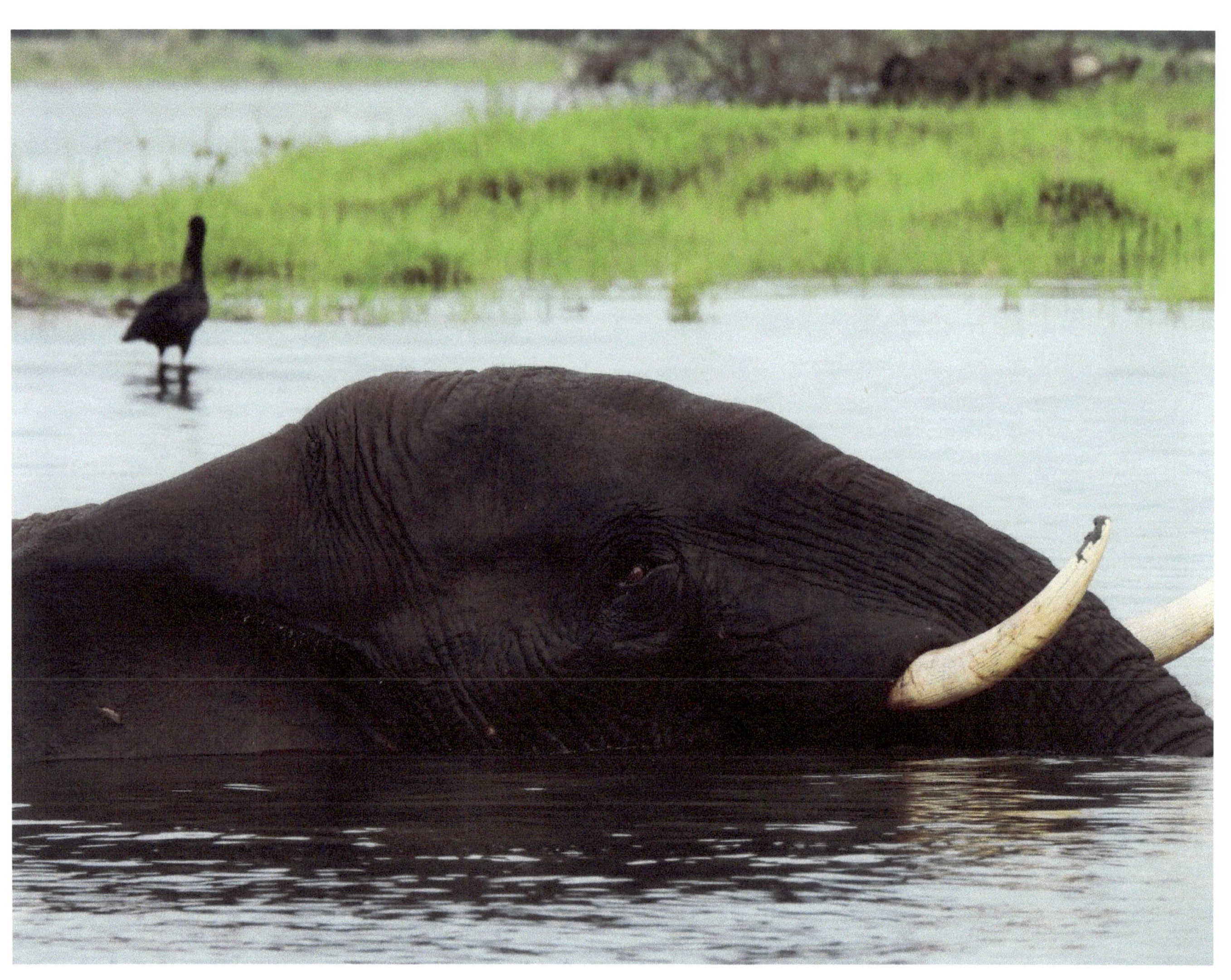

Elephants love water and are excellent swimmers.

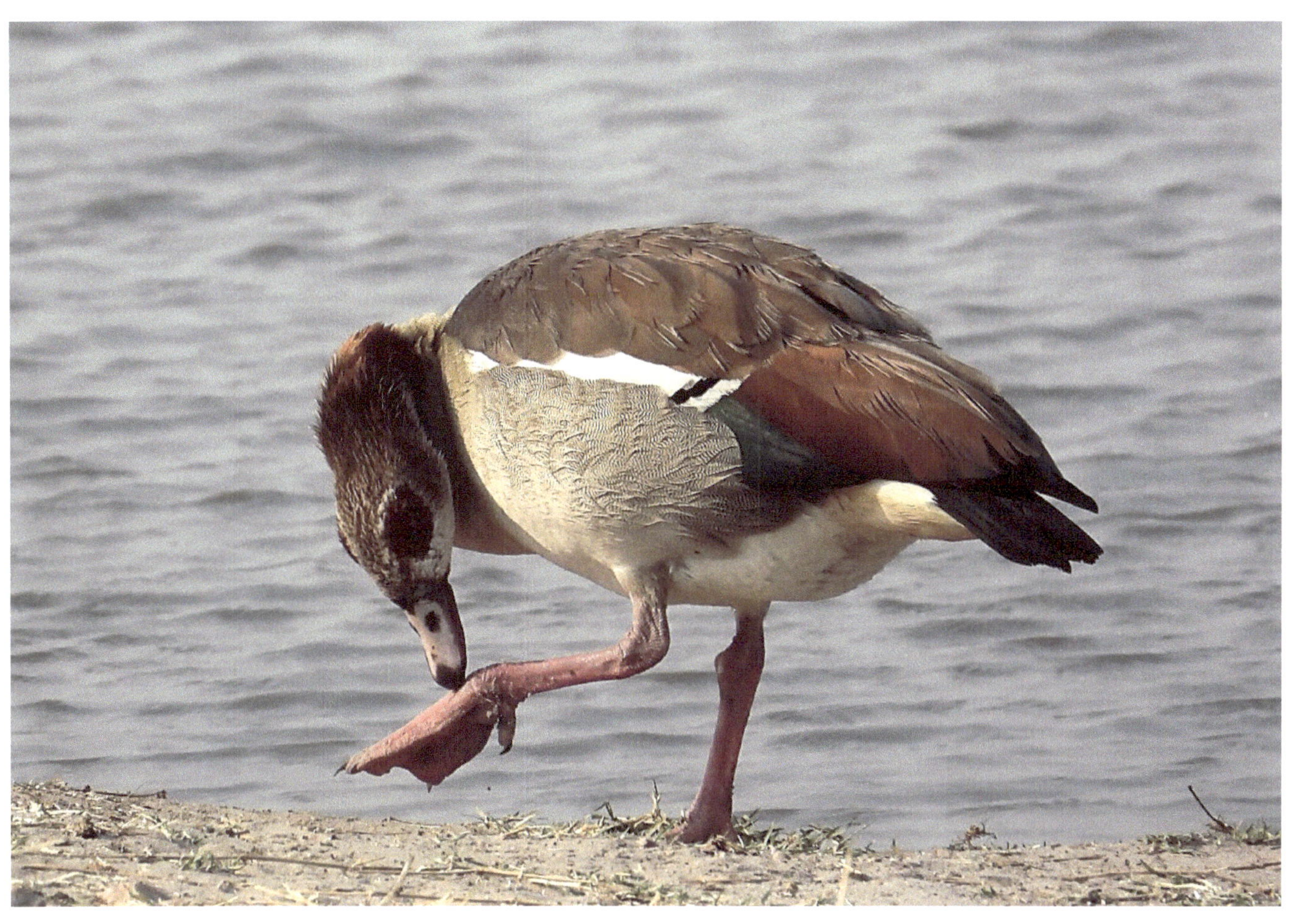

This Egyptian goose was checking out his webbed foot.

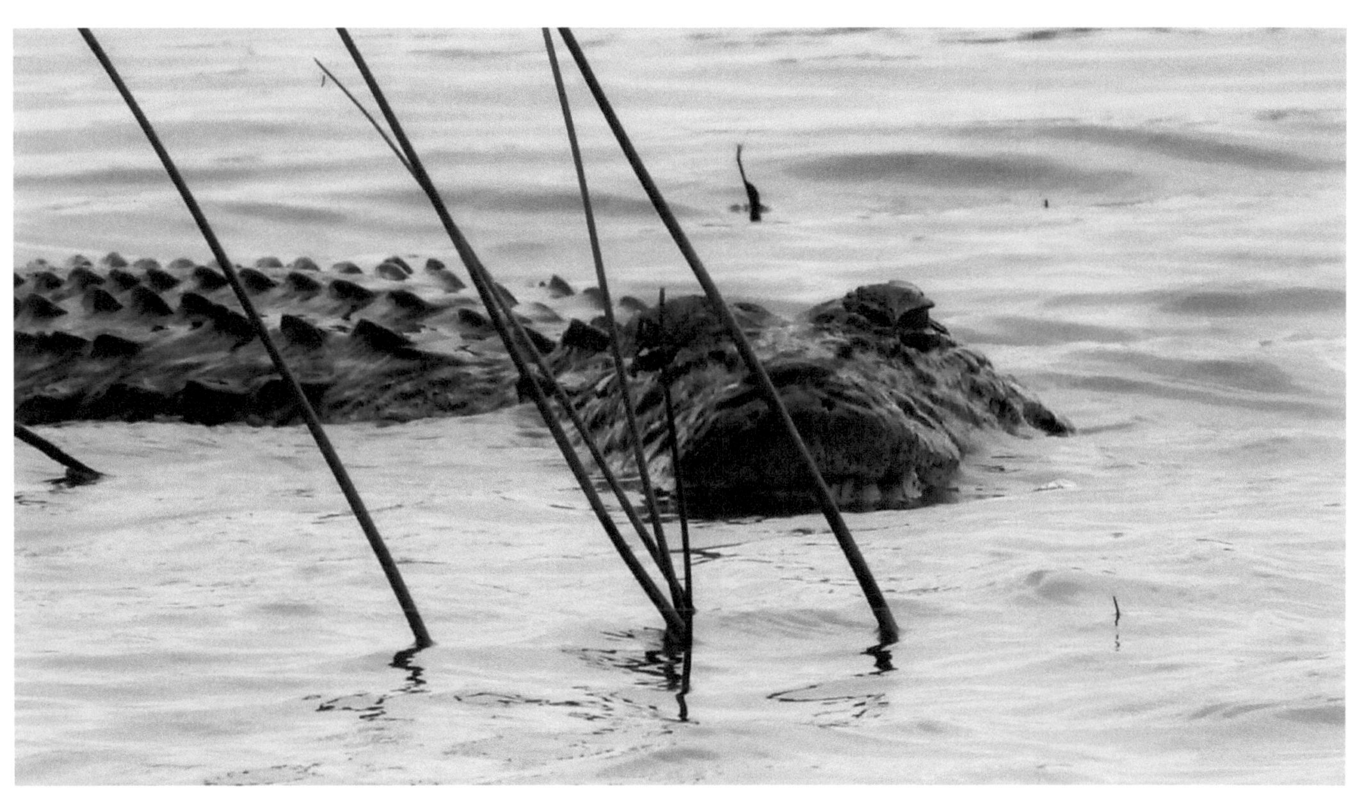

Never get this close to a Nile crocodile.

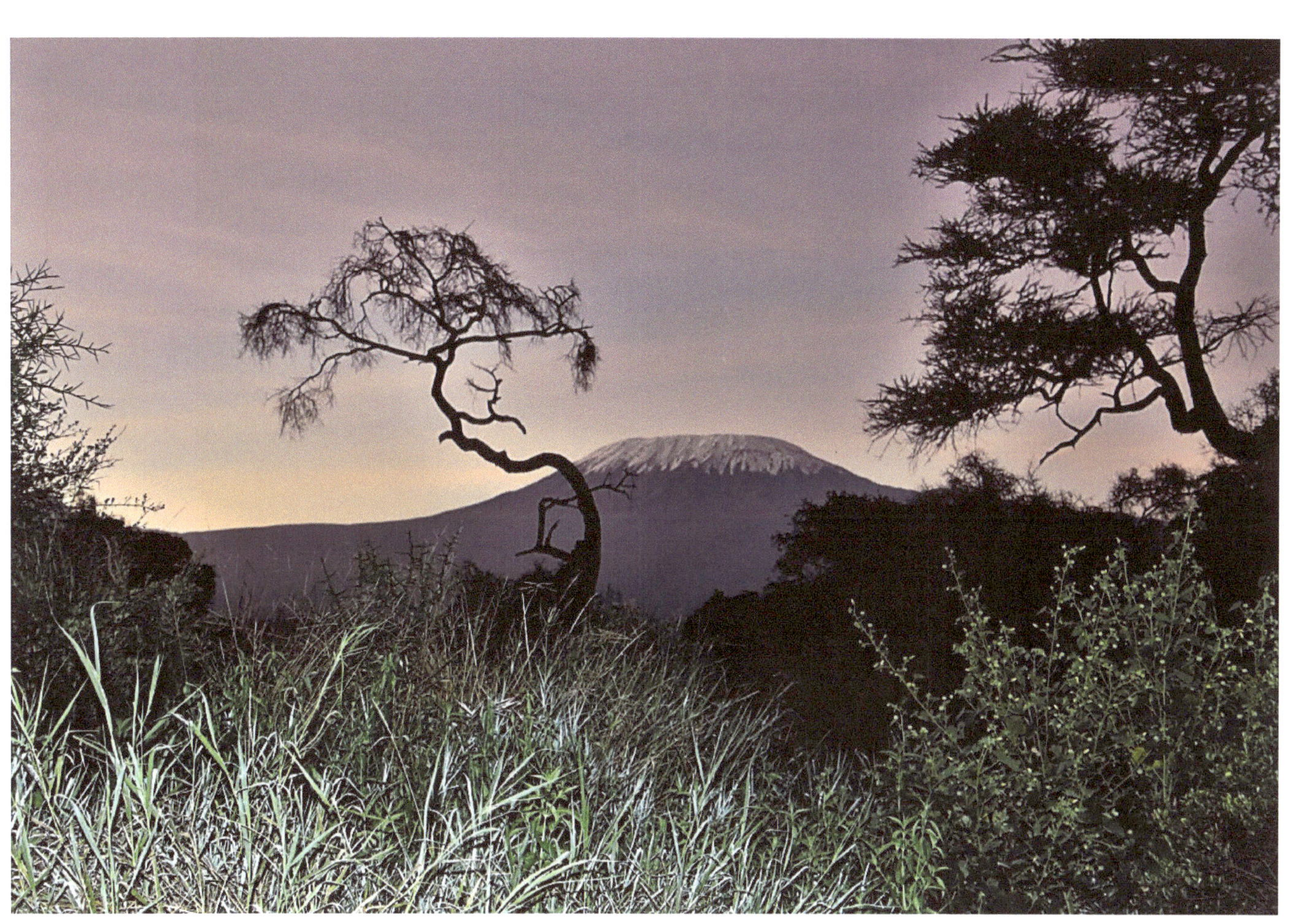

An evening view of the snows of Kilimanjaro

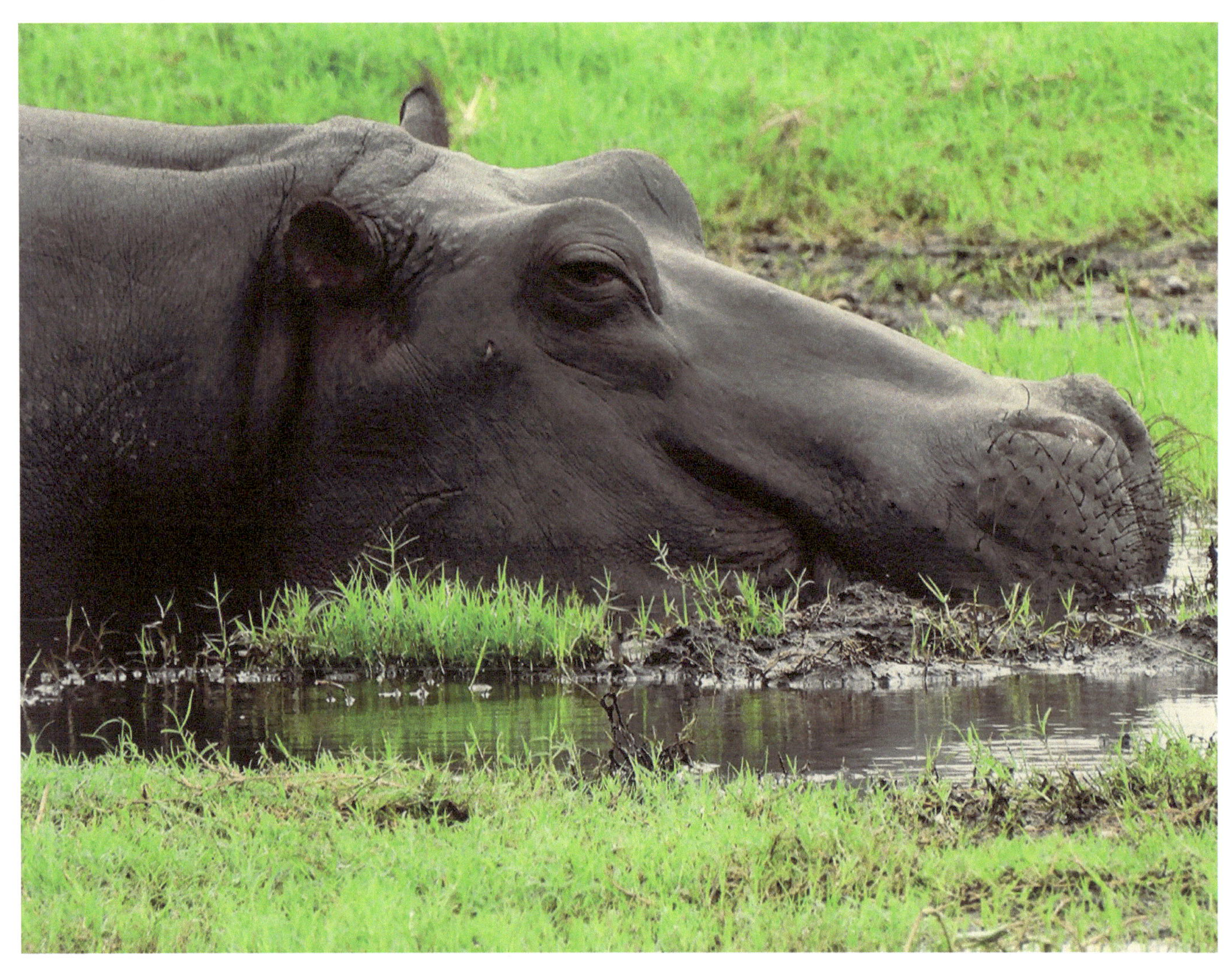

This hippo did not want to be disturbed.

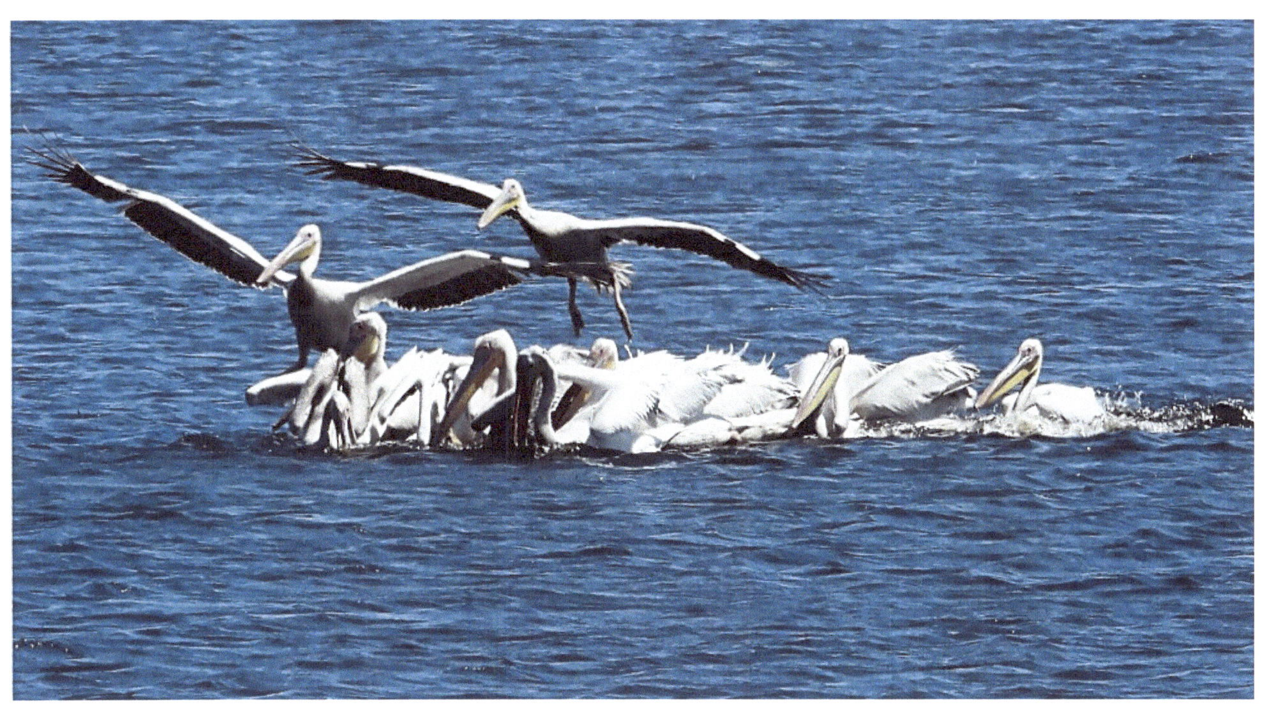

Great white pelicans gather in the shallow water of the Zambezi River in Zambia

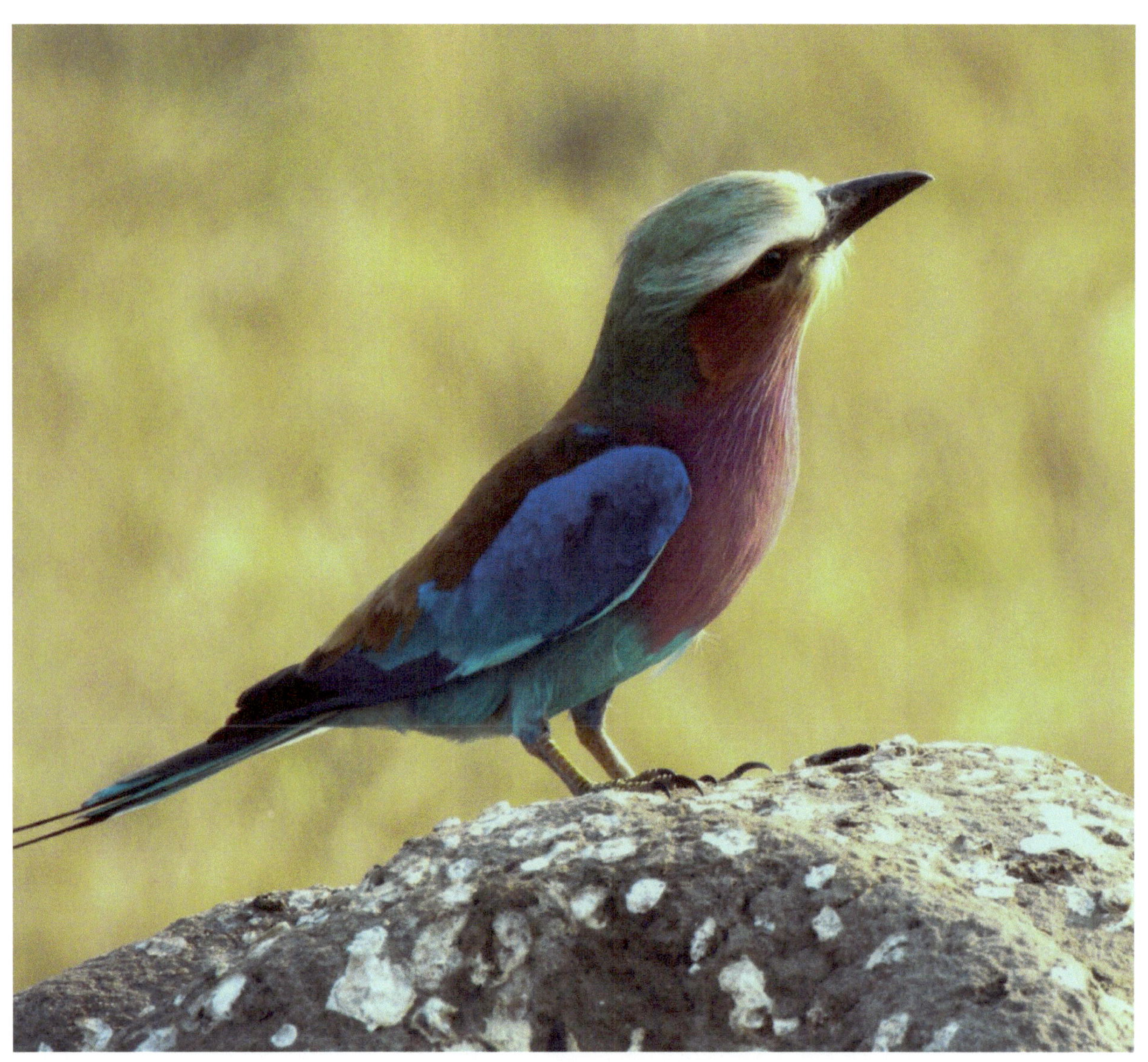

The lilac breasted roller, one of the most beautiful birds of Africa

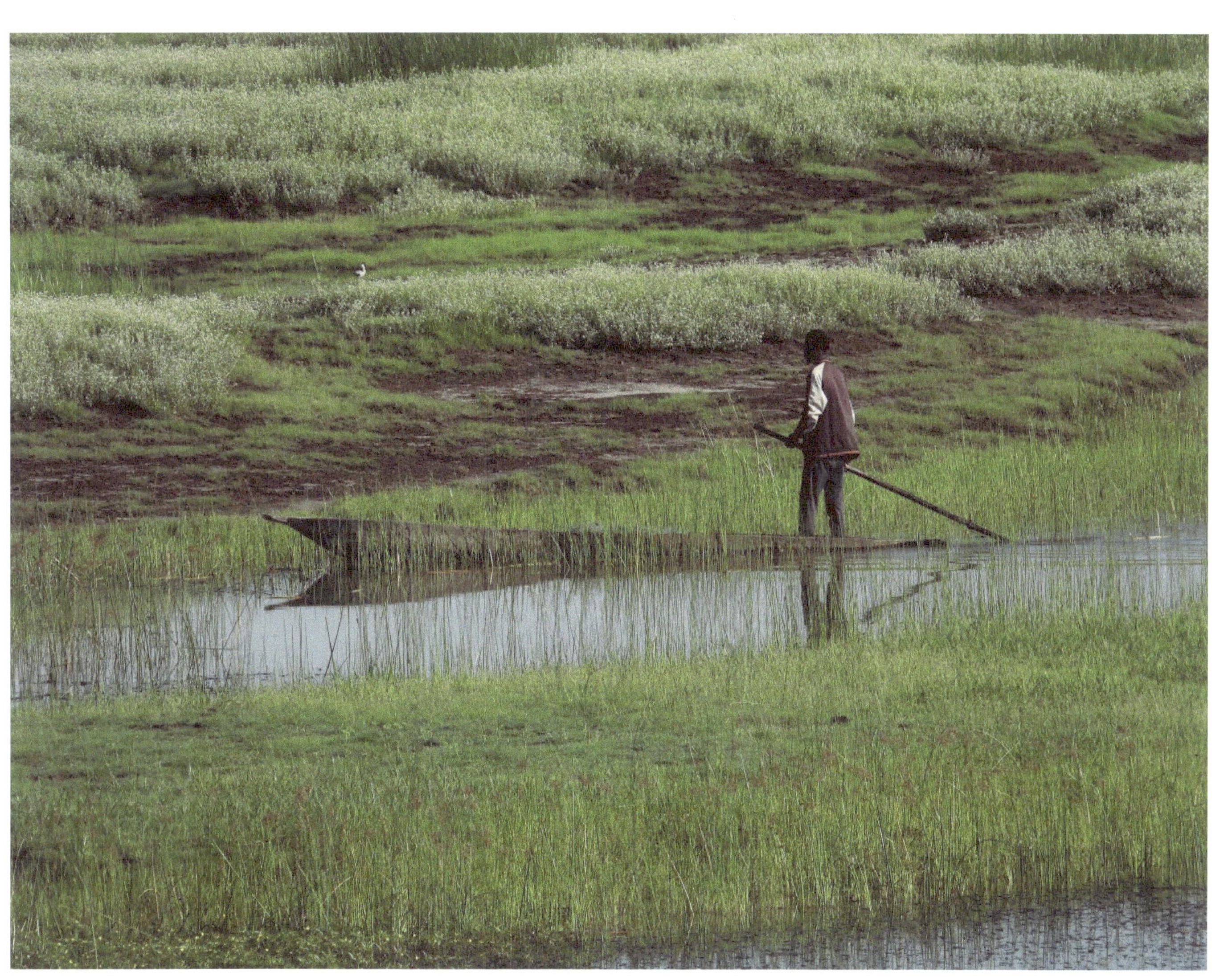

A lone fisherman hoping to catch dinner and avoid crocodiles and hippos

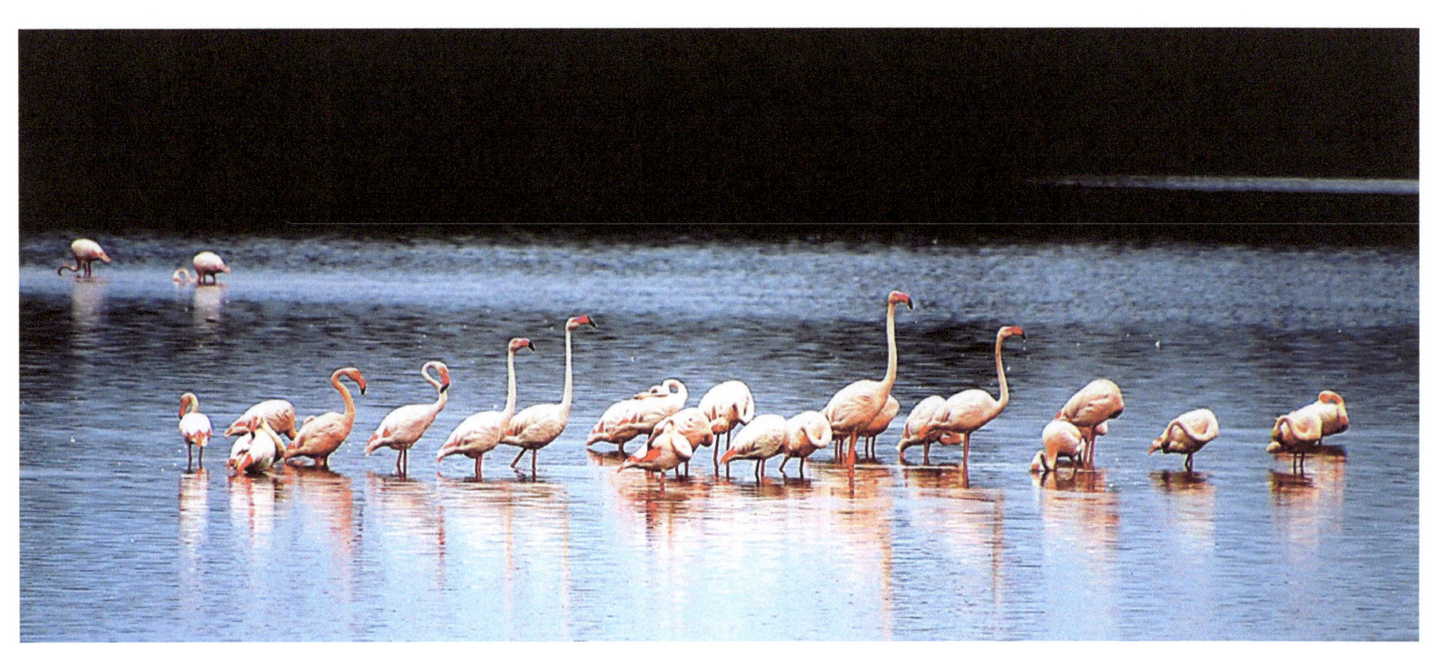

The lesser flamingo is the pinkest of this species. One day I would love to see them perform their distinct mating dance.

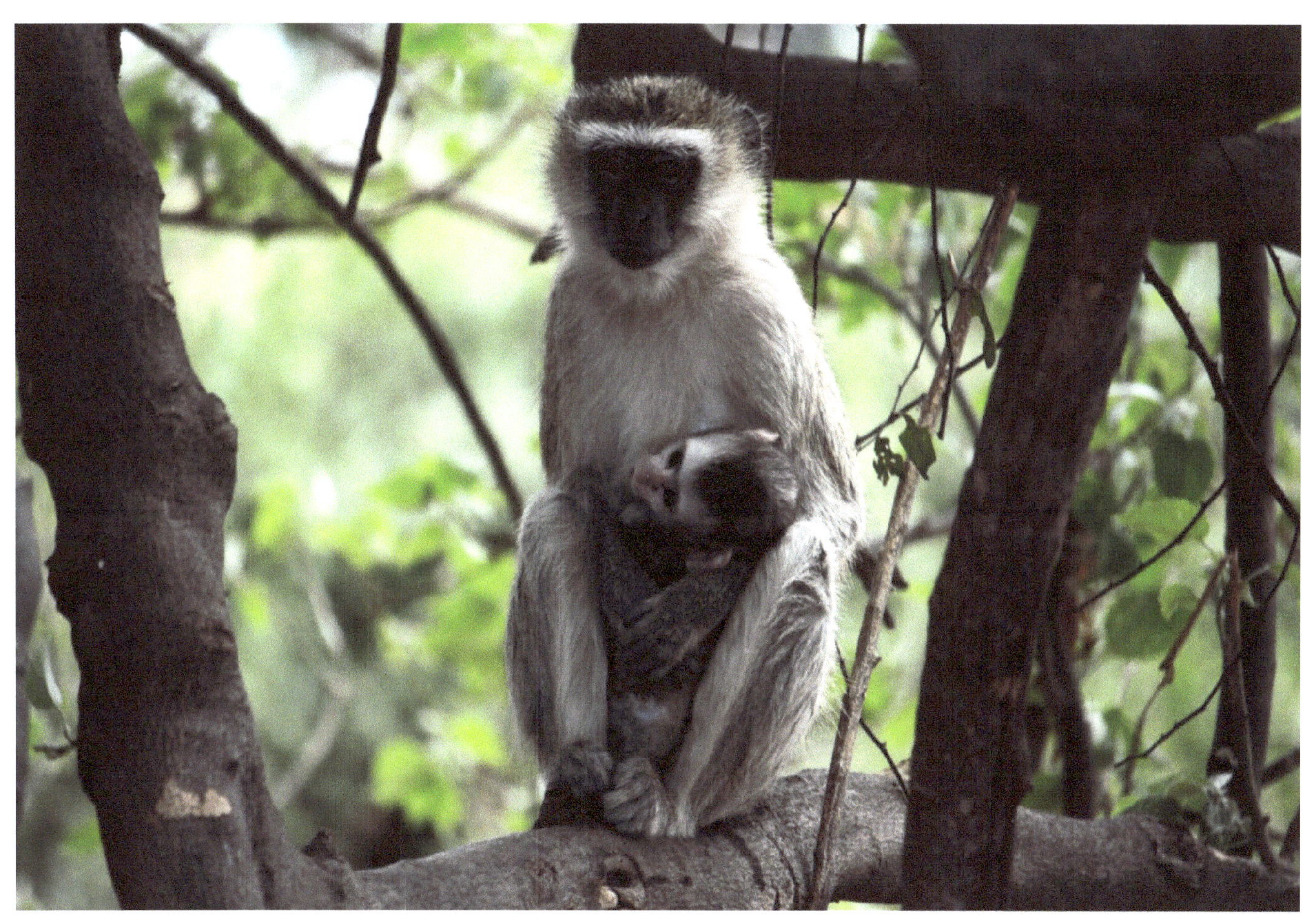

Velvet monkey mother and baby

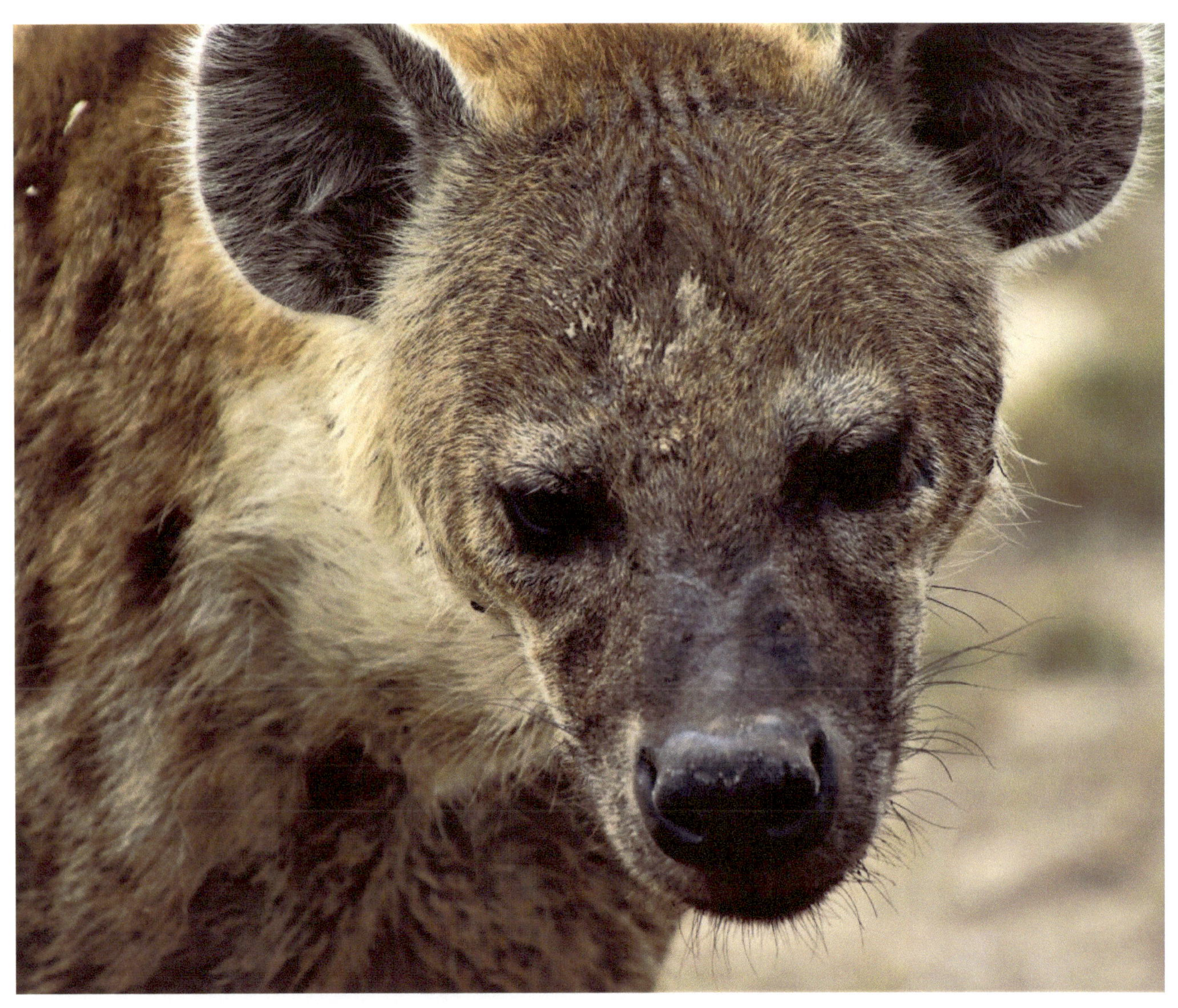

Spotted hyenas seem dog-like to me as they run in packs and a social hierarchy run by the female.

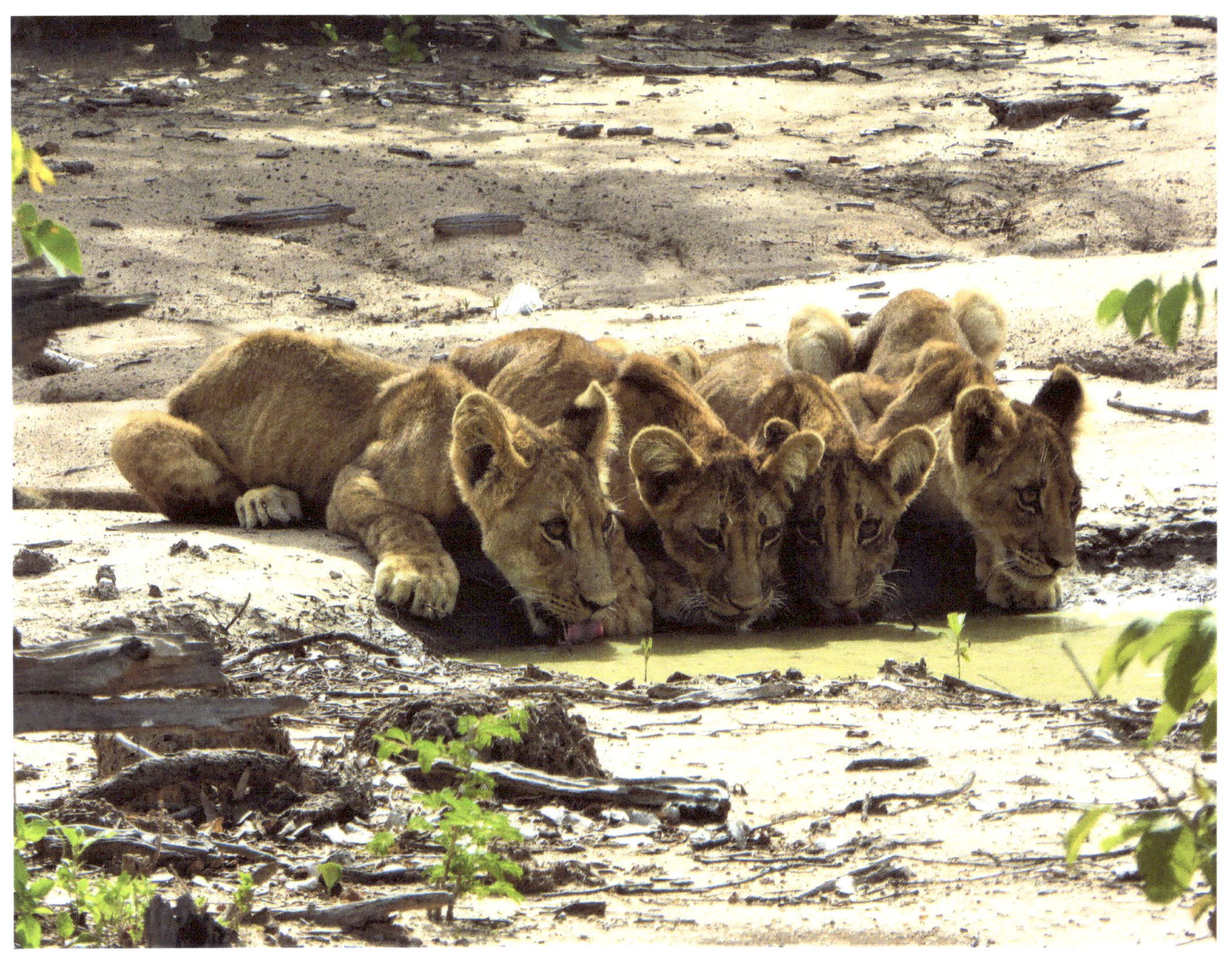

Lion cubs quenching their thirst on a hot and sunny day

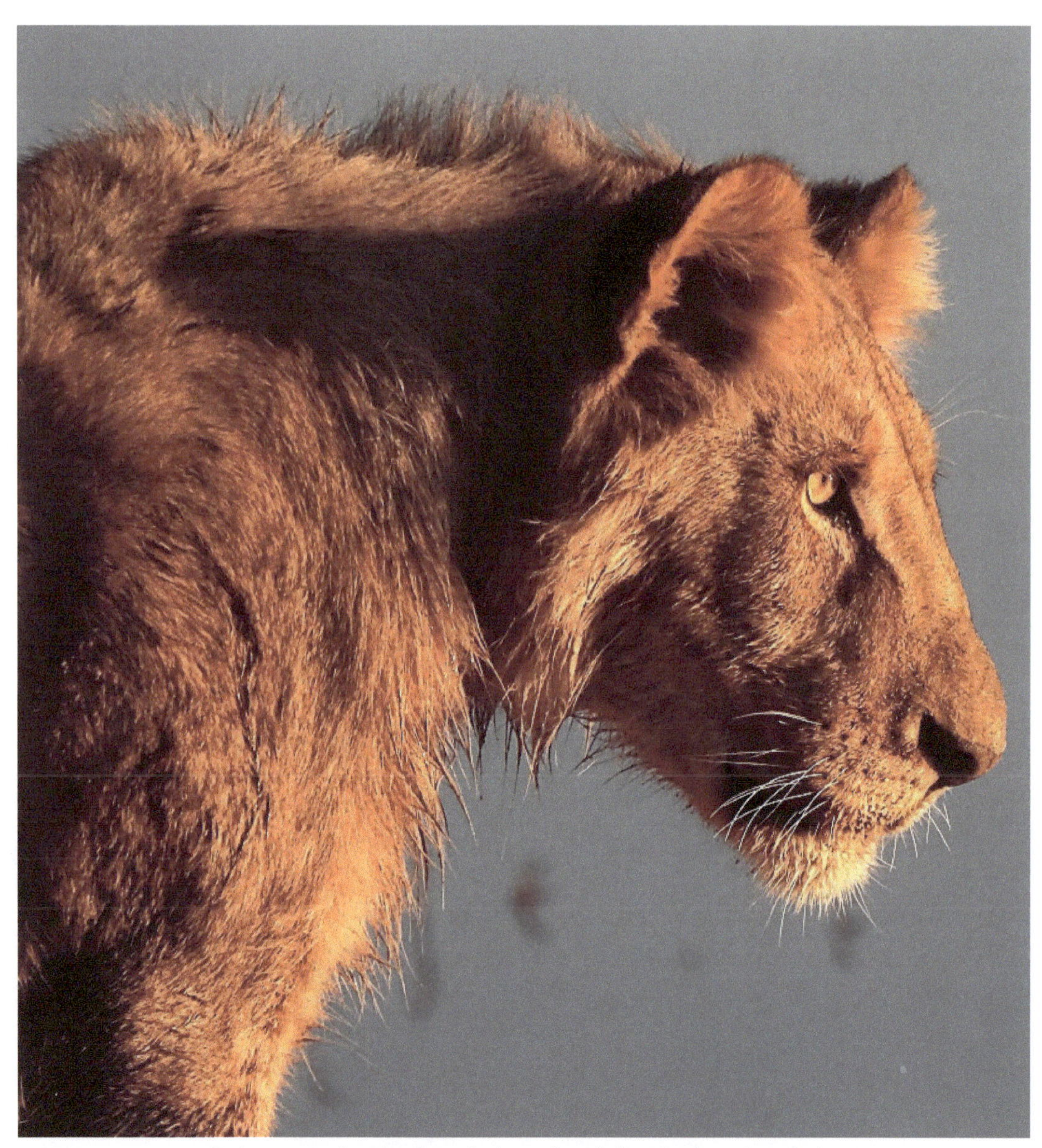

Early morning hunting face of a large female lion. Look out impalas!

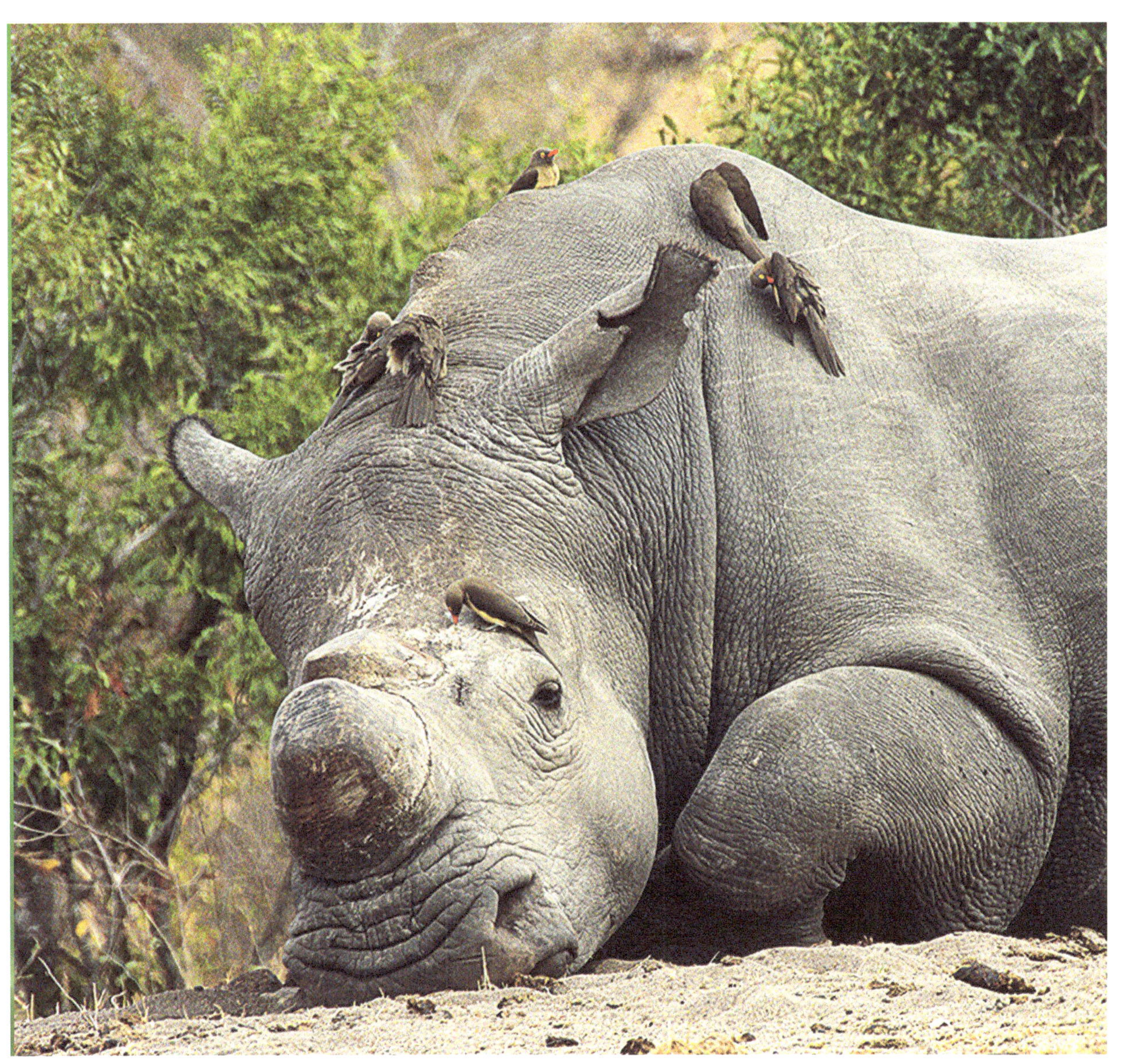

Lucky to see this sleepy rhinoceros while the friendly oxpeckers clear the insects from his hide.

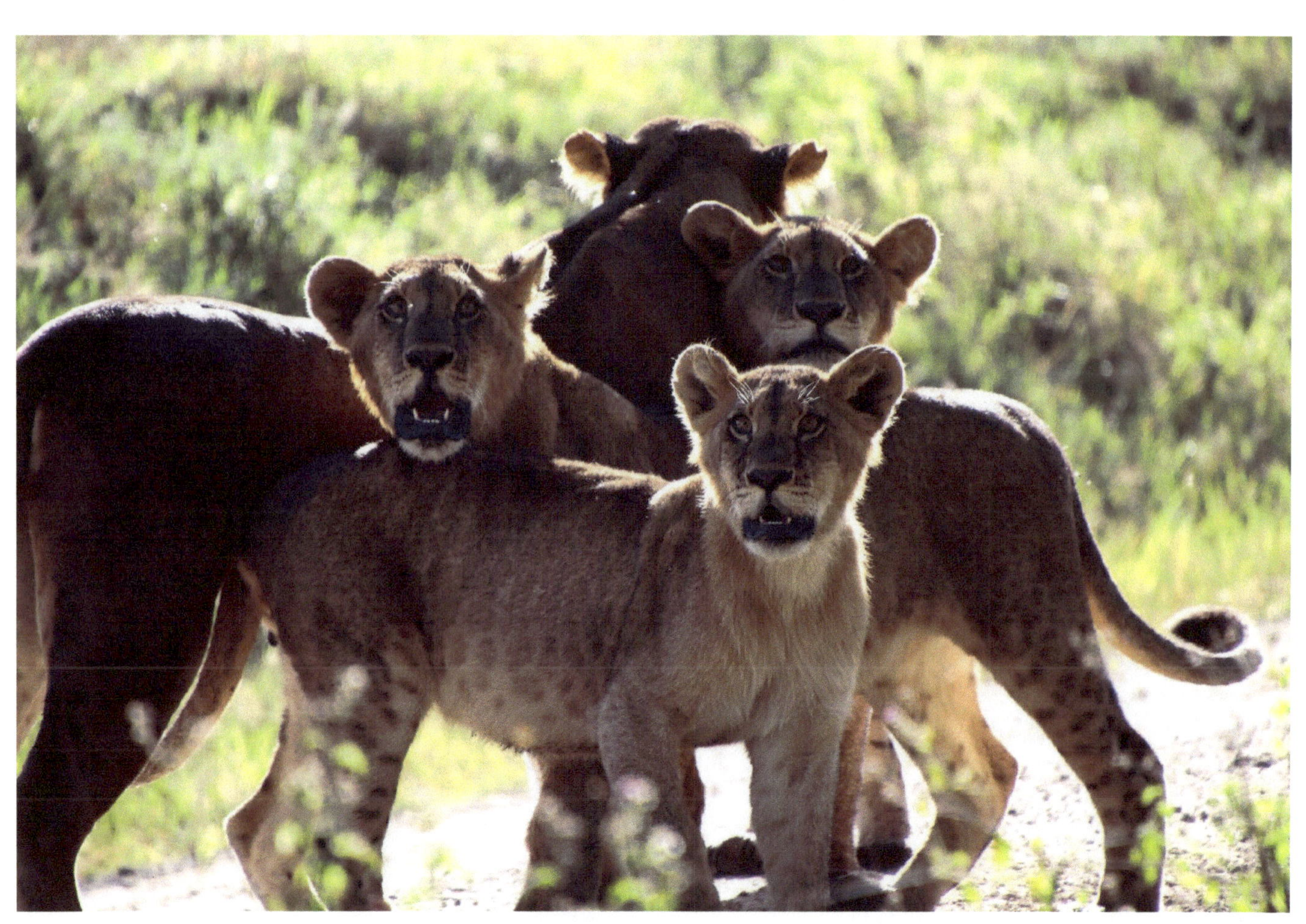

Did you see that? What's over there? Where's mom?

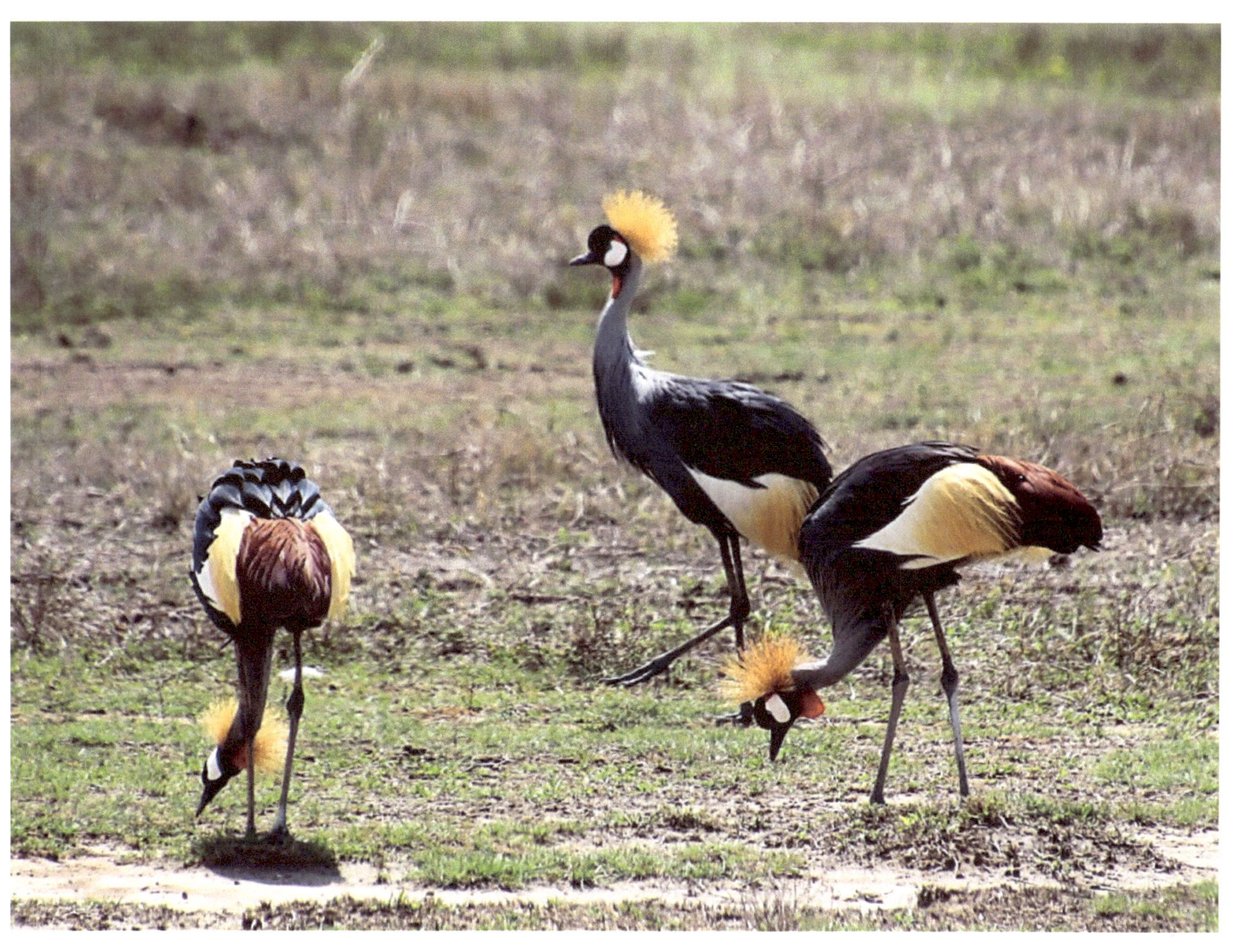

African grey crowned cranes foraging for insects and snakes!

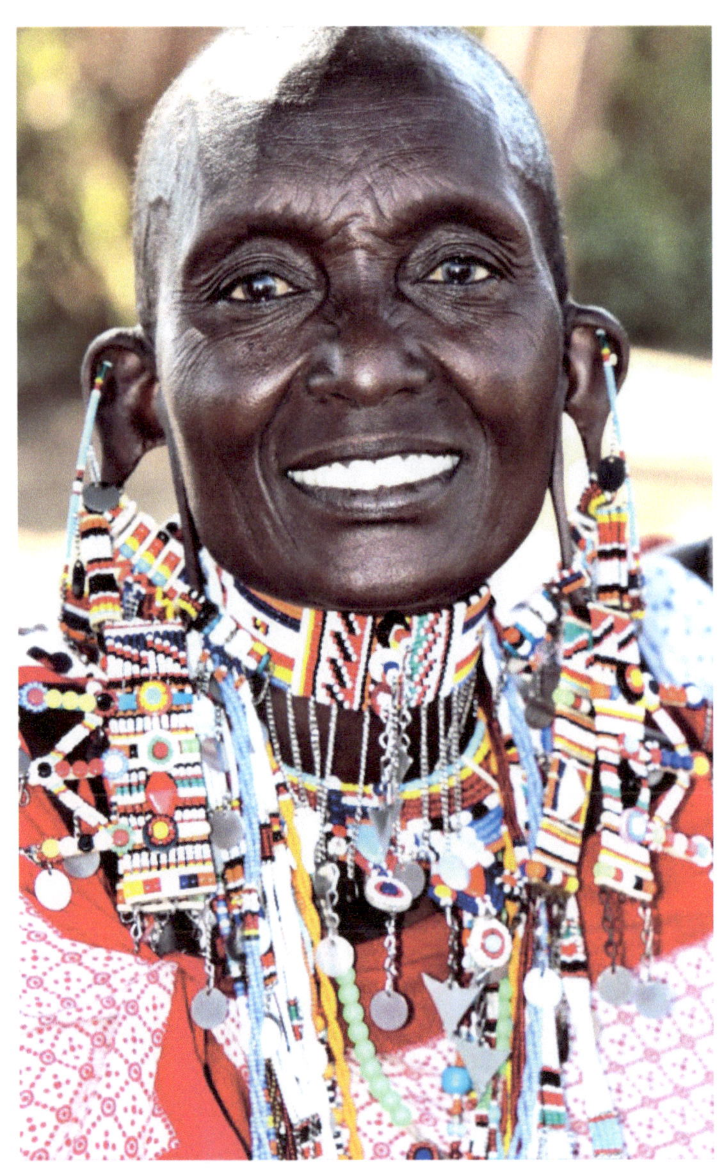

Beautiful Maasai woman wearing her intricate beaded adornments

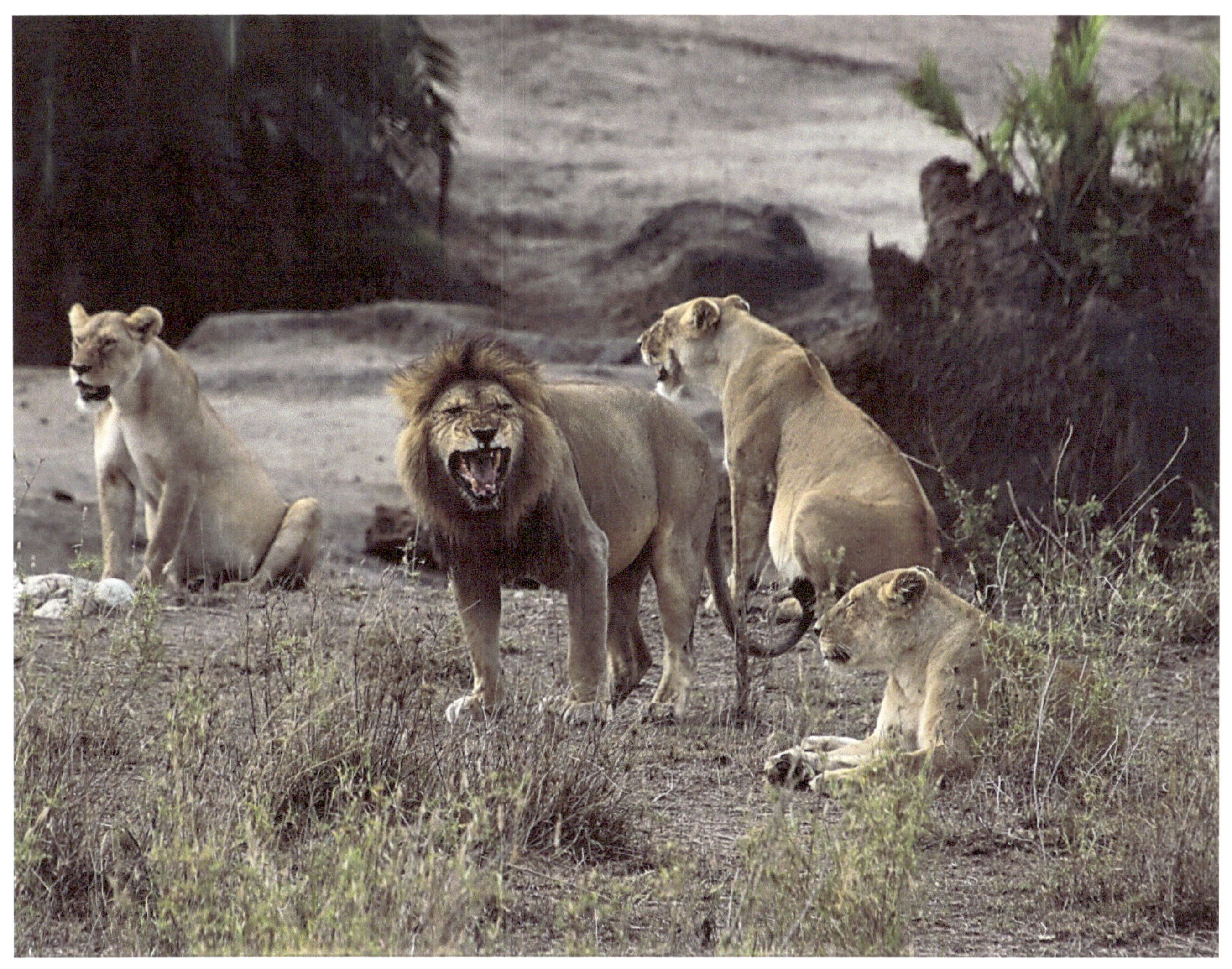

This male lion seems upset with his ladies.

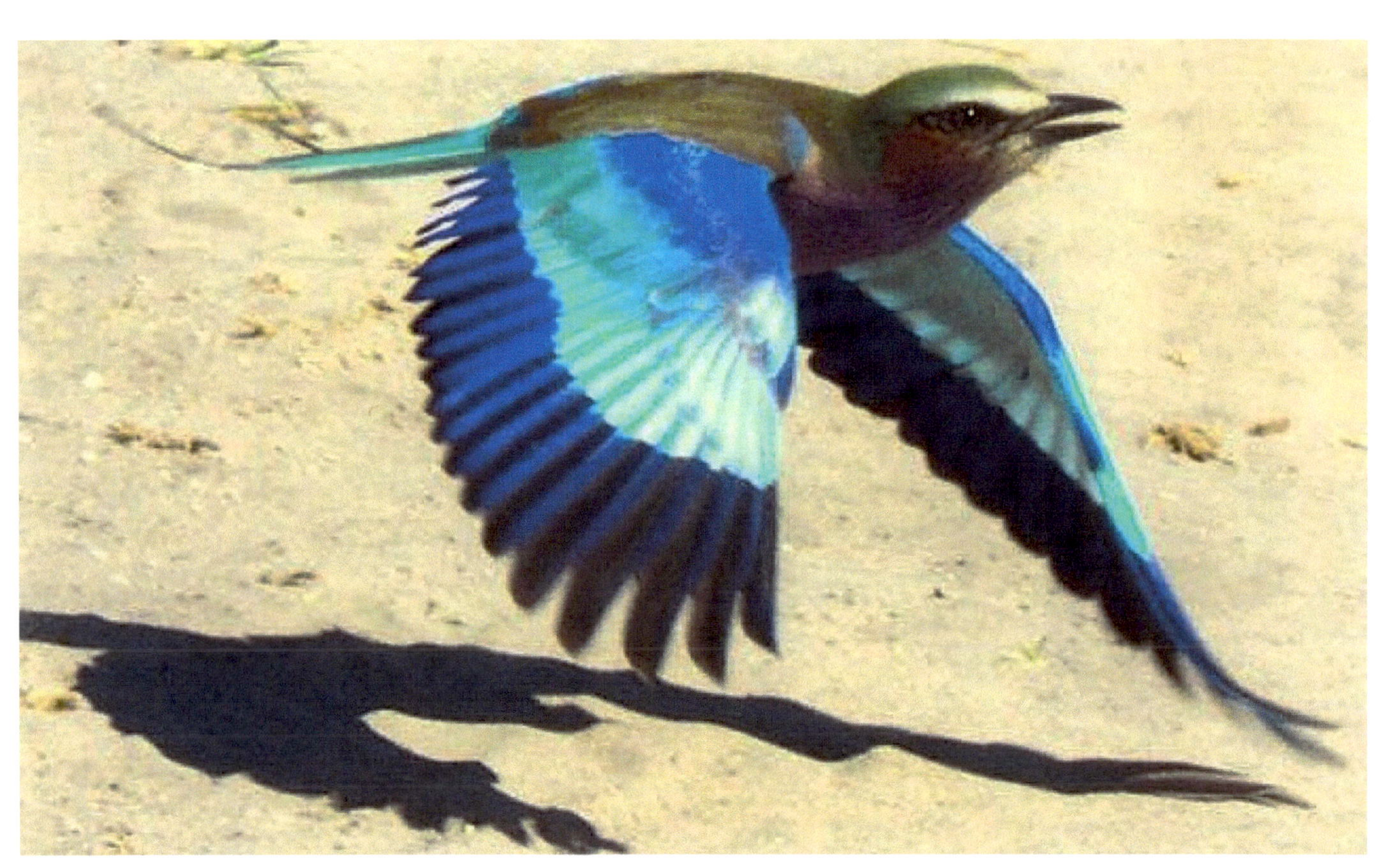

The famous lilac brested roller, one of the most photographed birds in Africa

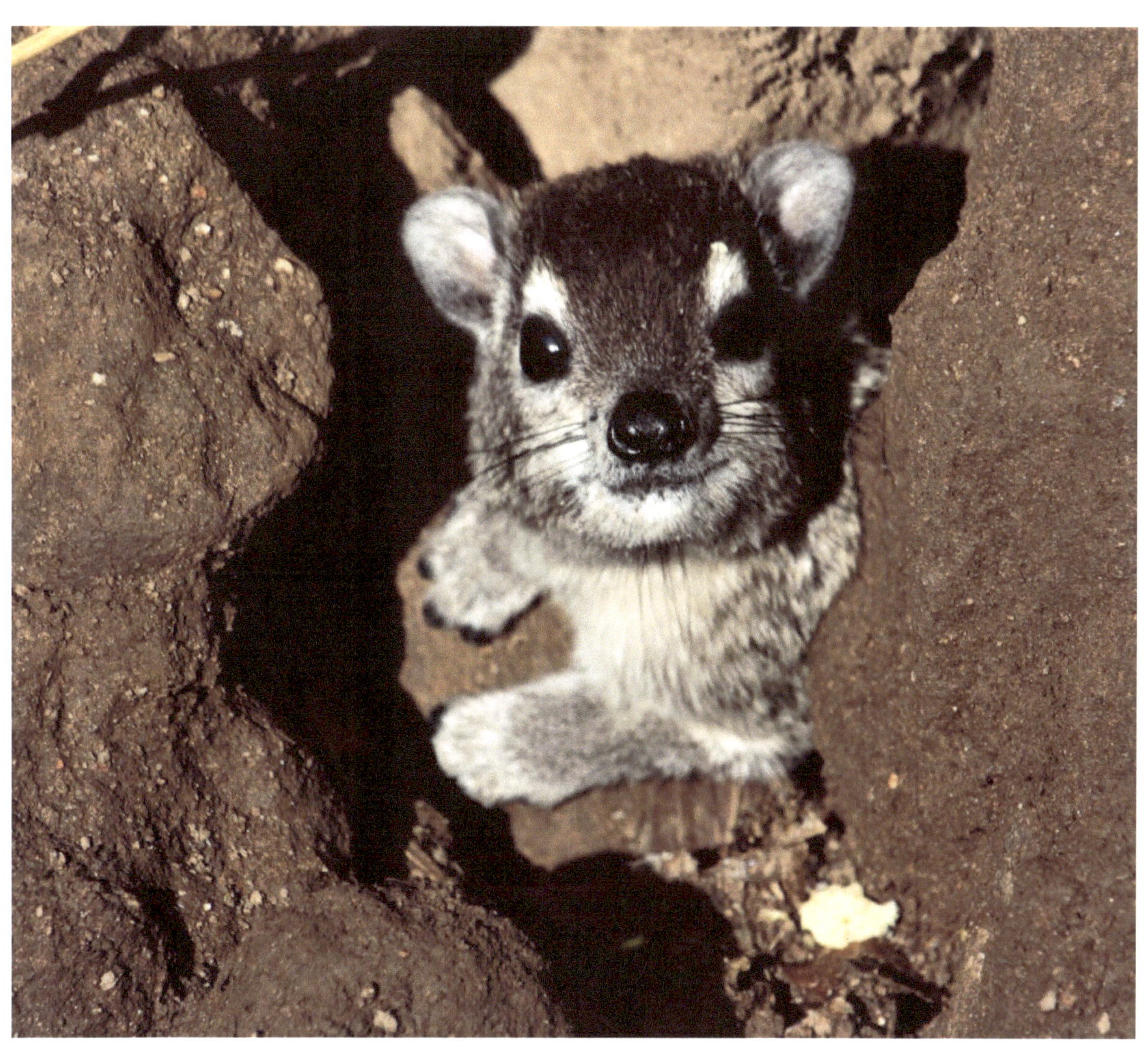

This is a young rock hyrax or "Dassie," a tiny furry animal that is closely related to the elephant.

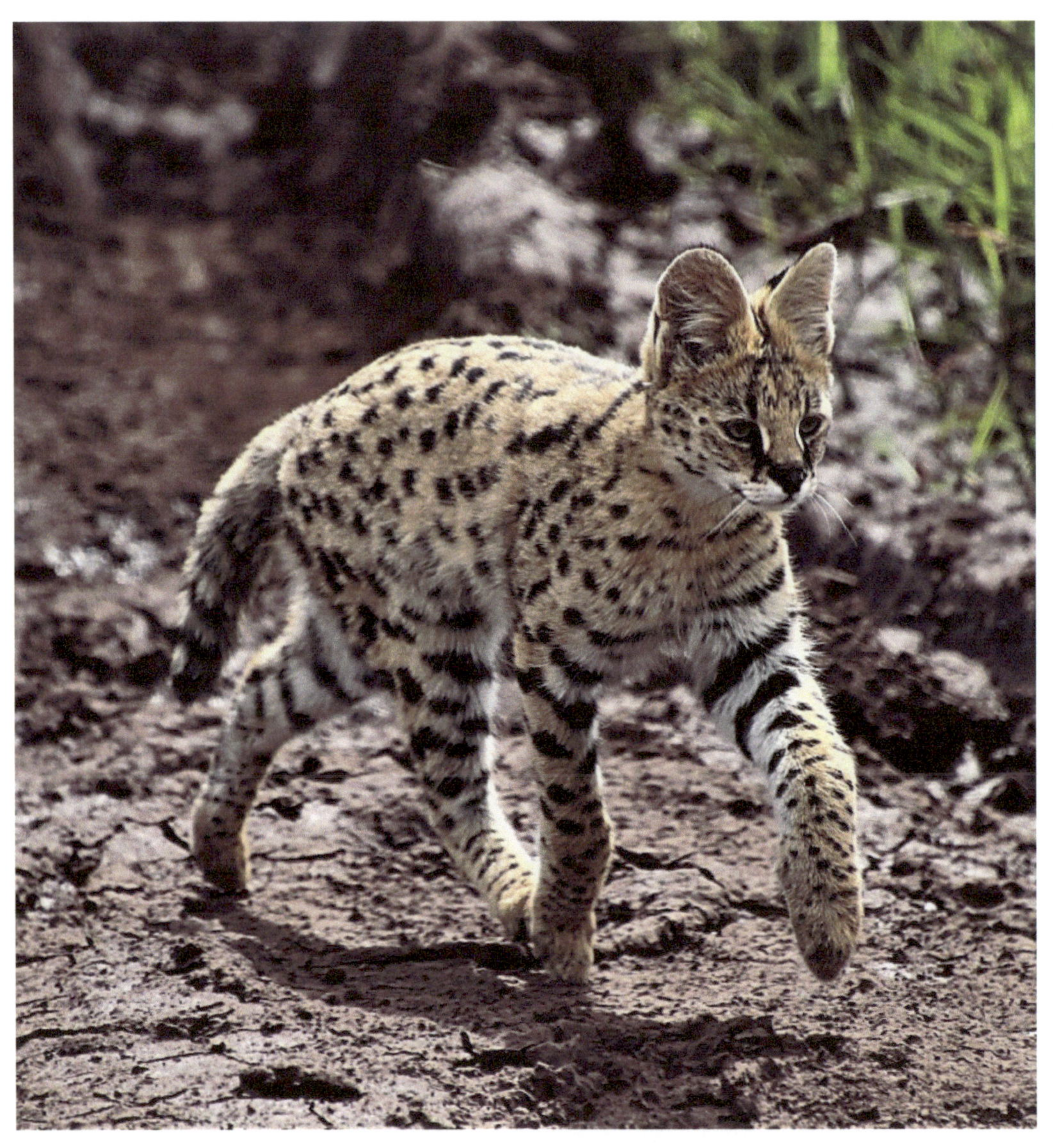

The serval is a medium-sized cat that eats rodents, birds, and small reptiles.

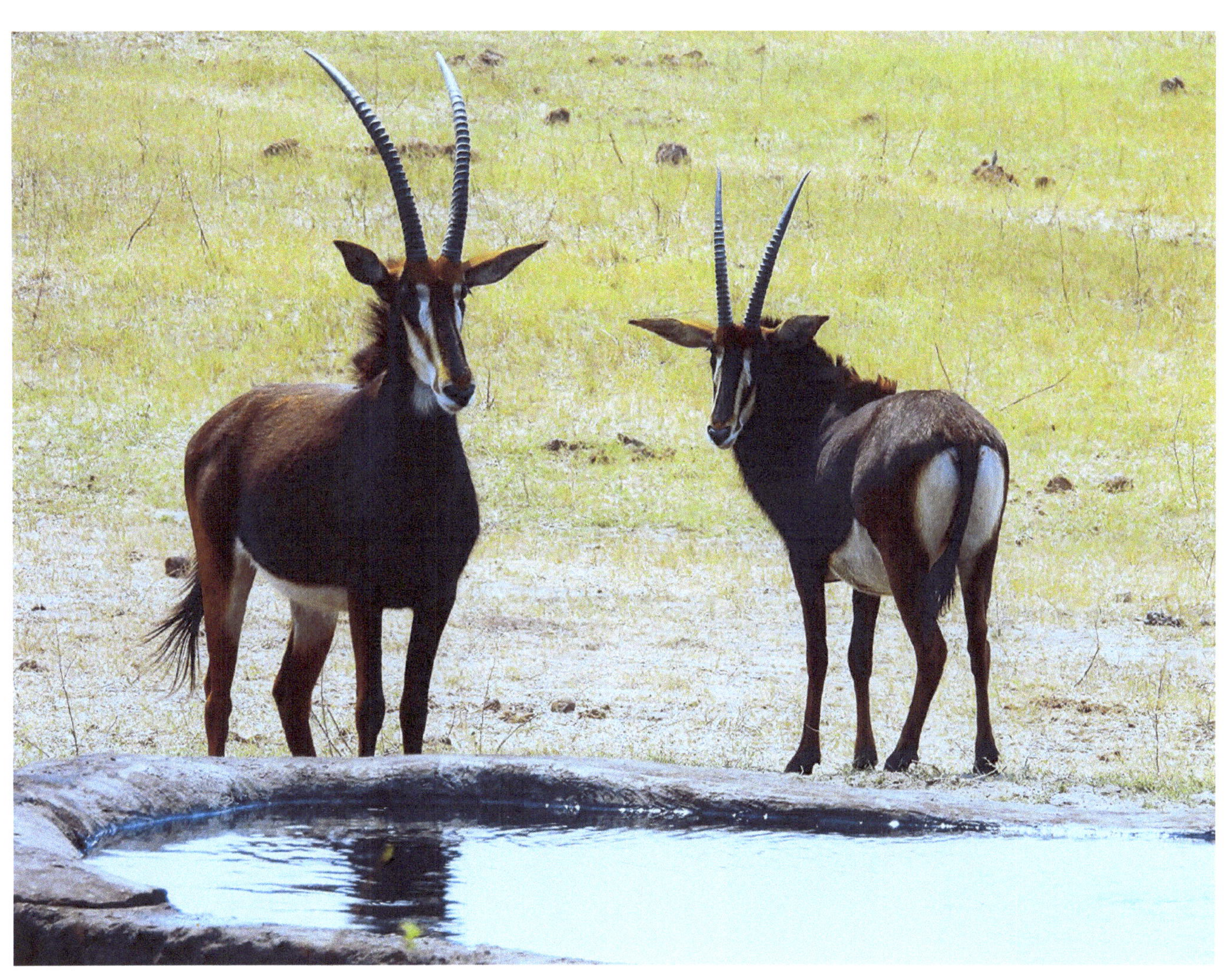

The beautiful sable antelope, once prized for its hide to make coats. Thank goodness they are now protected.

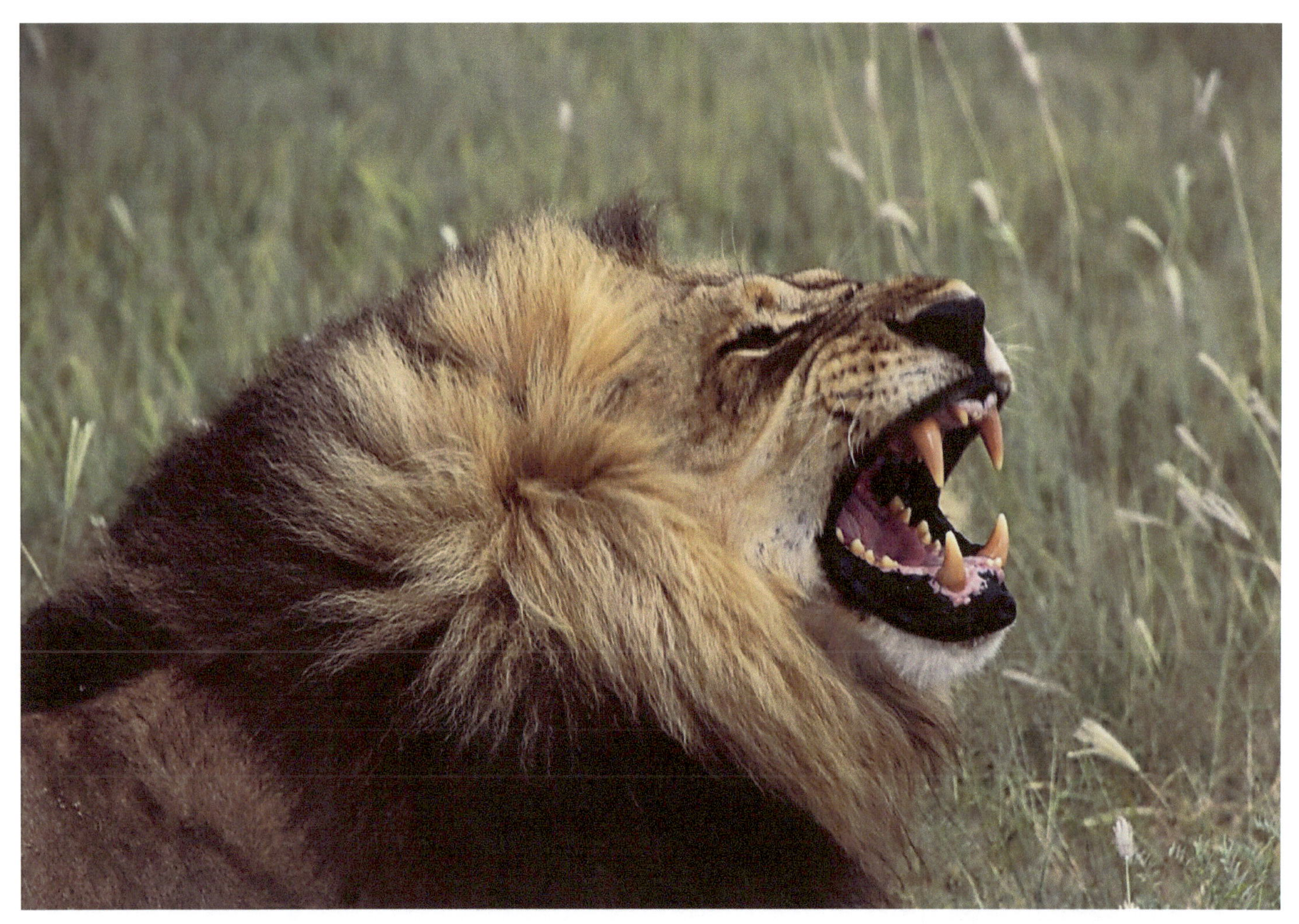

The lion roars!

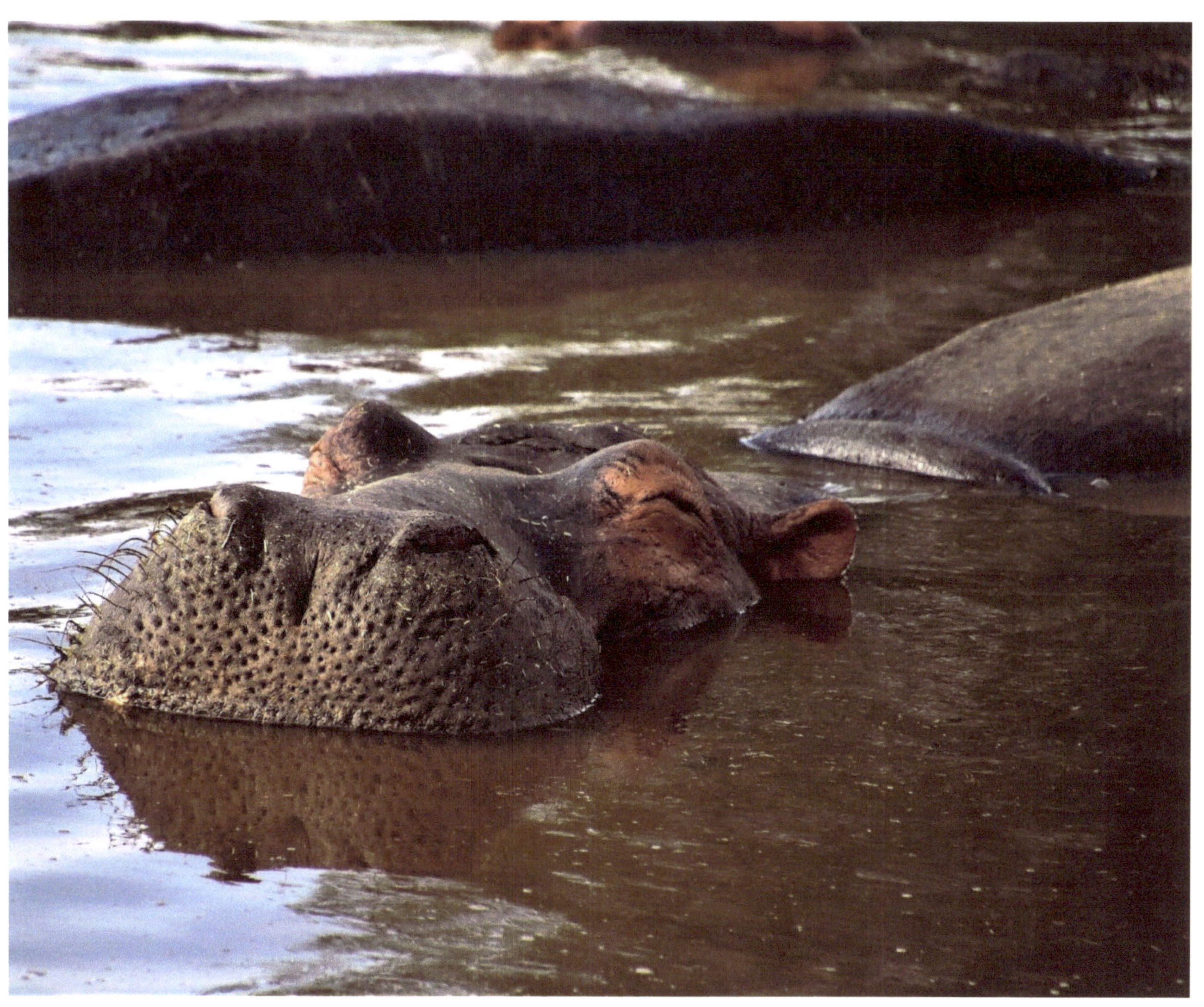

Hippos kill more people than any other African animal.

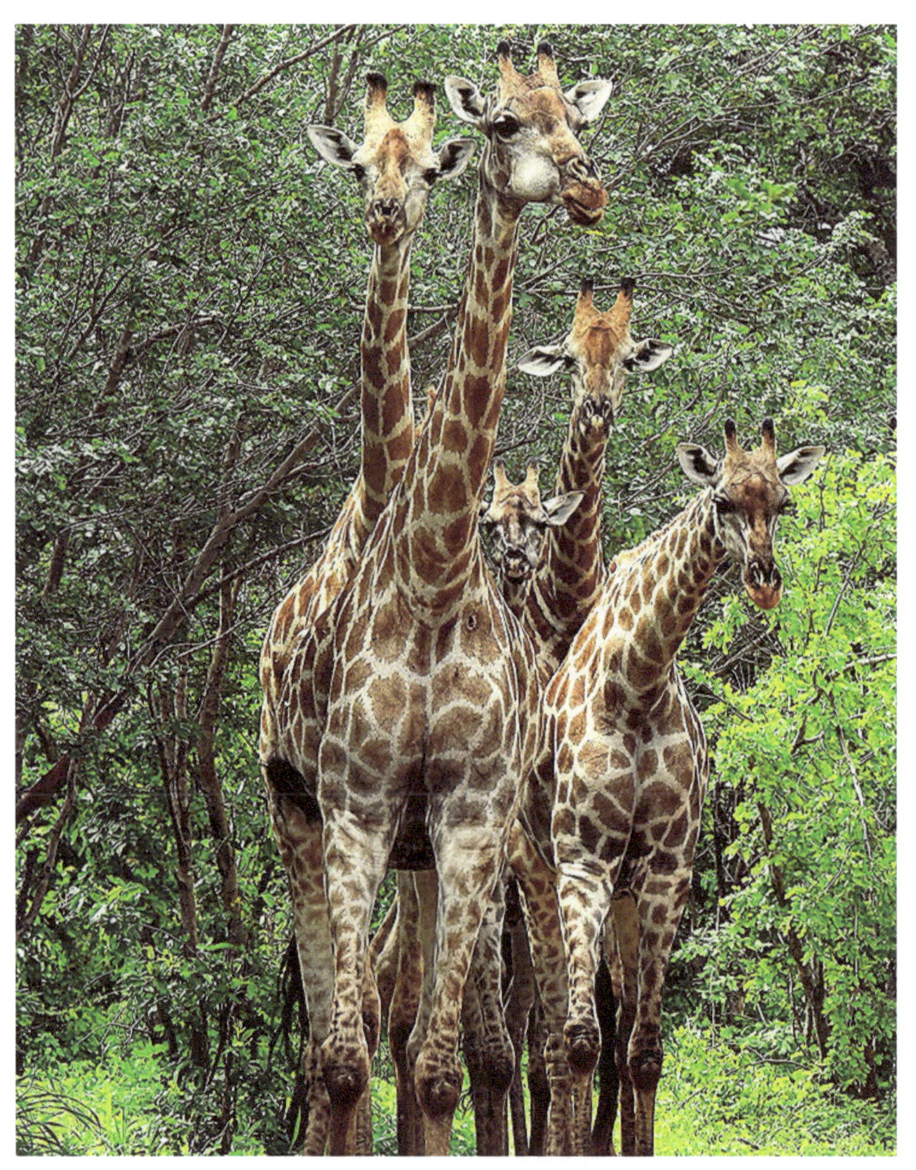

A group of giraffes is a "tower." If they are walking, they are a "journey."

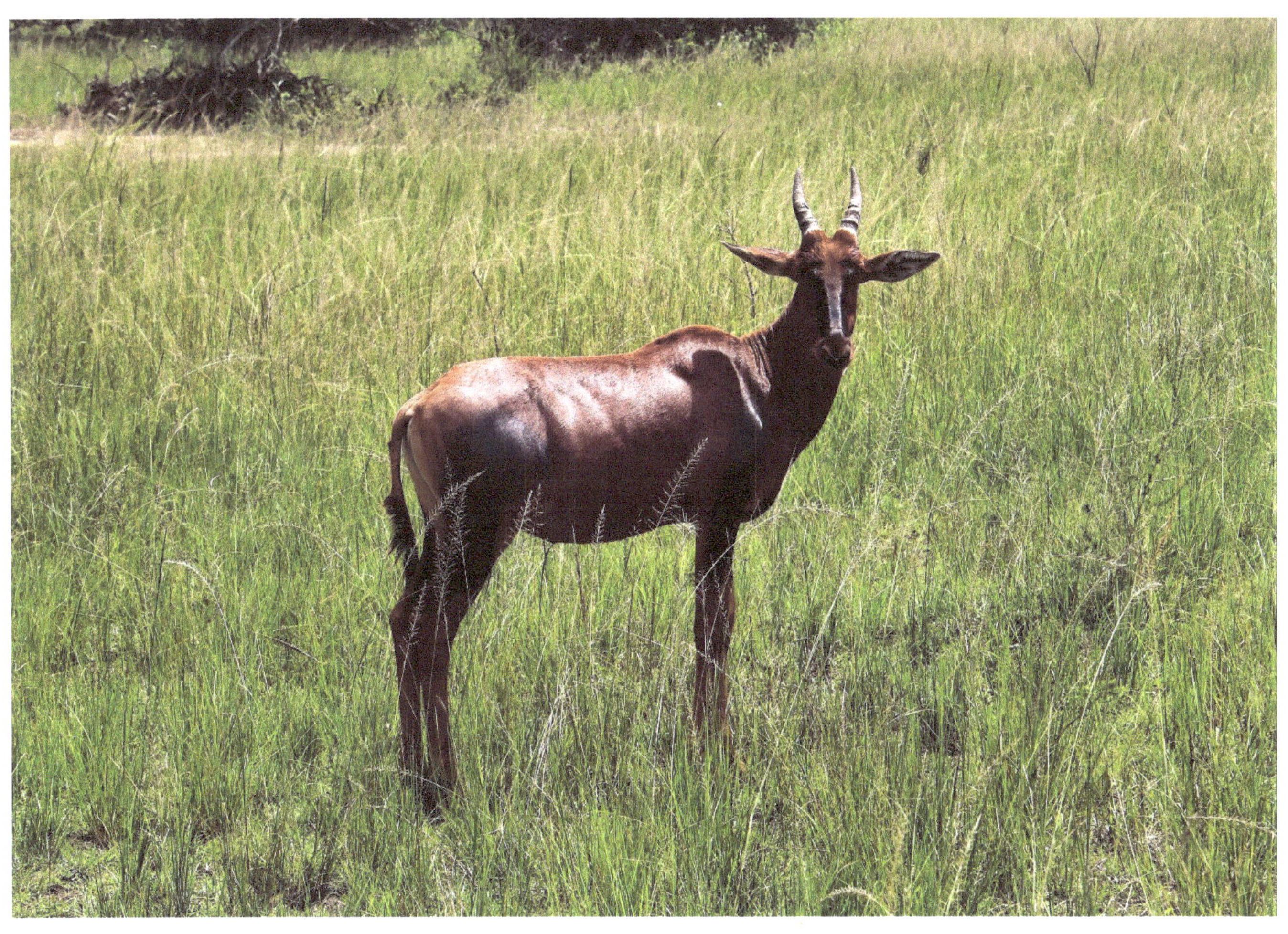

The topi, also known as the levi because of the denim coloring on its hips and thighs

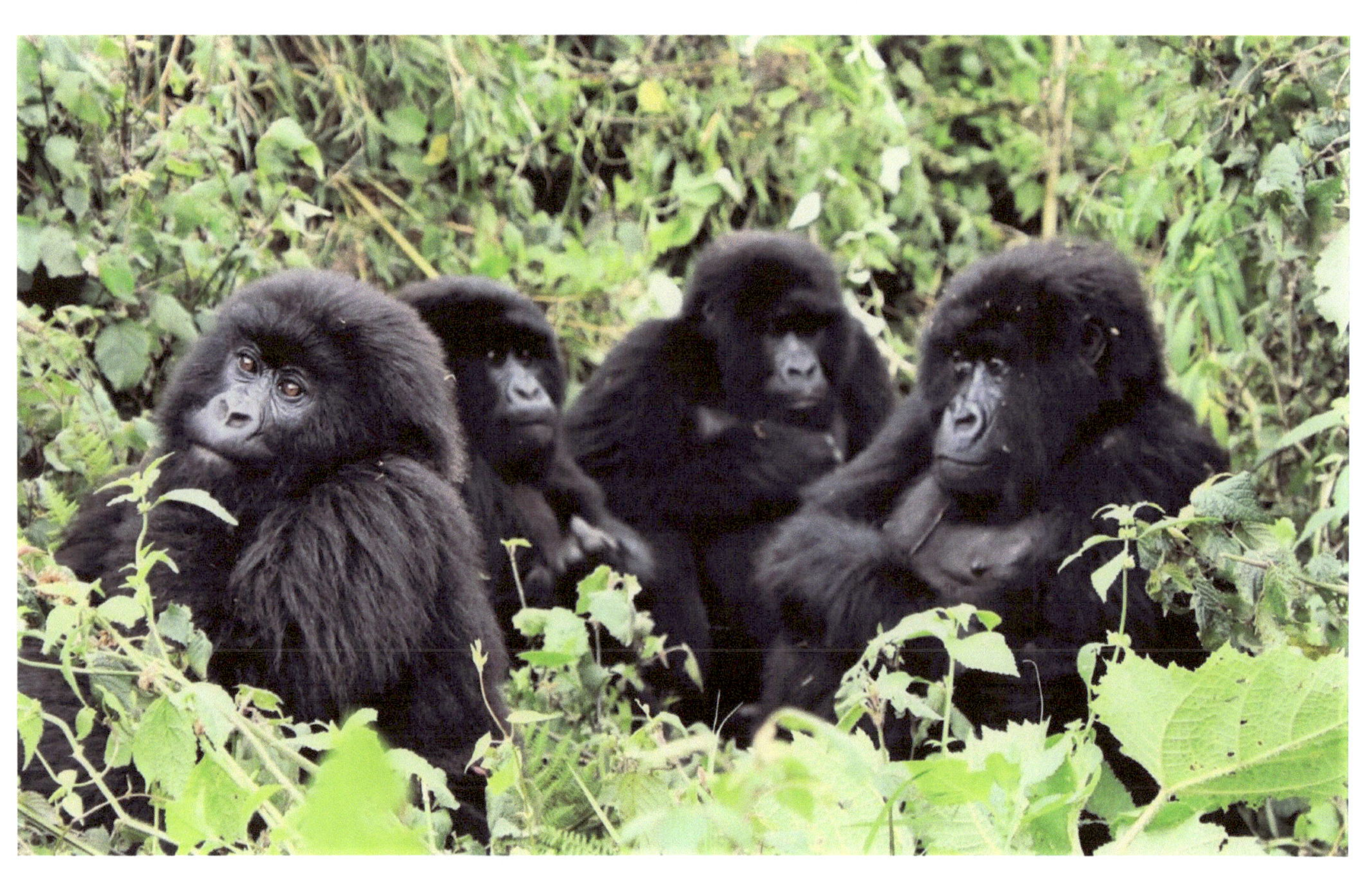

Mountain gorillas of Rwanda. They live in family units with a male silverback as the leader.

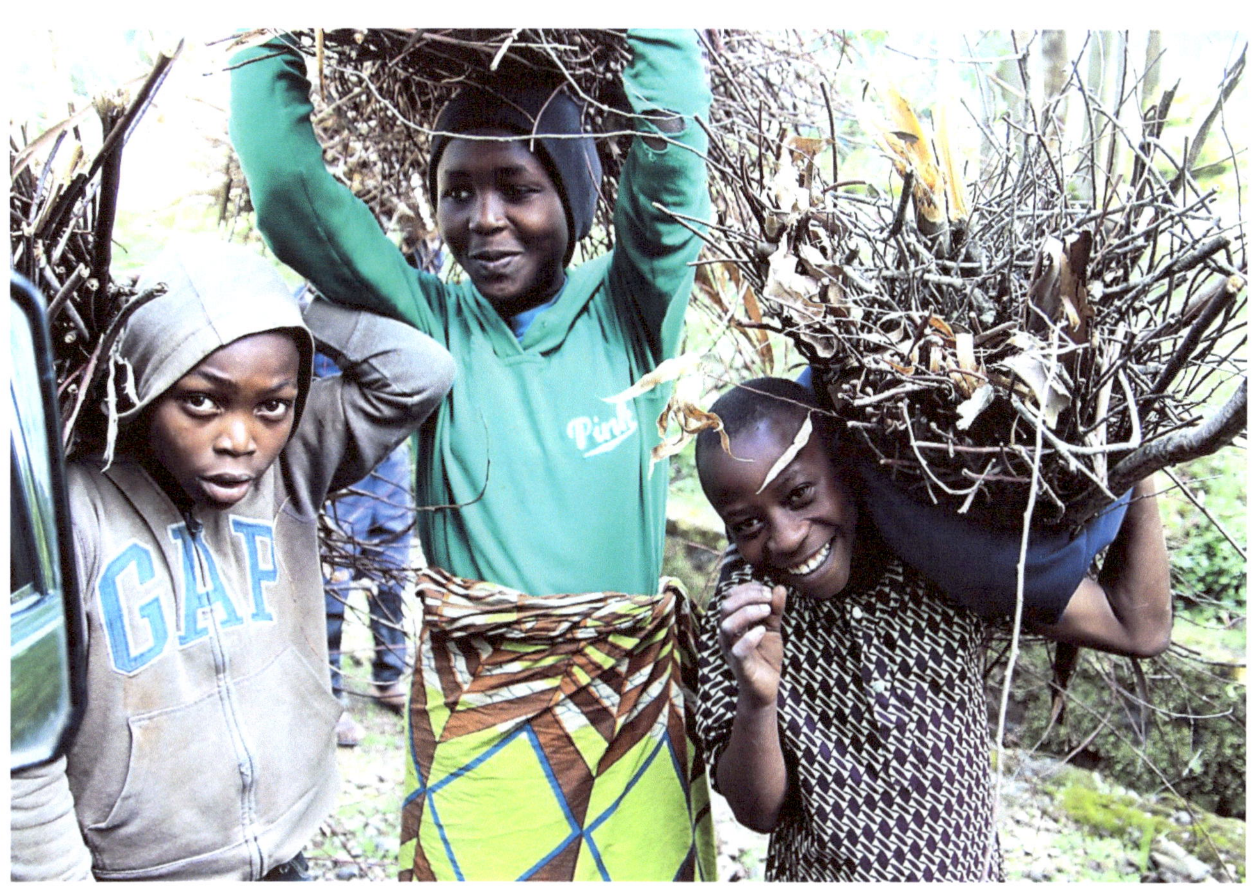

Children of Rwanda gathering wood for the evening fire

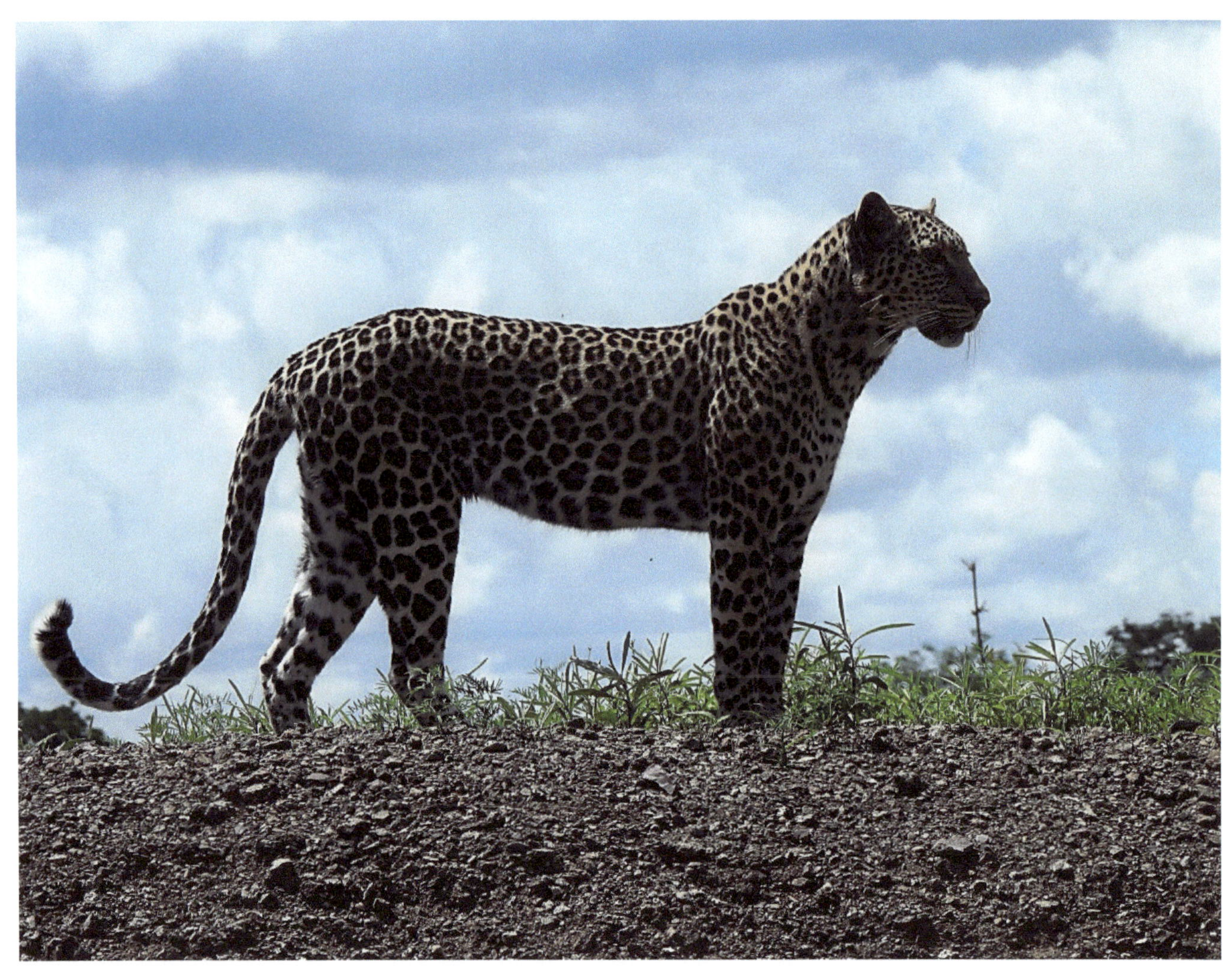

My favorite leopard photo!

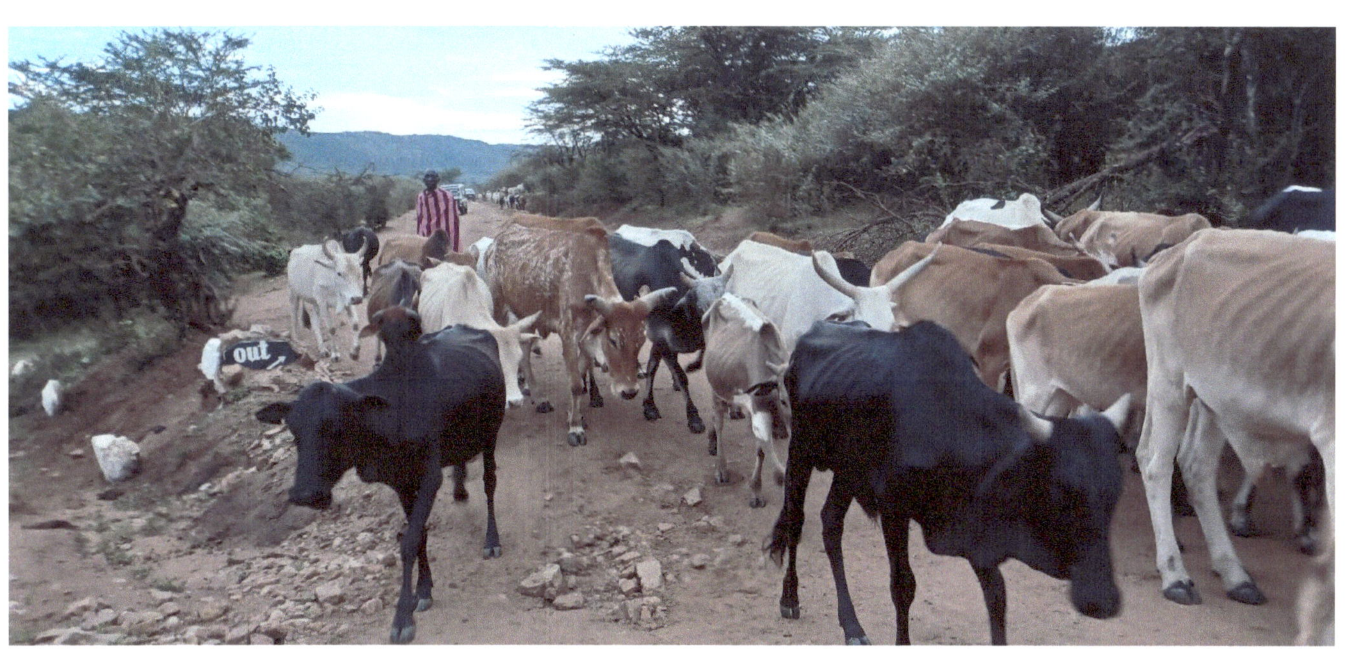

This is a typical road issue in the Maasai Mara, a cow jam!

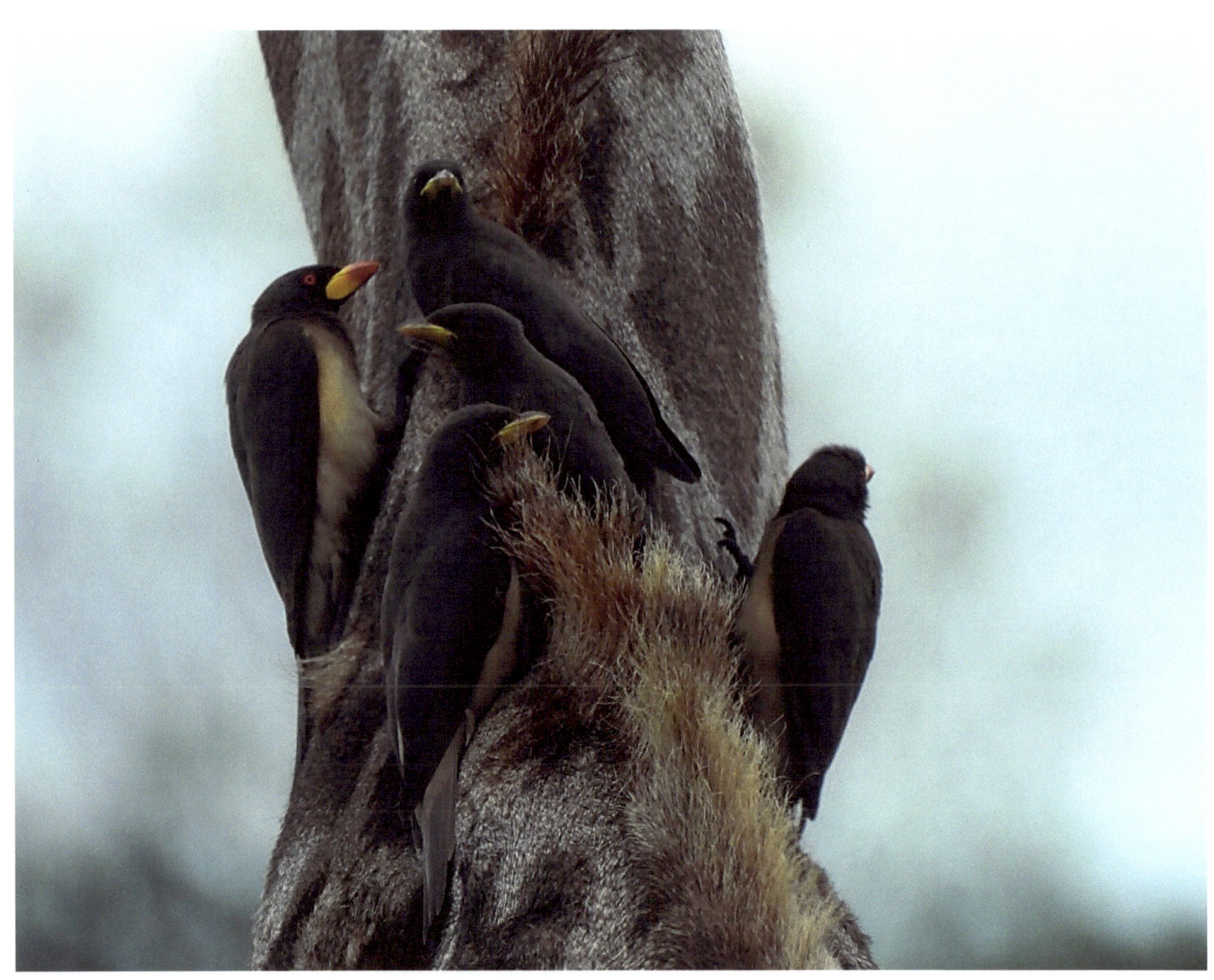

Oxpeckers buy eating insects on the long neck of a giraffe.

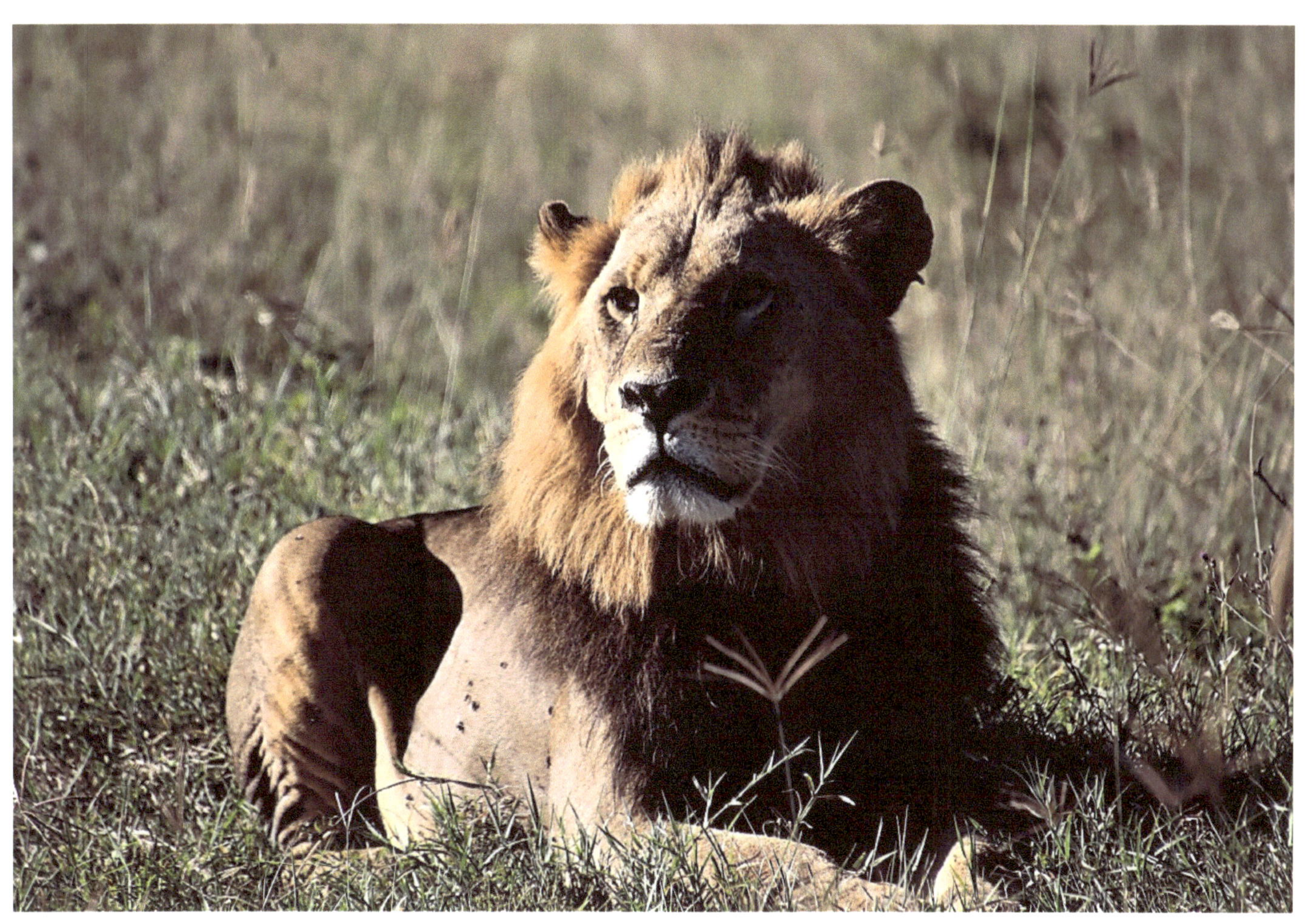

The majestic male lion in the evening light

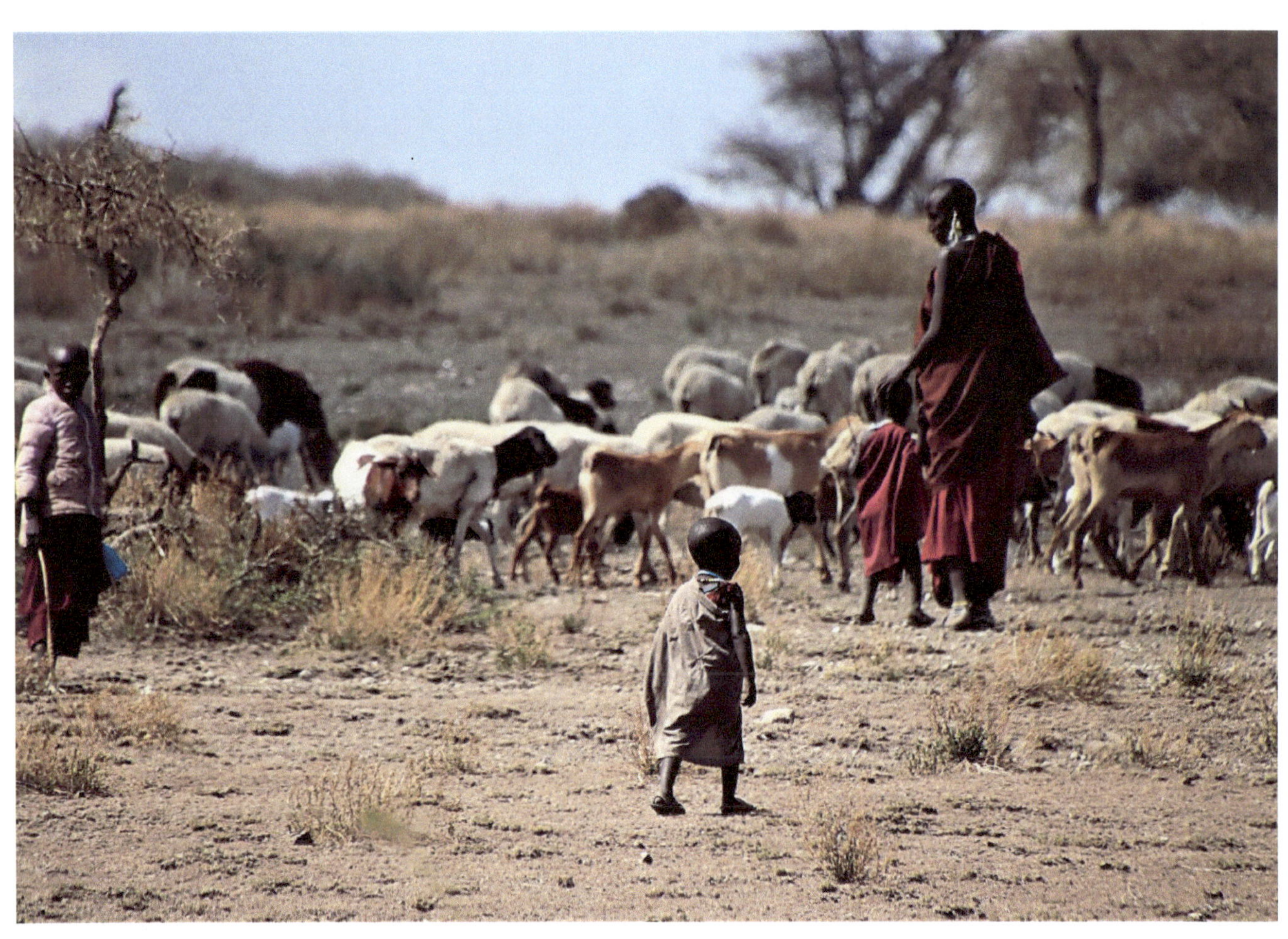

The Maasai tribe migrating to find food and water for the families and animal herds

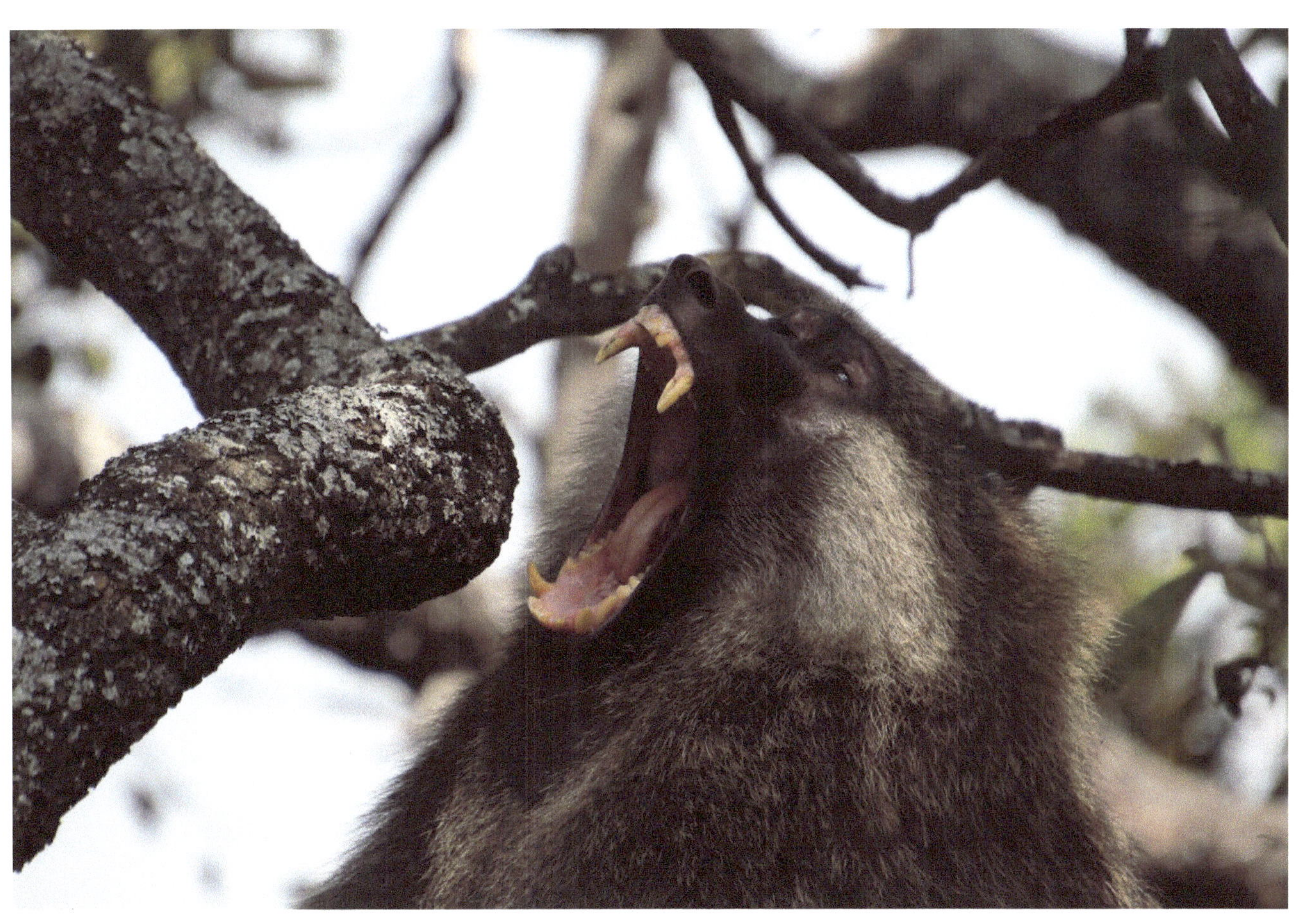

Baboon showing dominance to the congress. A group of baboons is called a congress!

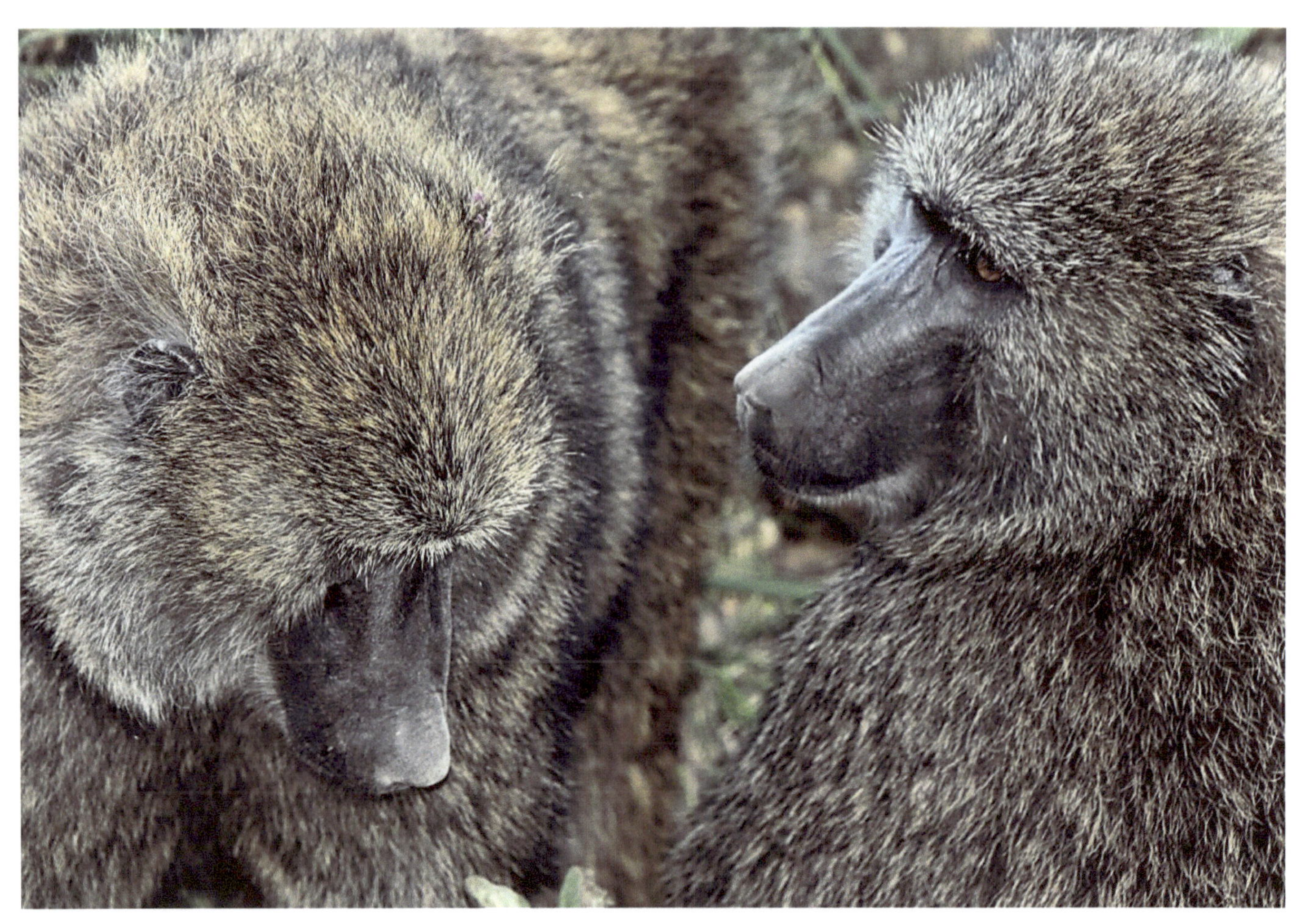

Two furry baboons

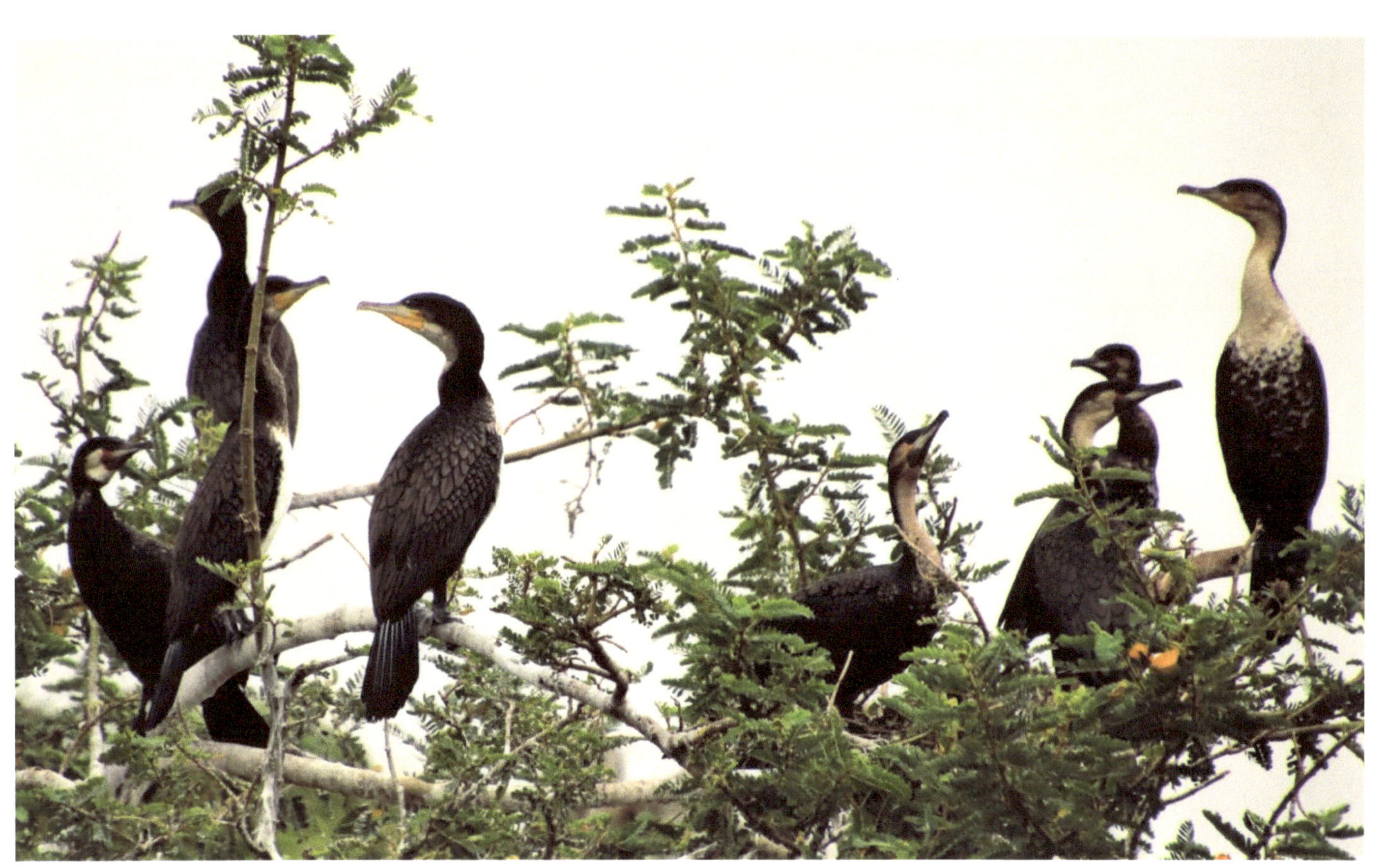

Eight African darters nesting for the night

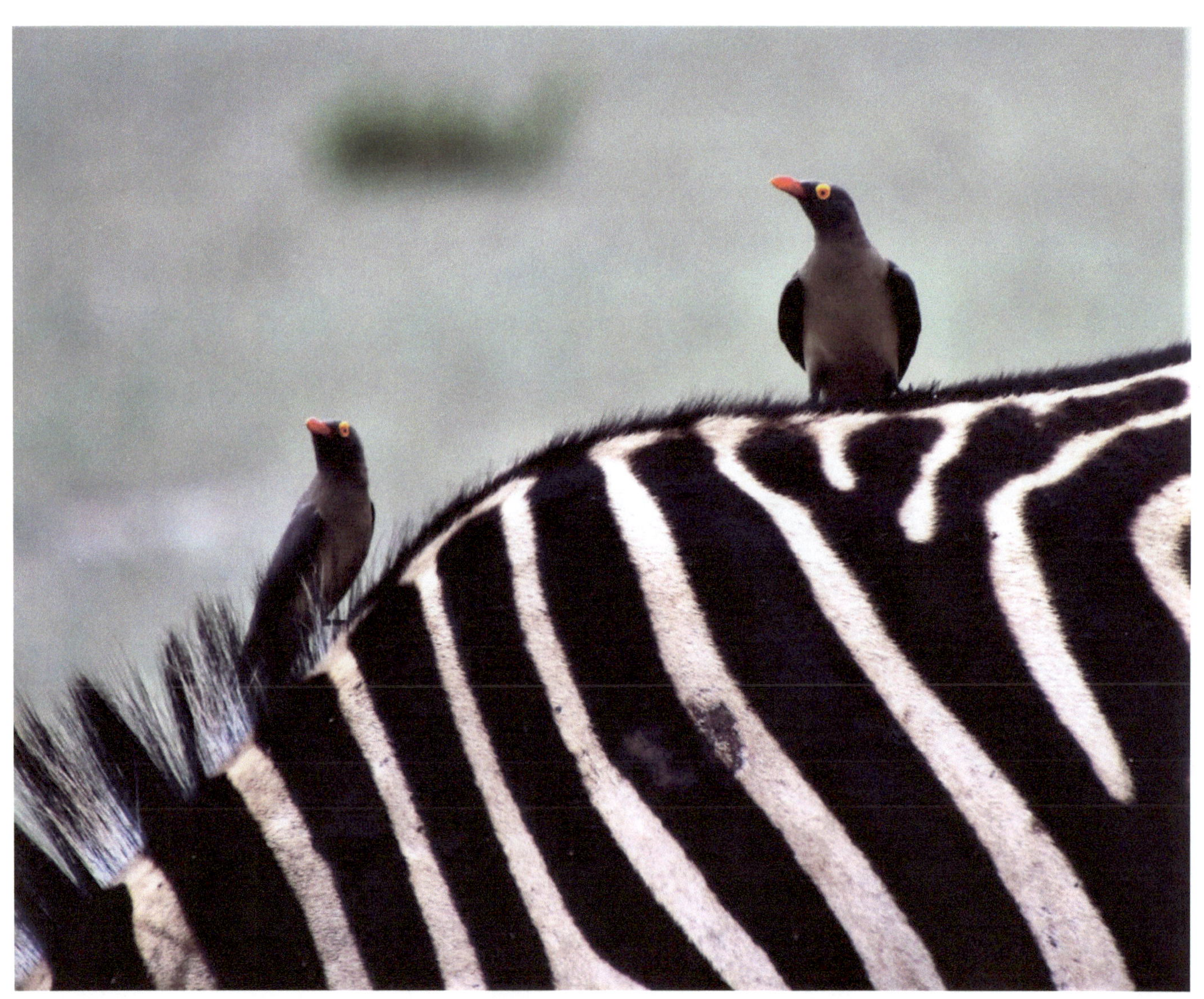

Oxpeckers hard at work on a zebra's back

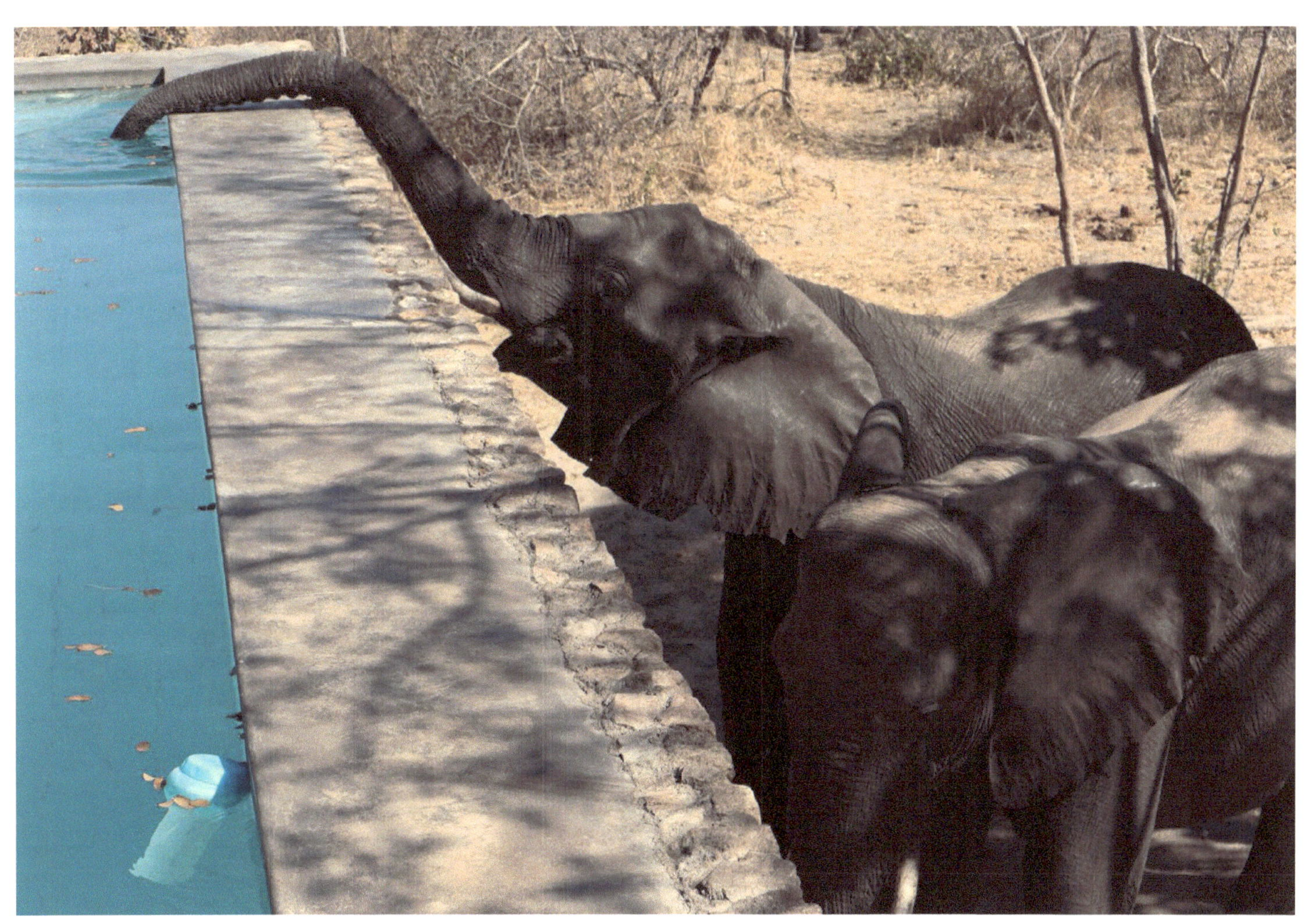

Only the tallest of the herd can reach the pool water.

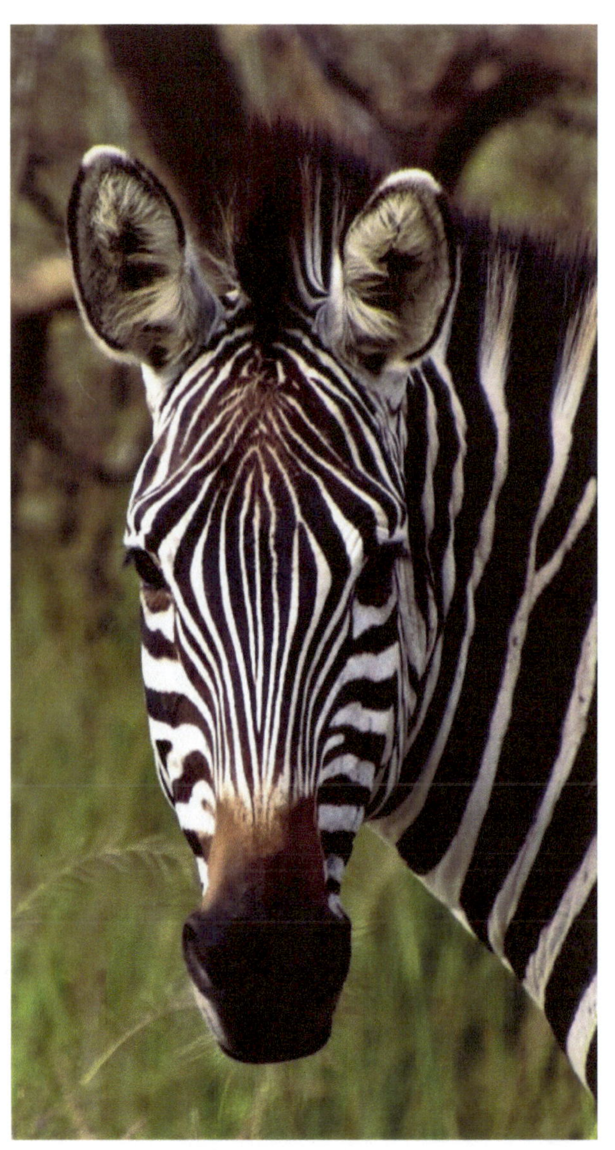

Beautiful face of a zebra

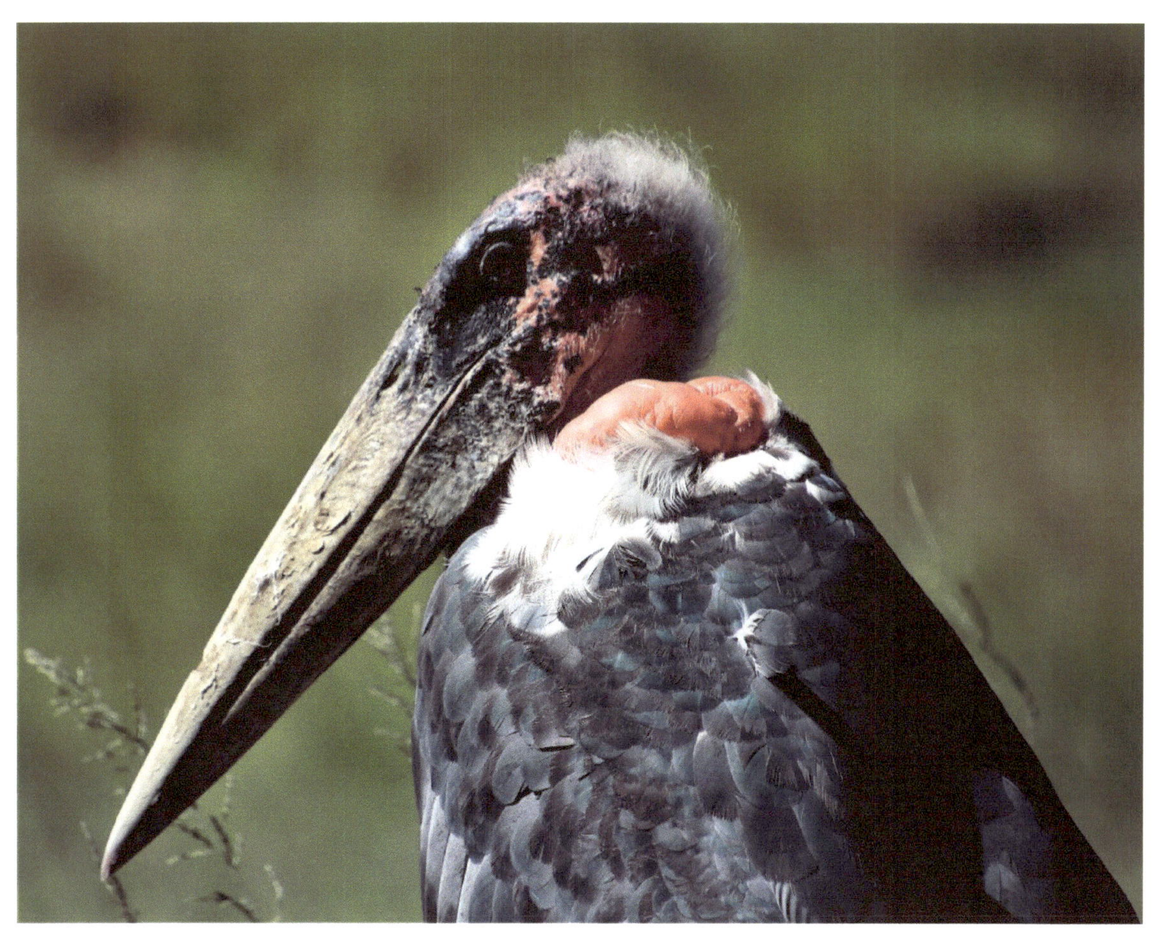

The marabou stork. One of the ugly five of Africa

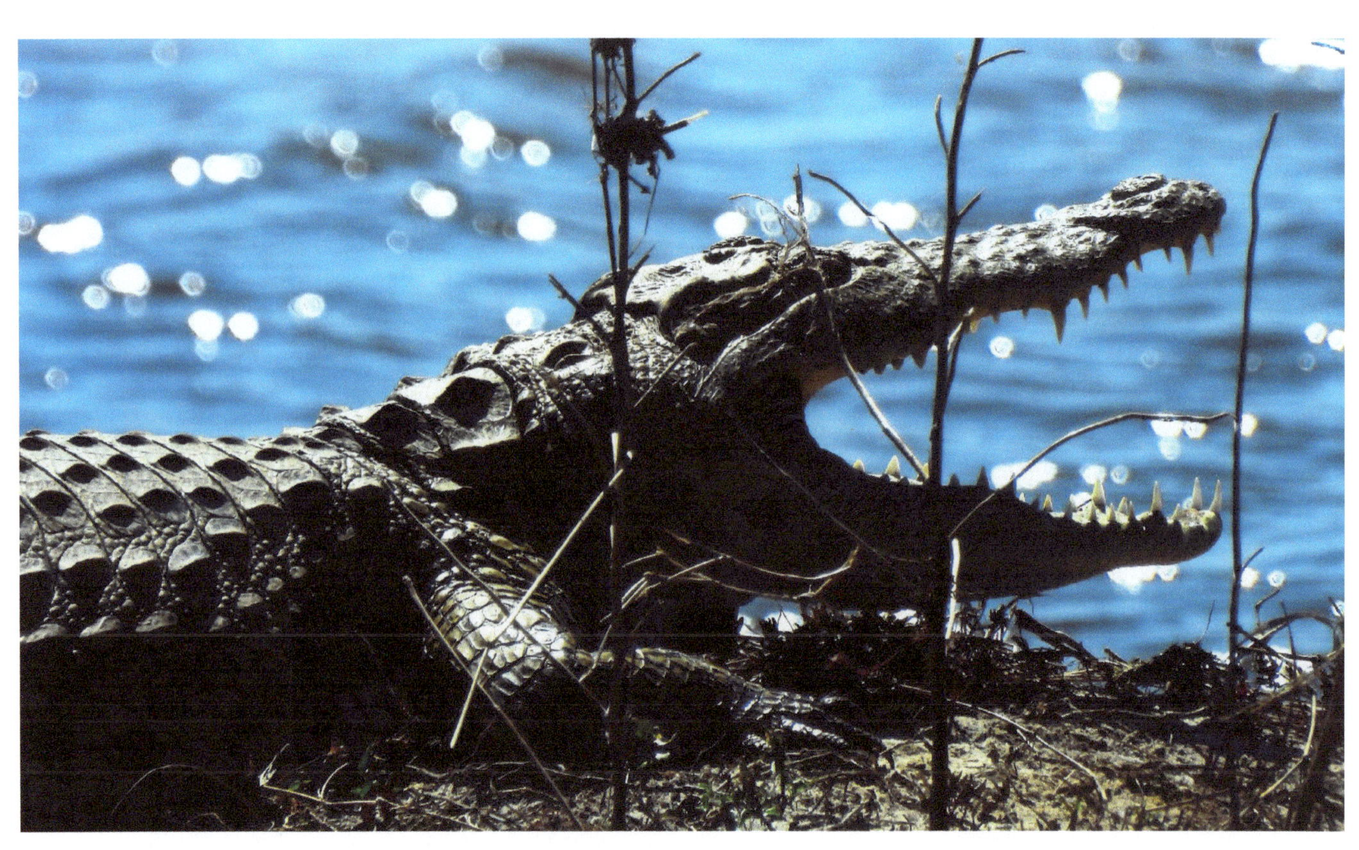

Crocodiles hold their mouths open to help regulate body temperature in the sun.

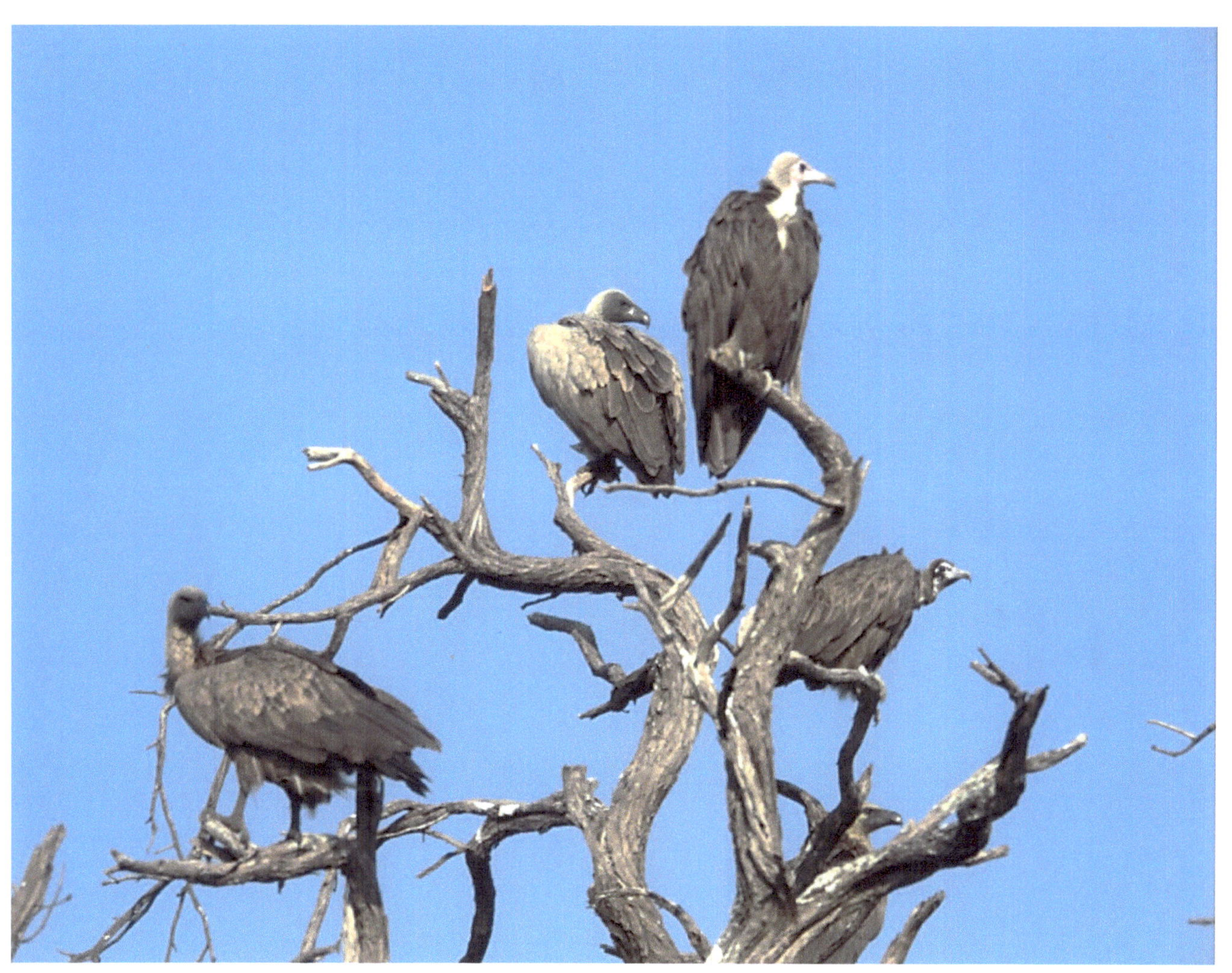

Vultures waiting their turn at the fresh carcass. They are the garbage cleaners of the wild.

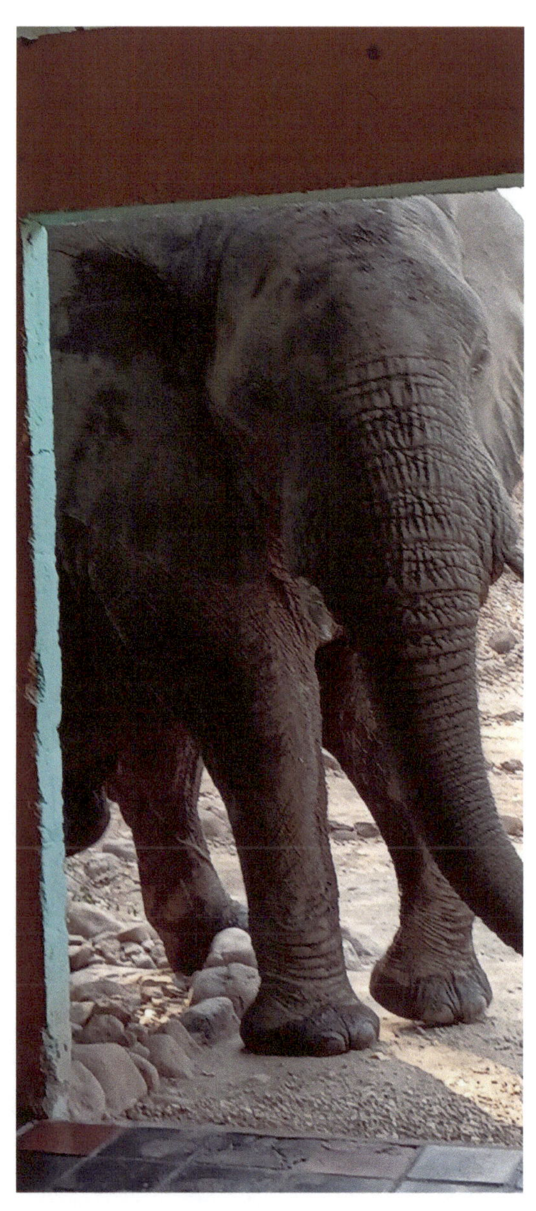

An elephant tries to enter the bar at the Warthog Lodge in Kariba, Zimbabwe!

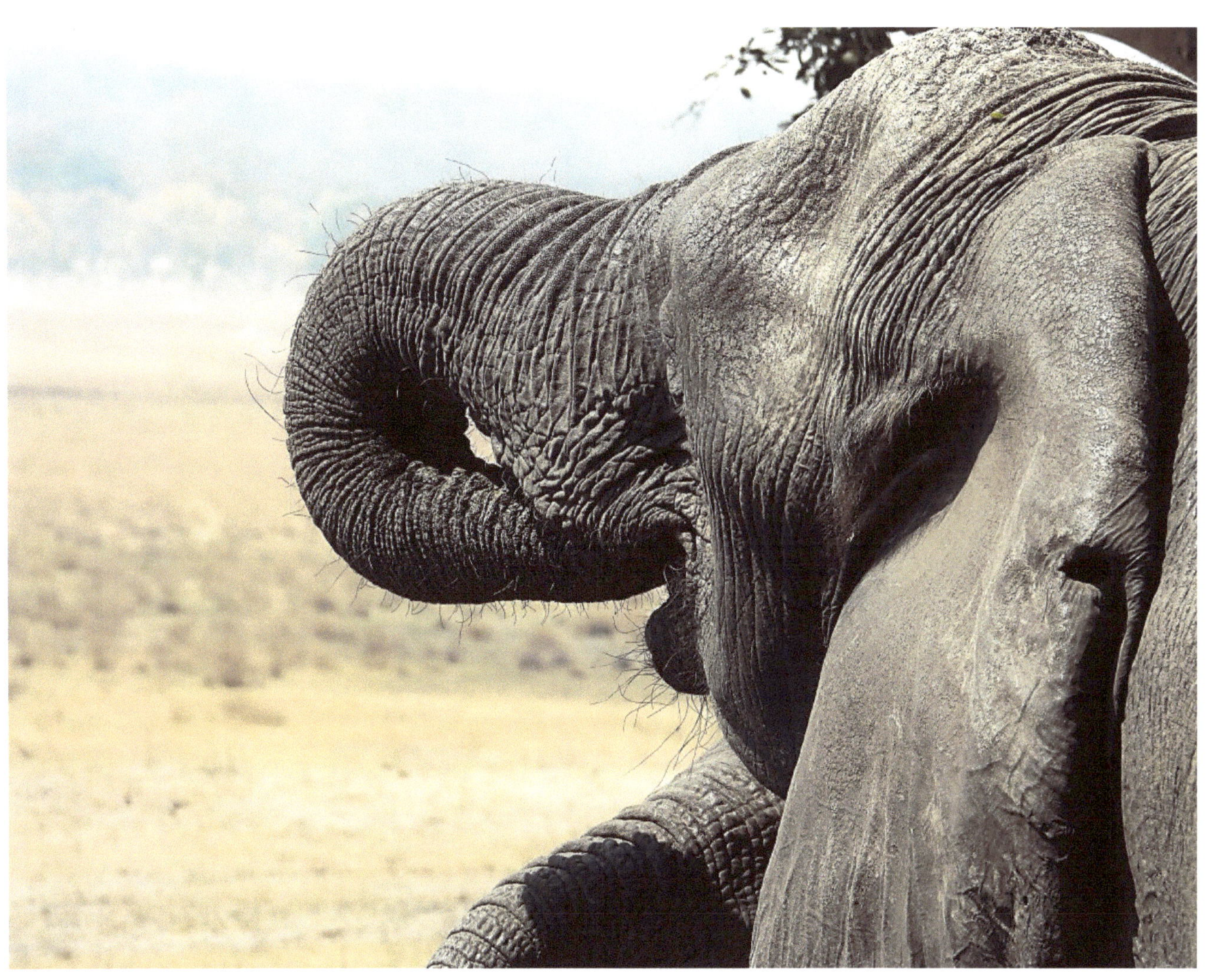

The elephant never knew I took his picture.

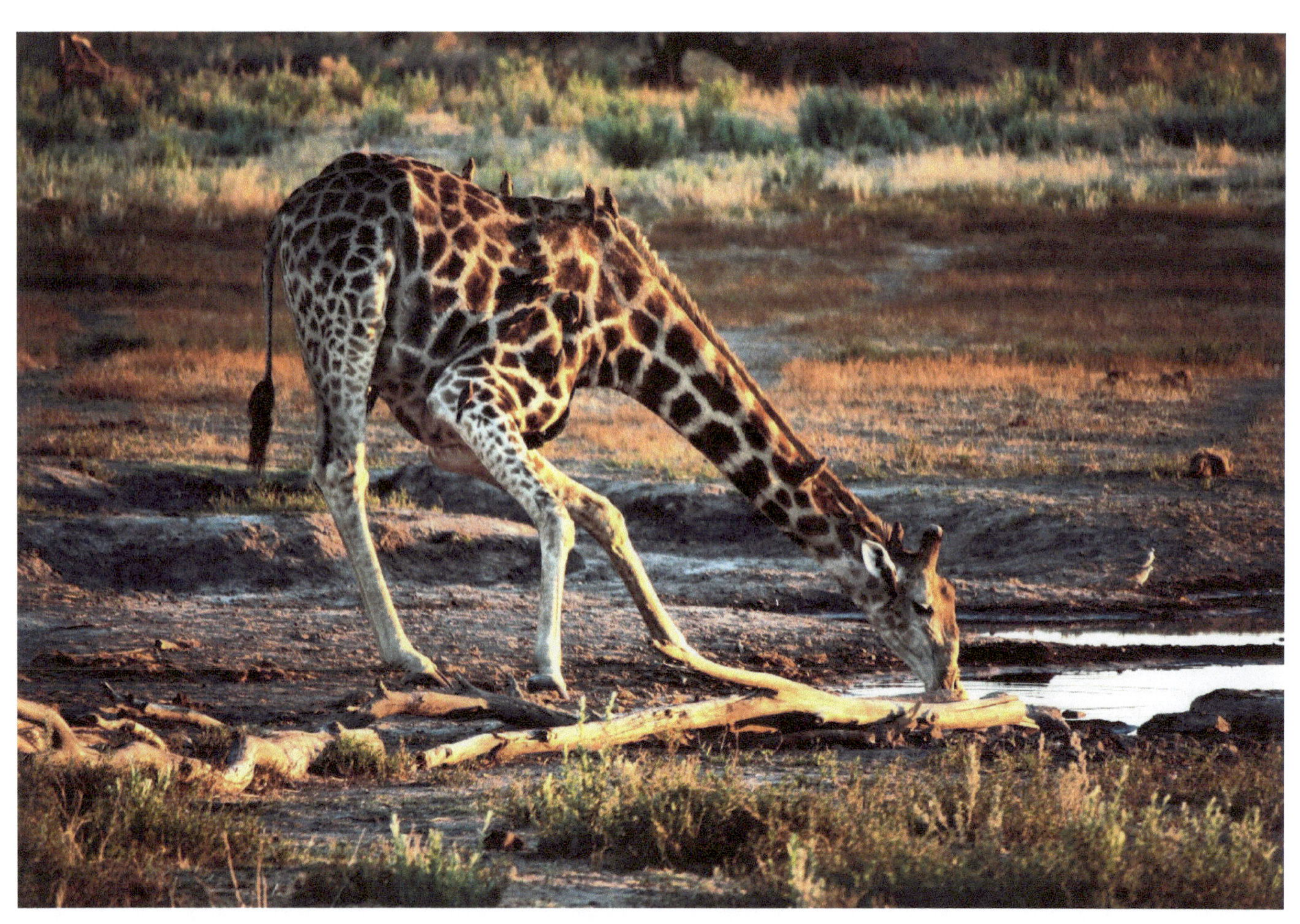

Giraffes are most vulnerable when leaning down to drink.

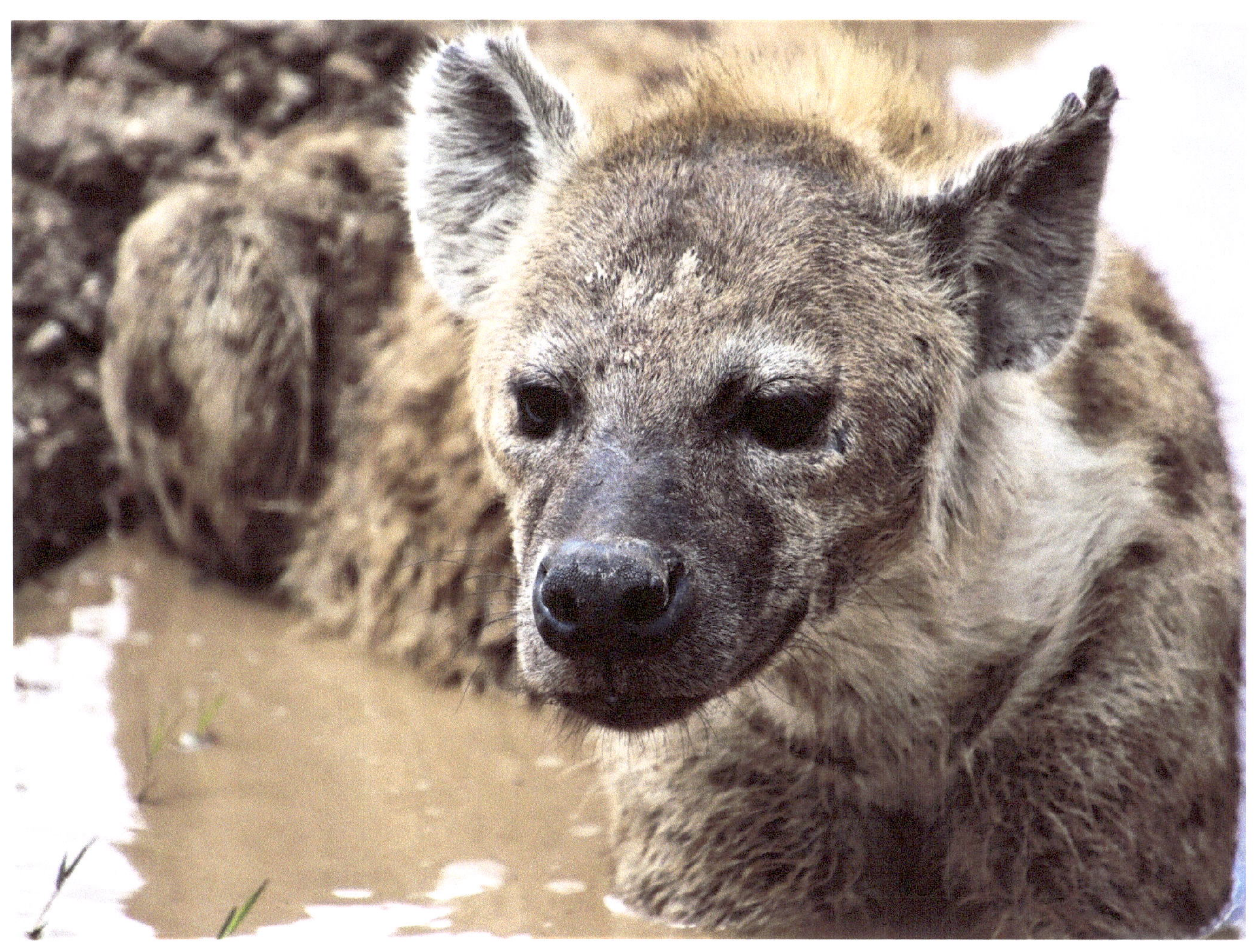

Hyena cooling off in a muddy puddle by the side of the road

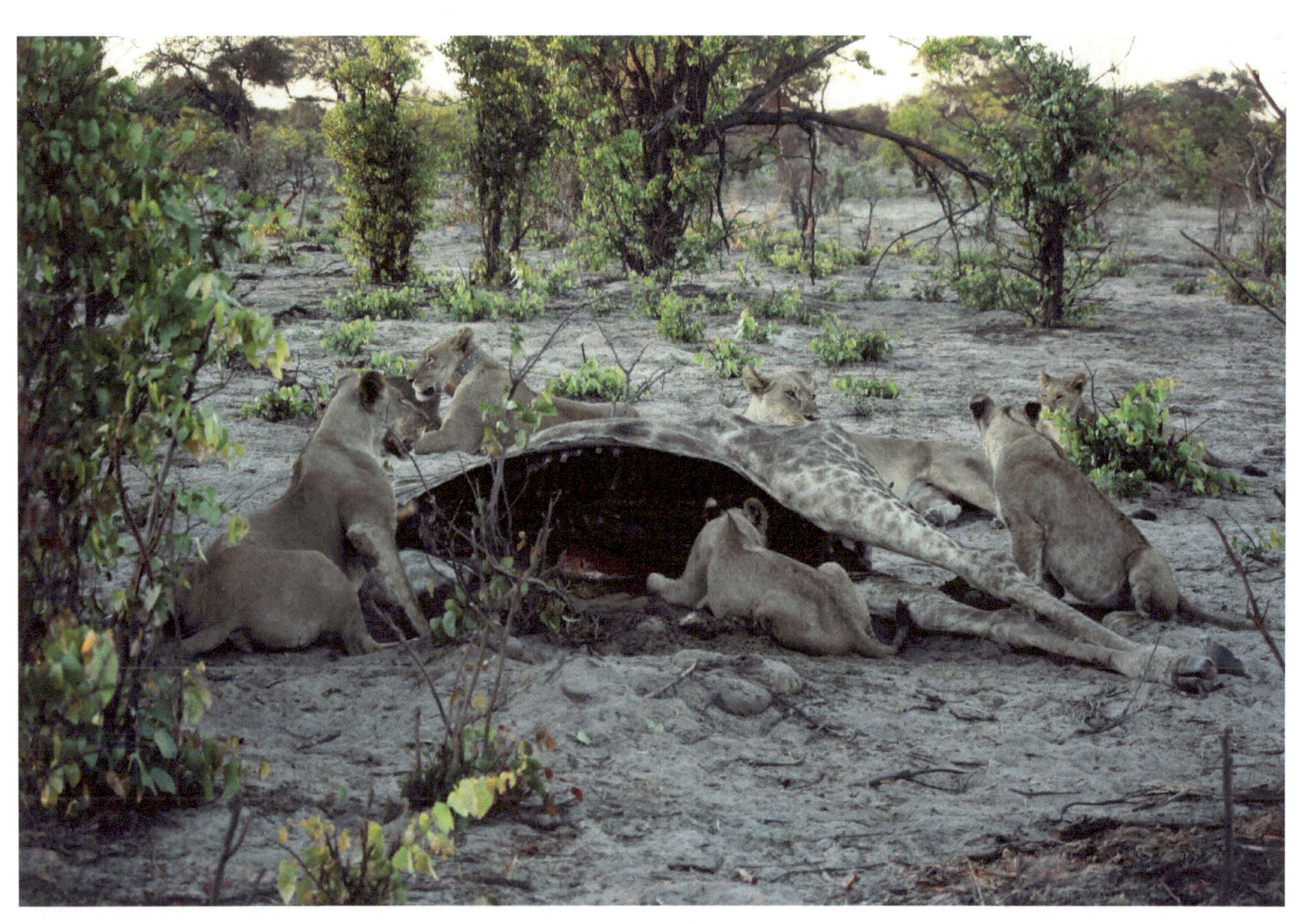

A gruesome sight, but this is nature in Africa. Predator and prey

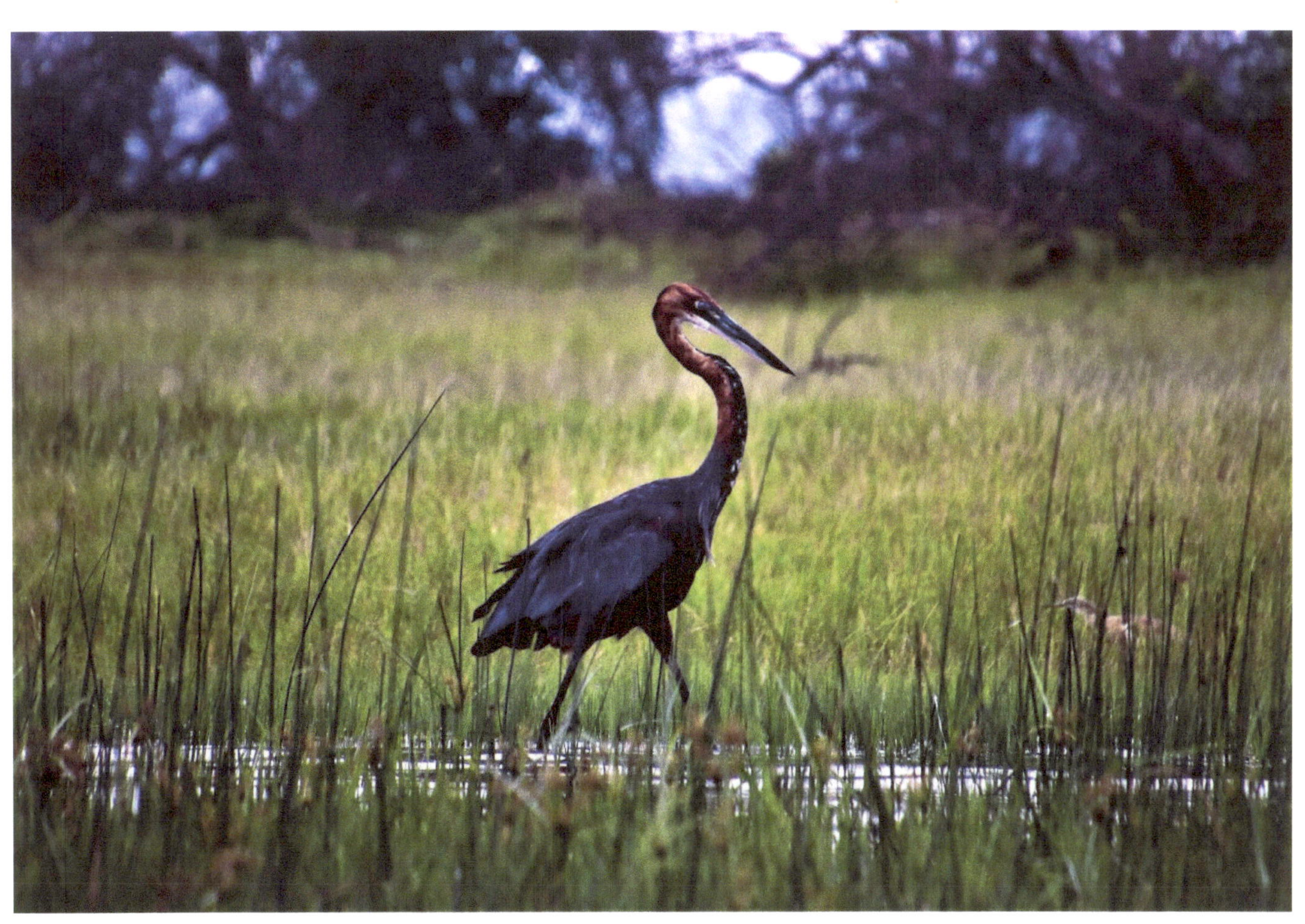

The goliath heron, the world's largest living heron, can stand from 3 to 5 feet tall.

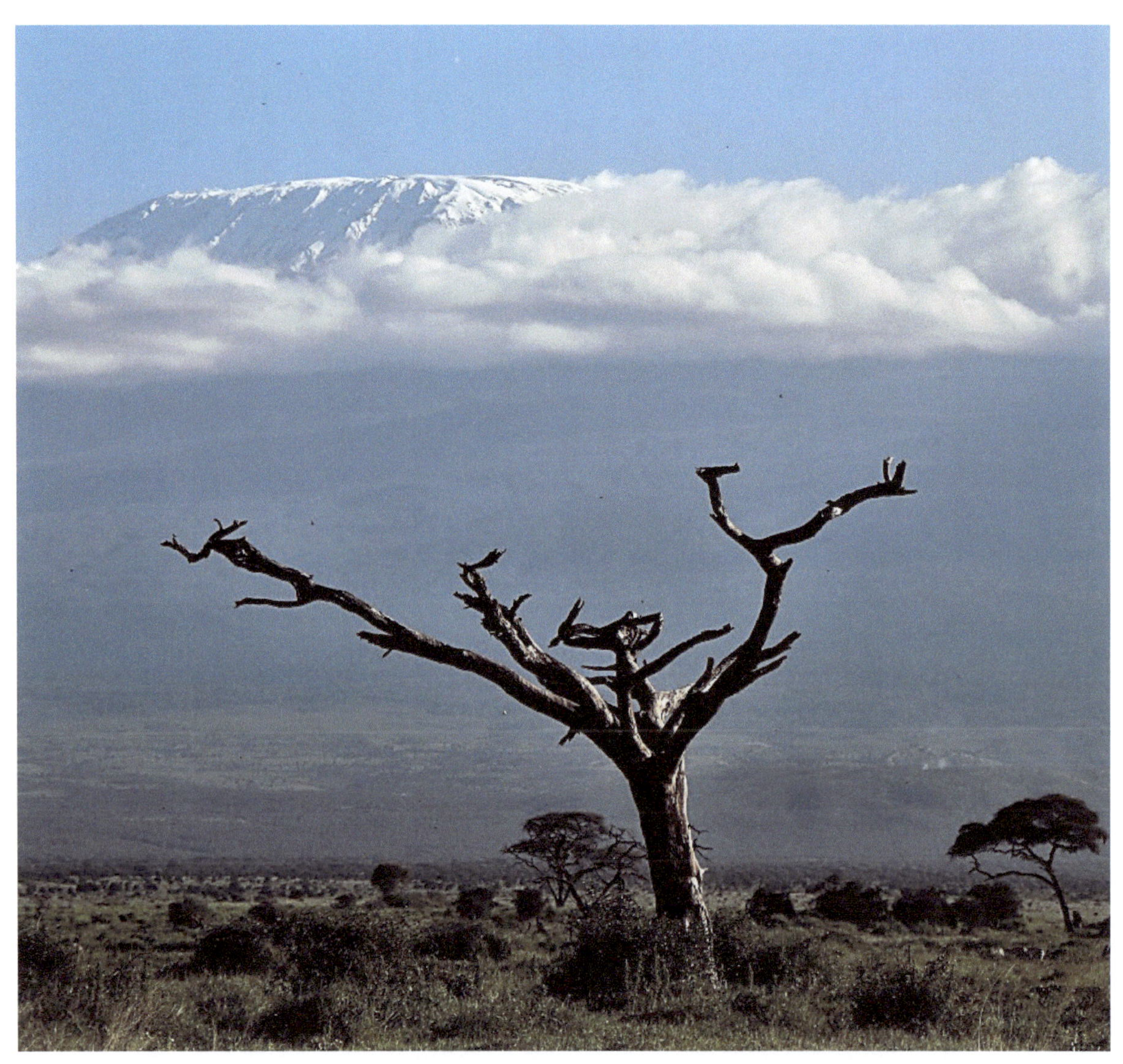

A view of snowcapped Kilimanjaro Mountain from the plains of Kenya

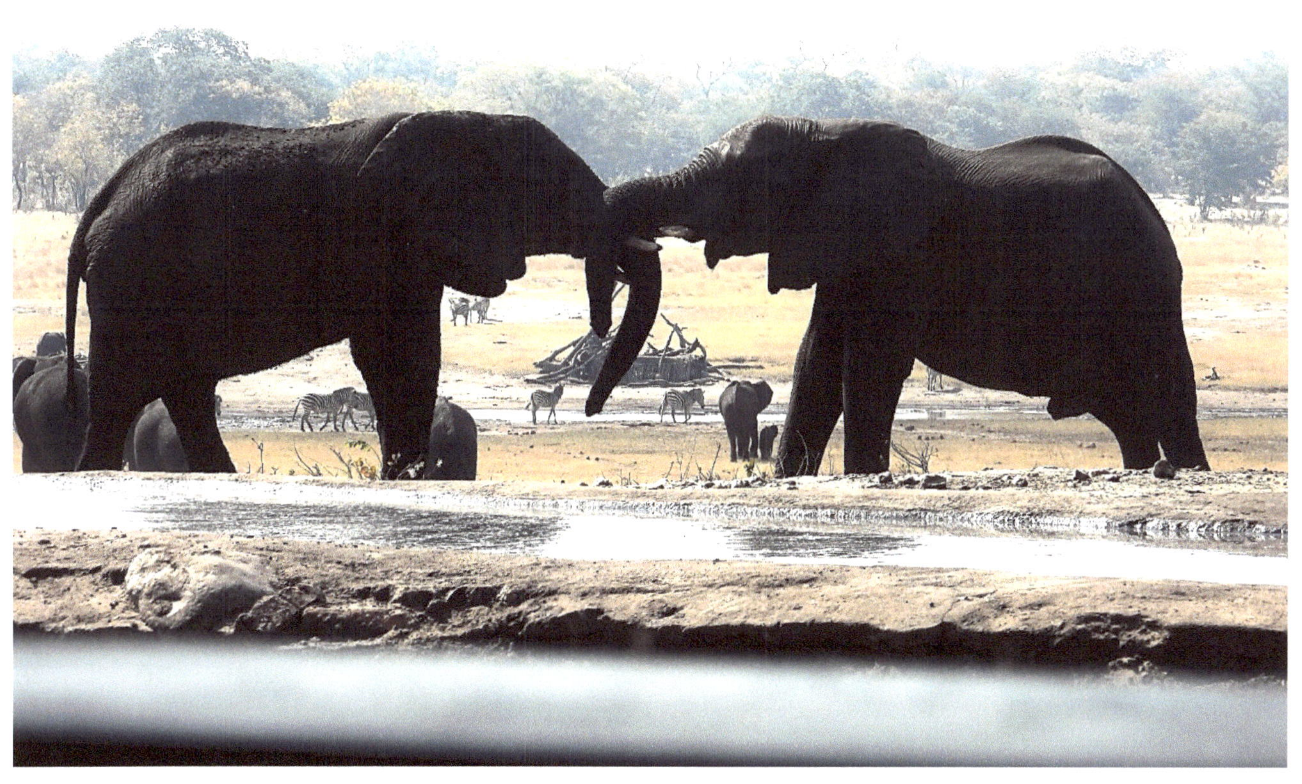

The view of the water hole from the hide at Sable Lodge, Hwange, Zimbabwe

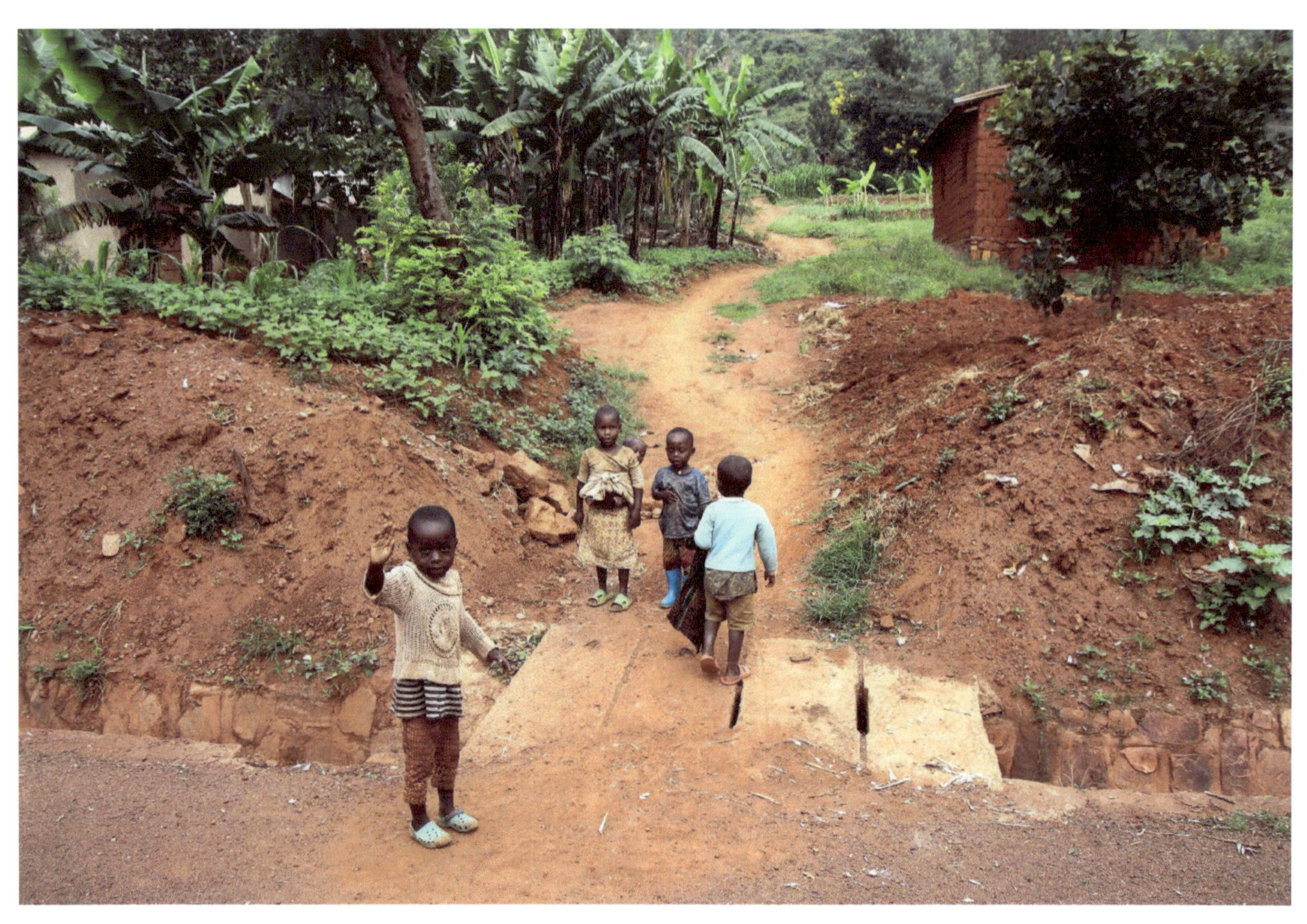

Kids wave as we pass by on the road in Rwanda

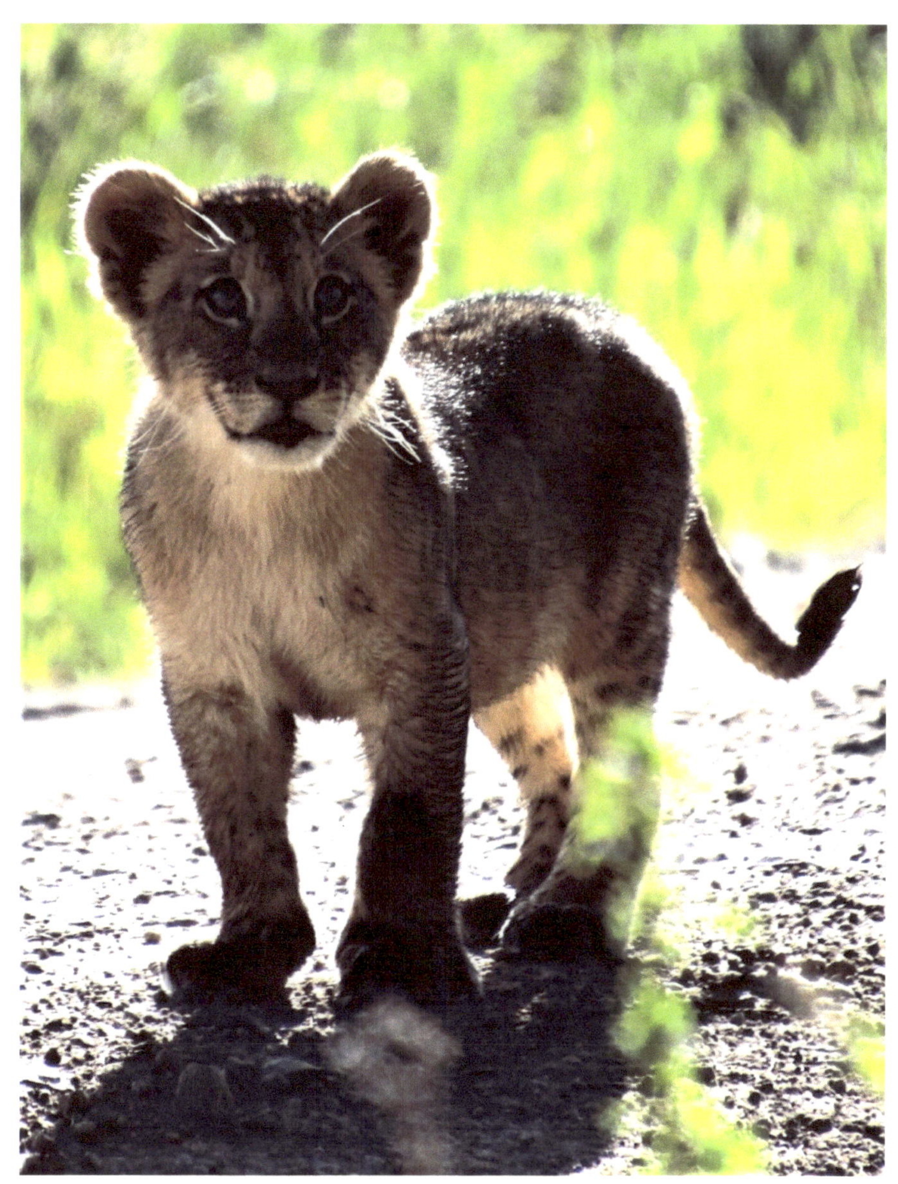

Adorable lion cub looks scared

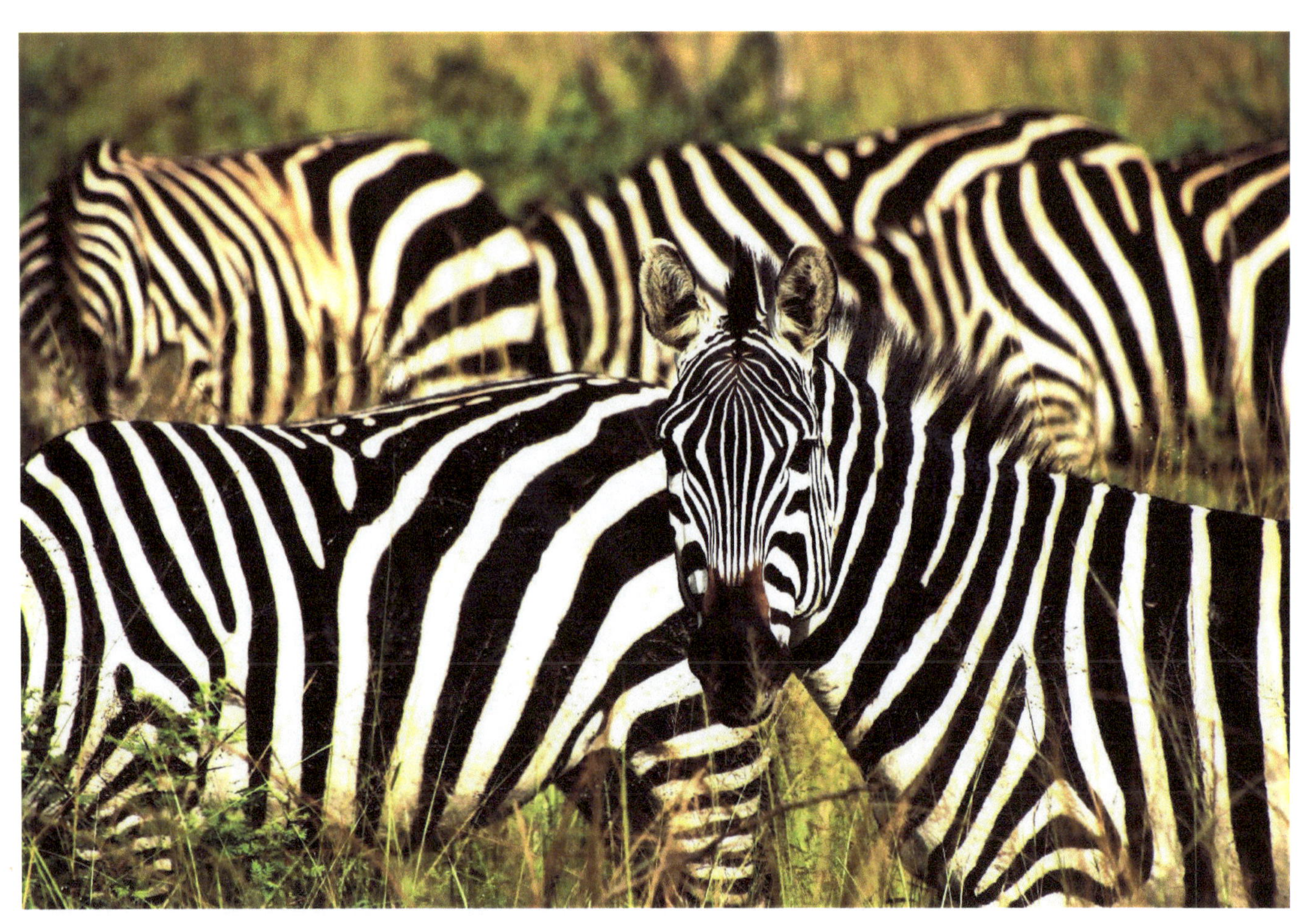

Can you see why they are called a dazzle when in a group?

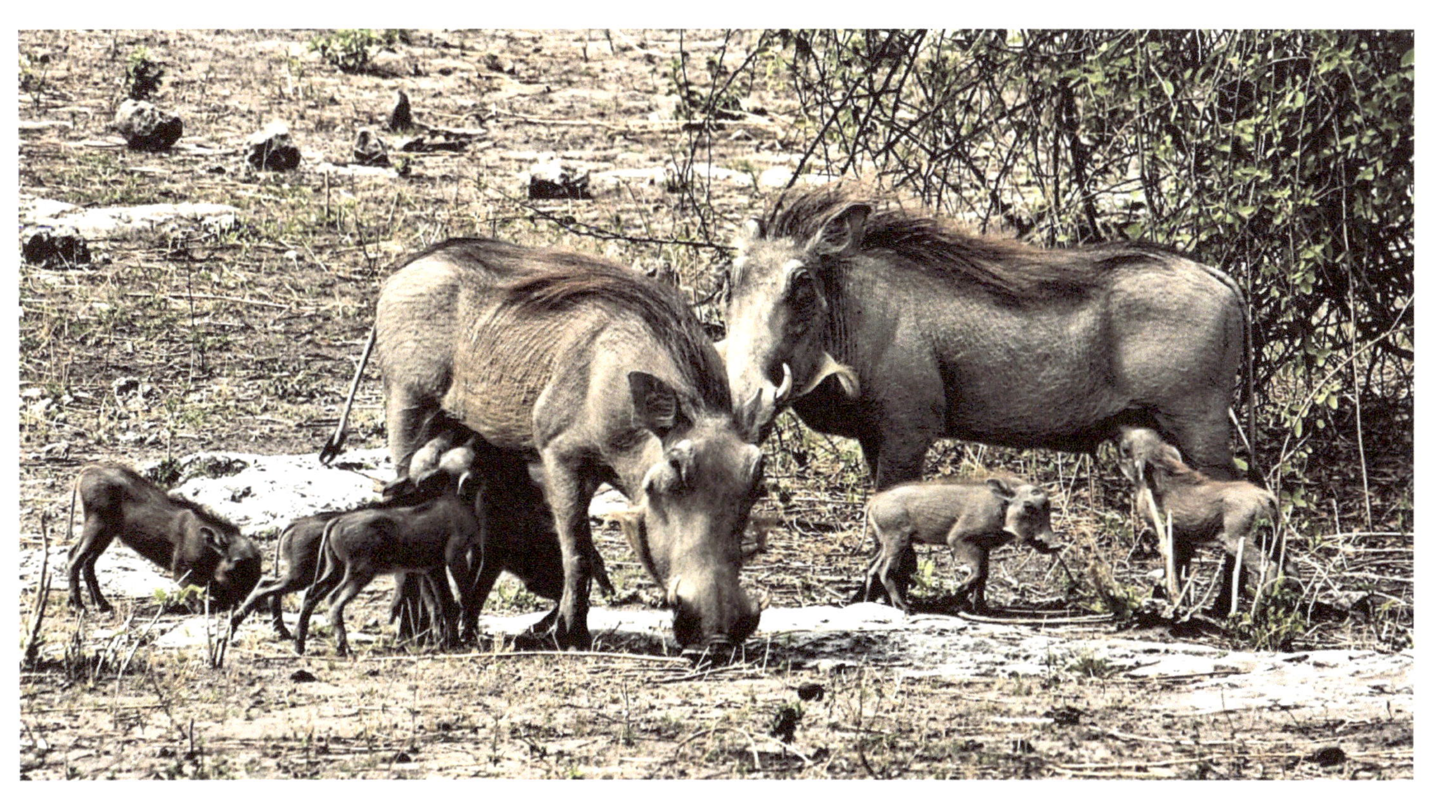

One of the ugly five. The warhog and their piglets. Also known as Mufasa!

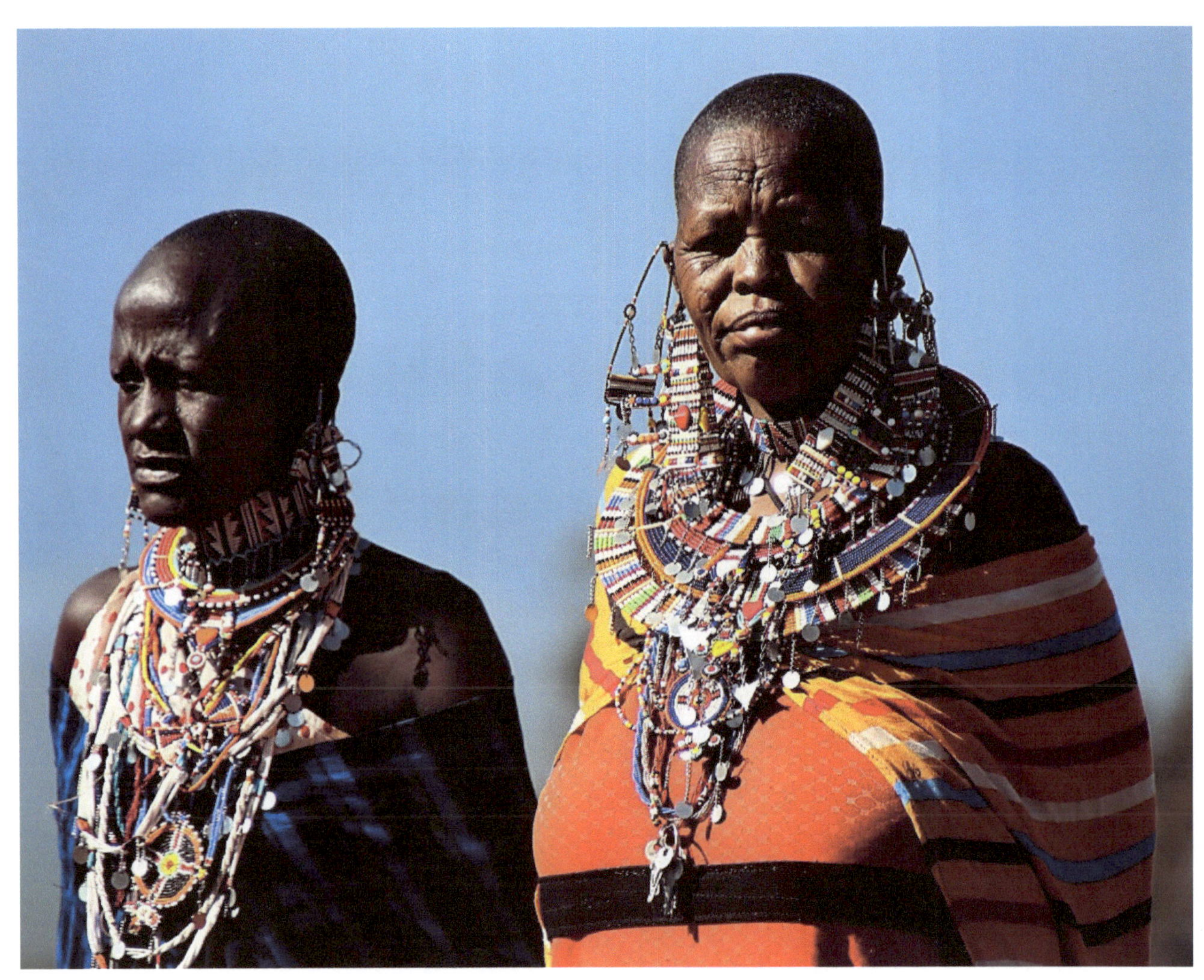

Maasai women wearing handmade beaded jewelry

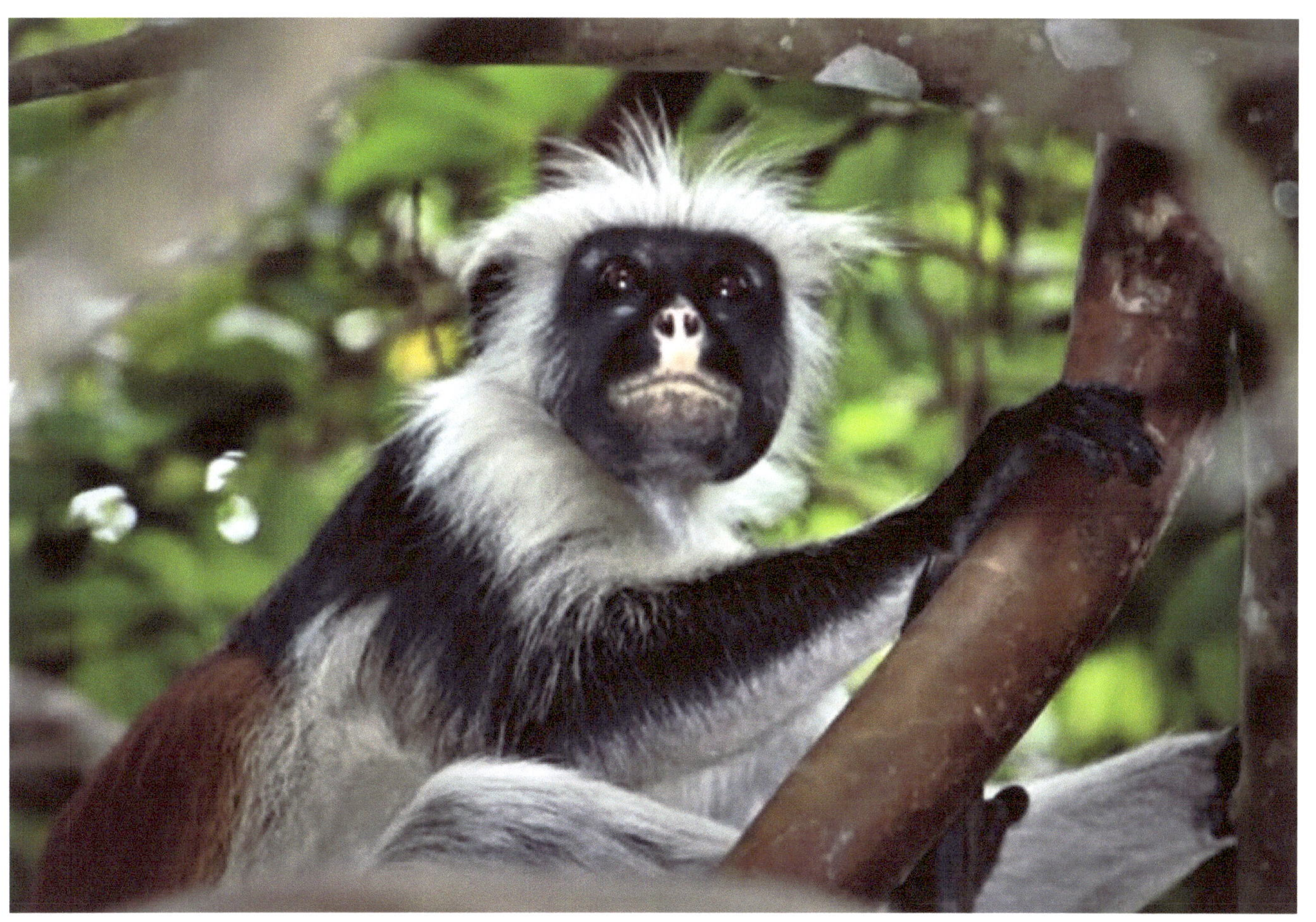

A surprised red colobus money checked me out as I raised my camera

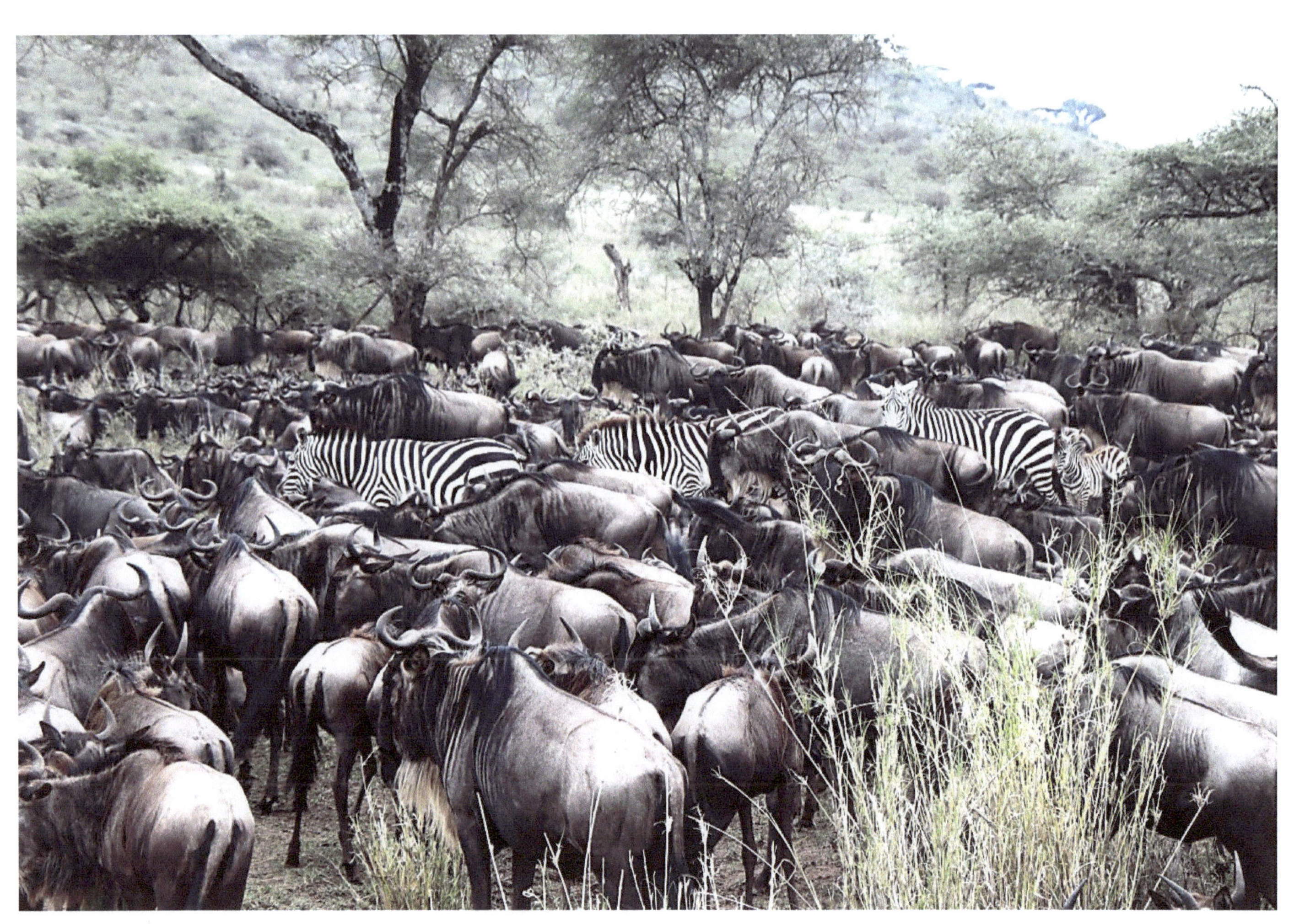

This is what "the great migration" looks like. Imagine a sea of animals that continuously flows from the horizon in the Serengeti National Park.

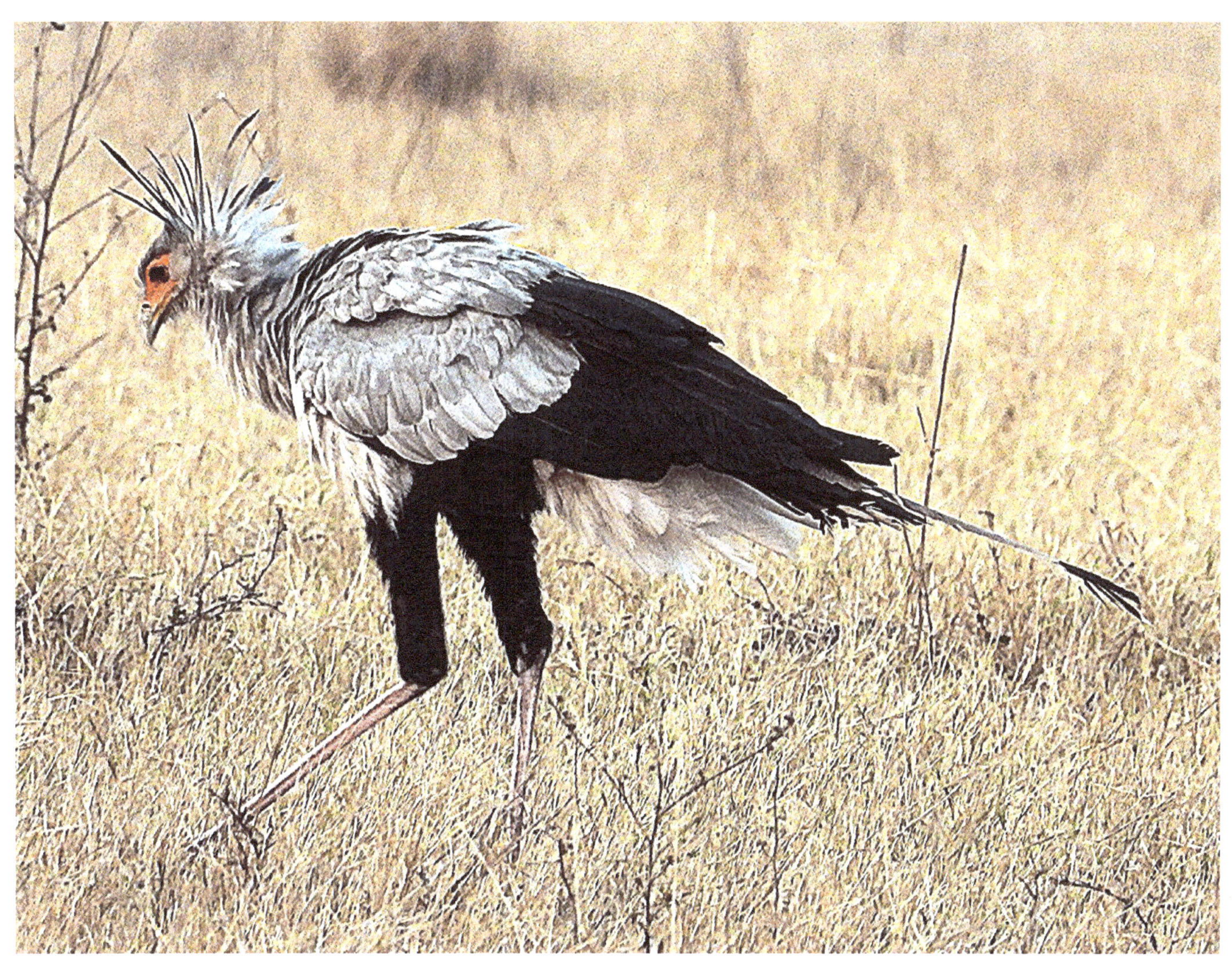

The secretary bird. Seeing him hunt and grab a snake, then swallowing it whole was an amazing sight.

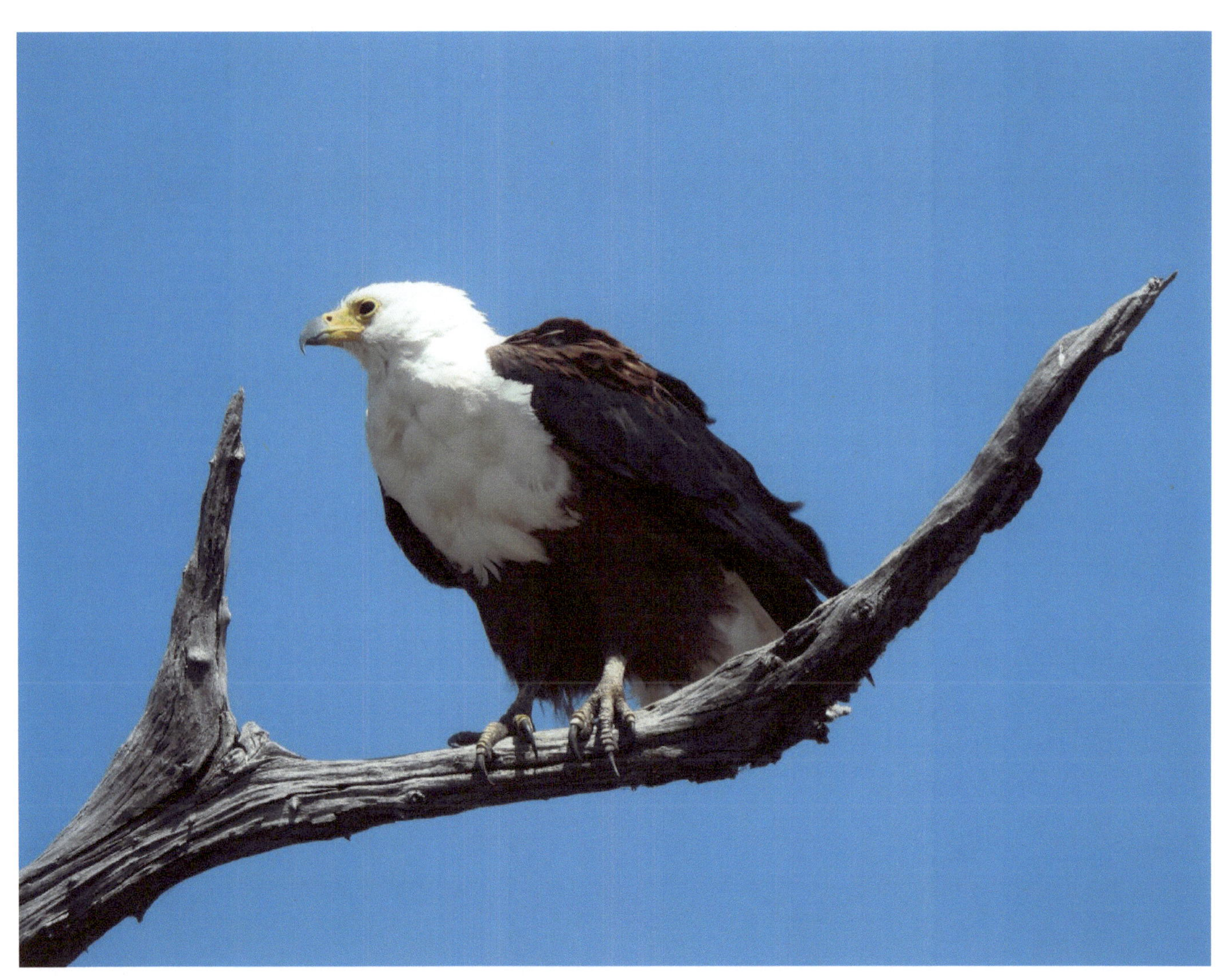

African king fisher spotting prey

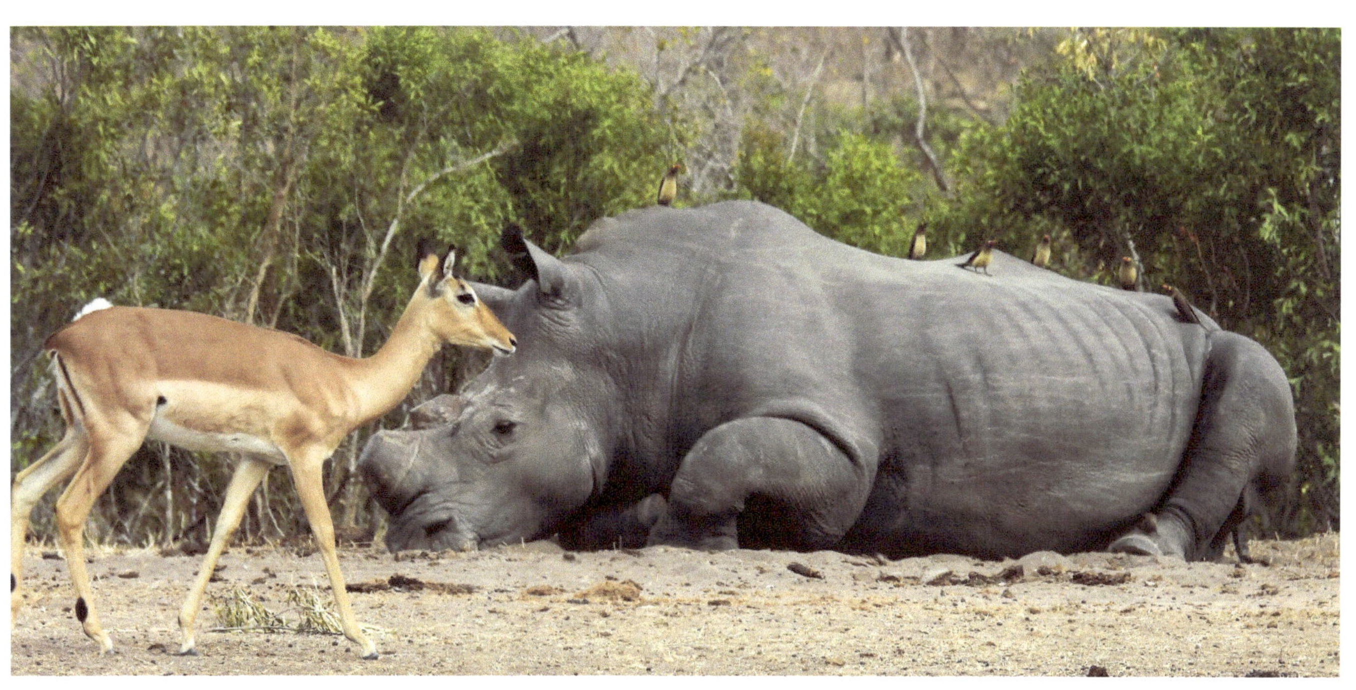

A Thompson impala, a rhino, and oxpeckers

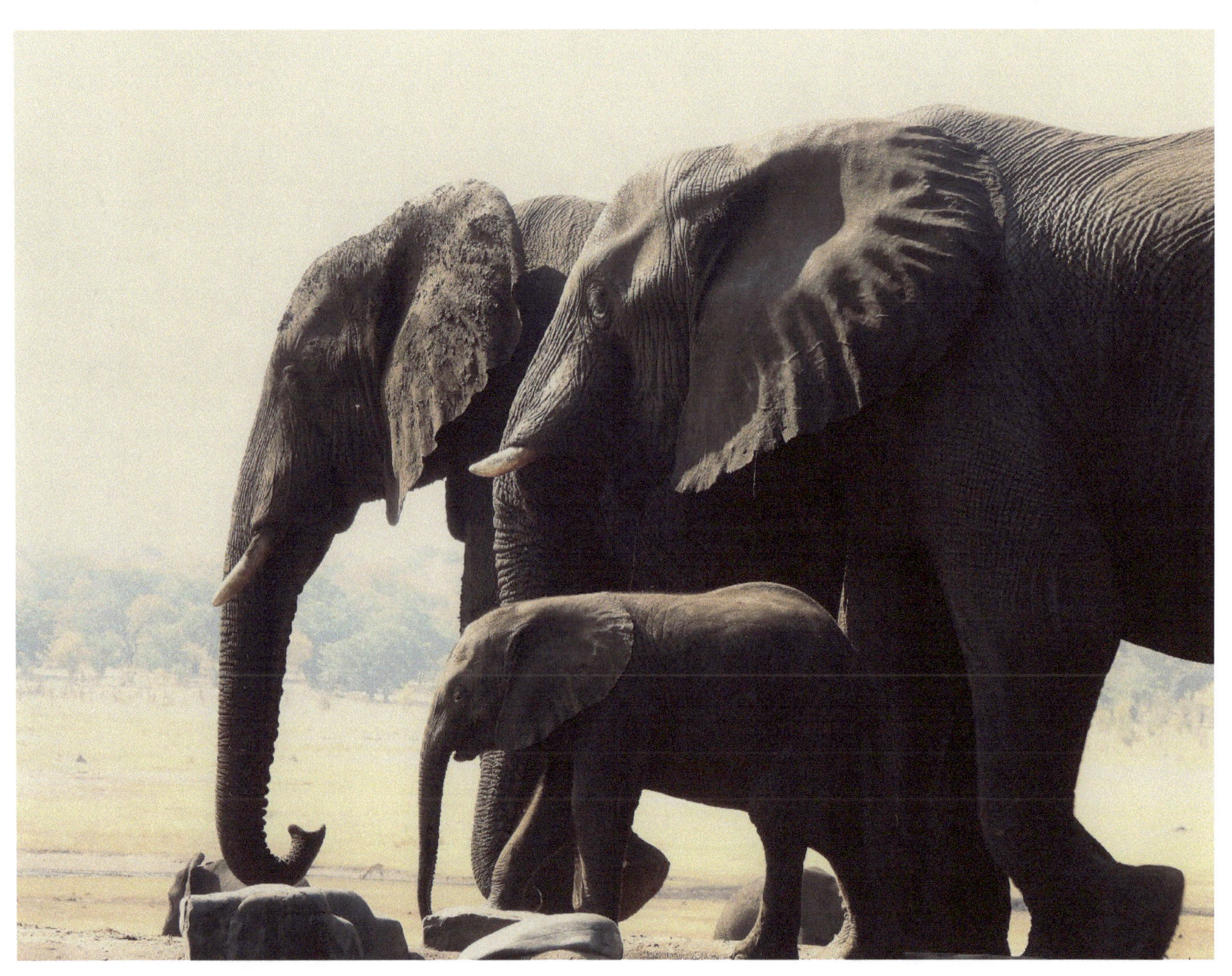

Imagine sipping a gin and tonic watching herds of elephants come and go to the water hole.

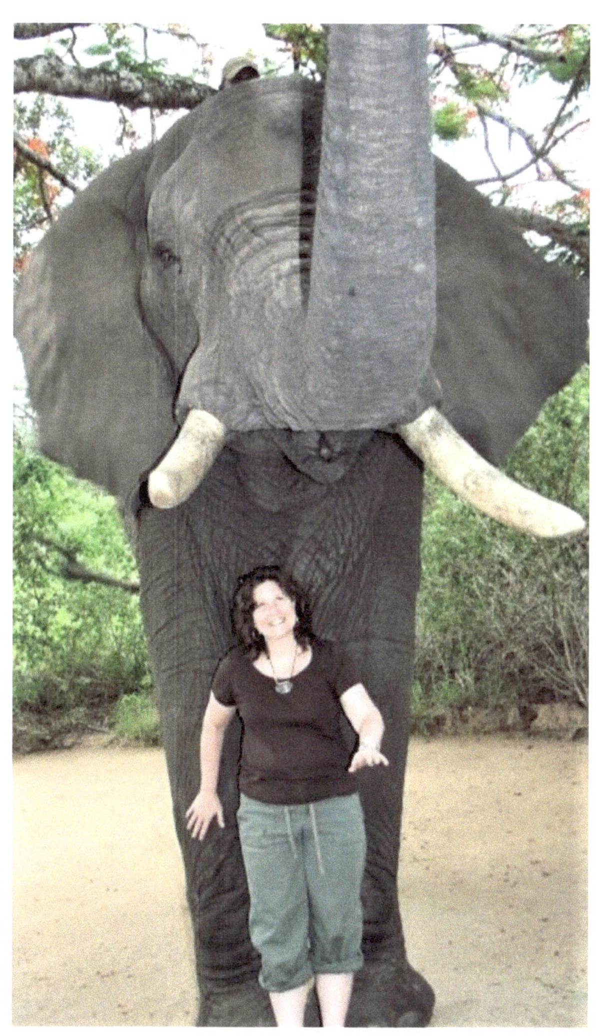

Yes, it's me under a big bull elephant in a sanctuary in South Africa (2017).
Note that I am 5'1". See how tall the elephant is.

If interested in traveling to southern Africa I highly recommend these two companies and these lodges for the best Safari adventures and game sightings.

Overseas Adventure Travel

www.oattravel.com
The leader in Small Group Travel and Small Ship Adventures.
Use my discount code to get $100 OFF when booking any trip.
Customer Number **2698400** (Sharon Smith)

For a more intimate travel experience with a minimum of only 4 adults
Reptor Tours and Transfers. (Yes this is Naume's company)
www.reptorsafaritoursandtransfers.com

Highly recommend these Lodges.
ZIMBABWE - www.amalindacollection.com
Ivory Lodge, Sable Valley Lodge, Khulu Lodge
Shearwater Explorers Village, Victoria Falls. https://explorersvillage.com/
SOUTH AFRICA -Buffalo Rock Lodge - https://www.buffalorock.co.za
BOTSWANA – Elephant Valley Lodge - https://elephantvalleylodge.com

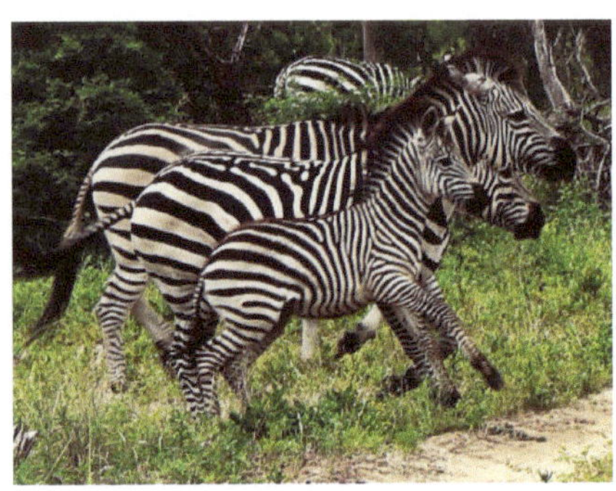
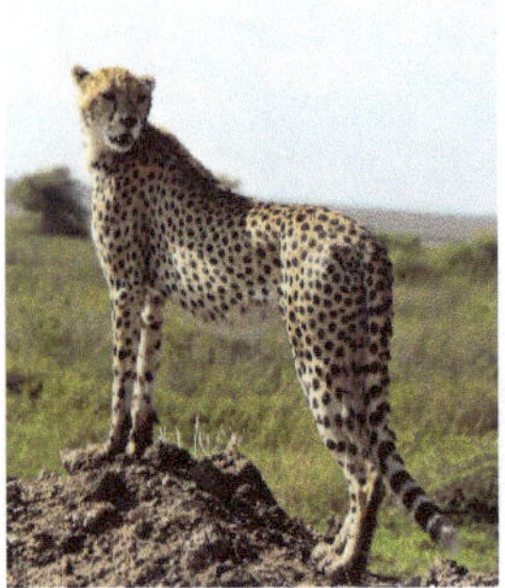
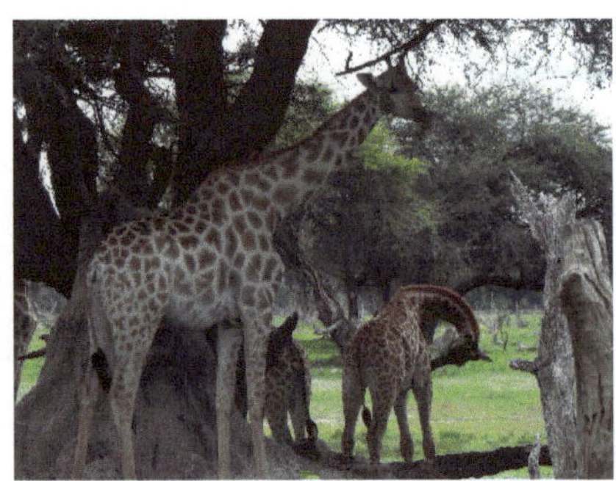

ABOUT THE AUTHOR

Sharon "Shaz" Smith is a traveler, adventurer, and photographer Her home base is in Allentown, Pennsylvania. Her first book, UNDER AFRICAN SKIES is an account of a romantic adventure she had in Africa. AFRICA: UP CLOSE AND PERSONAL, is her second book.

www.ingramcontent.com/pod-product-compliance
Lightning Source LLC
Chambersburg PA
CBHW040130240726
48664CB00002B/435